MOSES AND THE LAW
IN A CENTURY
OF CRITICISM SINCE GRAF

SUPPLEMENTS

TO

VETUS TESTAMENTUM

EDITED BY
THE BOARD OF THE QUARTERLY

G. W. ANDERSON - P. A. H. DE BOER - G. R. CASTELLINO
HENRY CAZELLES - E. HAMMERSHAIMB - H. G. MAY
W. ZIMMERLI

VOLUME XIX

LEIDEN
E. J. BRILL
1970

MOSES AND THE LAW
IN A CENTURY
OF CRITICISM SINCE GRAF

BY

R. J. THOMPSON
Dr Theol.

LEIDEN
E. J. BRILL
1970

To
the memory of
H. H. ROWLEY
whose
"Re-Discovery of the Old Testament"
first set the writer on this track
twenty years ago

CONTENTS

PART TWO

THE LAW CAME AFTER

THE GRAFIANS 1865-1925

PART THREE

THE LAW CAME BETWEEN

THE POST-GRAFIANS 1905-1965

ABBREVIATIONS

Periodicals

AJSL   *The American Journal of Semitic Languages and Literature*
ASTI   *Annual of the Swedish Theological Institute in Jerusalem*
BA   *Biblical Archaeologist*
BAR   *Biblical Archaeologist Reader*
Bibl   *Biblica*
BibSac   *Bibliotheca Sacra*
CBQ   *The Catholic Biblical Quarterly*
DLZ   *Deutsche Literaturzeitung*
EncJud   *Encyclopaedia Judaica*
ExpT   *Expository Times*
EvTh   *Evangelische Theologie*
HTR   *Harvard Theological Review*
HUCA   *Hebrew Union College Annual*
IEJ   *Israel Exploration Journal*
JAOS   *Journal of the American Oriental Society*
JBL   *Journal of Biblical Literature*
JBR   *The Journal of Bible and Religion*
JEA   *Journal of Egyptian Archaeology*
JNES   *The Journal of Near Eastern Studies*
JQR   *The Jewish Quarterly Review*
JR   *The Journal of Religion*
JSS   *Journal of Semitic Studies*
JTS   *The Journal of Theological Studies*
MGWJ   *Monatsschrift für Geschichte und Wissenschaft des Judentums*
NKZ   *Neue kirchliche Zeitschrift*
NTS   *New Testament Studies*
OTS   *Oudtestamentische Studiën*
PEQ   *Palestine Exploration Quarterly*
RB   *Revue Biblique*
RE   *Review and Expositor*
SEA   *Svensk Exegetisk Årsbok*
ThLZ   *Theologische Literaturzeitung*
ThR   *Theologische Rundschau*
ThStKr   *Theologische Studien und Kritiken*
ThZ   *Theologische Zeitschrift*
VT   *Vetus Testamentum*
VTSuppl   *Vetus Testamentum Supplements*
ZAW   *Zeitschrift für die alttestamentliche Wissenschaft*
ZDMG   *Zeitschrift der deutschen morgenländischen Gesellschaft*
ZKWL   *Zeitschrift für kirchliche Wissenschaft und kirchliches Leben*
ZThK   *Zeitschrift für Theologie und Kirche*

Other Abbreviations

ATD   *Das Alte Testament Deutsch*
BK   *Biblischer Kommentar*
DB   *Dictionnaire de la Bible*
DBSuppl   *Dictionnaire de la Bible Supplements*

EBrit	*Encyclopaedia Britannica*
ERE	*Encyclopaedia of Religion and Ethics* edited by James Hastings
HDB	*Dictionary of the Bible* (5 vols) edited by James Hastings
HZAT	*Handbuch zum Alten Testament*
IB	*Interpreter's Bible* edited by G. A. Buttrick
IDB	*The Interpreter's Dictionary of the Bible* edited by G. A. Buttrick
ICC	*The International Critical Commentary*
ISBE	*International Standard Bible Encyclopaedia* edited by James Orr
KEH	*Kurzgefasstes exegetisches Handbuch zum Alten Testament*
KS	*Kleine Schriften*
NBD	*The New Bible Dictionary* edited by J. D. Douglas
NHDB	*Dictionary of the Bible* (One Volume) edited by James Hastings, revised by F. C. Grant and H. H. Rowley
PRE	*Realencyclopädie für protestantische Theologie und Kirche*
Cf	Compare
ed.	edition
(ed.)	editor
ET	English Translation
A.T.	Altes Testament
O.T.	Old Testament
ff	following
N.F.	Neue Folge
N.S.	New Series
rec.	recension
Rev.	Review
Rev. ed.	Revised edition

CHAPTER ONE

PROLOGUE

The English reader of the Old Testament beginning his King James Version at Genesis is met by the title "The First Book of Moses Called Genesis". The German reader has it simply as "First Moses" (*Erste Mose*), and similarly "Second Moses", "Third Moses" and so on for the following books of the Pentateuch. It is likely that it was from Luther that the titles were taken over by the English translators. Luther himself followed the church tradition, which was also that of the Jews, although no such titles occur in the Hebrew Bible.

The Jewish tradition of the Mosaic authorship of the first five books of the Bible is extremely old and predates Luther by about two thousand years. It is contained in the Talmud, and in Jewish writers contemporary with the New Testament like Philo and Josephus. It was shared by the New Testament writers, and apparently by our Lord Himself, when He asked "Did not Moses give you the law (Jn 7: 19)"? For most Christians this has seemed conclusive, except where the nagging question of the nature of our Lord's human knowledge made itself heard. Could it have been otherwise, if He shared the human life of His time? [1] What if in His incarnation He had consented not to know what His contemporaries could not know on such matters? [2]

Just what then is the strength of

THE TRADITION

"The law given by Moses .." Jn 1: 17

While the famous Talmud testimony "Moses wrote his book and the passage dealing with Balaam and the Book of Job" [3] suggests a question as to what the "book" of Moses was if Num. 22-24 required

---

[1] Charles Gore seems to have been one of the first to raise this question in England in connection with our Lord's witness to the Old Testament. In his preface to the tenth edition of *Lux Mundi* he wrote "Unless He had violated the whole principle of the Incarnation, by anticipating the slow development of natural knowledge, He must have spoken of the Deuteronomist as 'Moses', as naturally as He spoke of the sun as 'rising'." (p. xxvi).

[2] Cf. his admission of limited knowledge on the date of the Parousia in Mk 13: 32.

[3] Cf. I. Epstein (ed.) *The Babylonian Talmud* Bab. Bathra I, London (1935) p. 71.

separate mention, Rabbinic literature nowhere else questions that the book of Moses was the whole Pentateuch. [1]) The only questions that were asked were as to whether any laws could have been given after Moses, [2]) whether the law was rightly ascribed to Moses or God, [3]) and whether God handed the heaven-inscribed law-book to Moses entire, or volume by volume. [4]) Commenting on the Deuteronomy text "This commandment is not in heaven", Midrash Rabbah records, " 'Do not say: "Another Moses will arise and bring us another Torah from Heaven"; ... it is not in Heaven, that is to say, no part of it has remained in Heaven' ". [5])

It is the more surprising, therefore, on turning to the Old Testament to find just how slight are the roots for the Jewish tradition there. When the Old Testament books are classified chronologically into the three periods, late, middle and early, the following striking facts emerge—

> the *later* books of the Old Testament speak of ritual and laws as "commanded in the book of Moses" and the reference is to the Pentateuch (Ezra 3: 2, 6:18; 2 Chron. 23:18, 30:16, 35:12);
> the *middle* books of the Old Testament refer to laws as "commanded in the book of Moses", but the reference is only to Deuteronomy (1 Kings 2:3; 2 Kings 14:6, cf. Dt. 24:16);
> the *earlier* historical and prophetic books have no such reference, except that the Pentateuch itself does say "Moses wrote" of the stages of the wilderness march (Num. 33:2), and of certain laws (Exod. 24:4, 34:27).

---

[1]) Except of course for the last eight verses of Deuteronomy assigned in the following clause to Joshua in defiance of much other Rabbinic tradition. One must assume that the Balaam reference relates to some ancient discussion, or is merely inserted for ornament.

[2]) The answer was in the negative, even the Feast of Purim from the time of Esther being found hinted at in the law. Cf. "The Responsa of the Babylonian Geonim as a source of Jewish History" by J. Mann in *JQR* IX (1918-1919) pp. 139-50 for the method in the tenth century A.D. of justifying late laws by earlier allusions—the two days of Rosh-ha-shana by 1 Sam. 20:27, the prohibition of carrying burdens and common talk on the sabbath by Jer. 17:22 and Is. 58:13, and shoe testimony, female inheritance and returning a present in the Jubilee Year by Ruth 4:7; Job 42:15 and Ezek. 46:17.

[3]) Against the claim that some rabbis held that the curses in Deuteronomy were by Moses himself, L. Jacob cites Baraita Sanhedrin 99a to the effect that the whole Torah was from heaven, and not even a single verse uttered by Moses himself. (*Conservative Judaism* XX (1965) pp. 68-69).

[4]) For references see B. H. Branscomb, *Jesus and the Law of Moses*, New York (1930) pp. 22, 27.

[5]) H. Freedman and M. Simon (ed.) *Midrash Rabbah Deuteronomy*, London (1939) p. 153.

The conclusion that is forced upon one is that the tradition is a growing one, the connection to Moses being extended from some laws, to Deuteronomy, to all the laws, to the whole Pentateuch. [1]) In fact the terms "Moses" and "the law" are extended in popular usage to include also the Psalms (Jn 10: 34, 15: 25) [2]) and the prophets (1 Cor. 14: 21 quoting Isaiah). The rabbis indeed go further, and make Moses the author of the oral tradition, and even of the Hebrew vowel points, which although not added until the sixth century A.D., are traced back to Moses on Sinai. [3])

The following statistics of the mention of Moses given by J.L. McKenzie [4]) indicate the growing tradition—twice in 1 Samuel, five times in the Prophets, eight times in the Psalms, ten times in 1-2 Kings, thirtyone times in Chronicles, Ezra, Nehemiah, eighty times in the New Testament, and hundreds of times in the Talmud. From his role as leader in the Exodus to which the reference is limited in the first three of the above, extension is made to that of lawgiver in the middle group, and author, first of the written, and later of the unwritten tradition, in the later. [5])

The Jewish tradition then, instead of settling the question, raises it more acutely. It is separated from the time of Moses by many hundreds of years, and against this vital gap its later perpetuity is of little consequence. As W.H. Bennett wrote in 1893: "A guess made centuries after the period it refers to does not become contemporary evidence by being repeated for two thousand years". The guesses of the Rabbis regarding the authorship of Old Testament books are centuries later than the books and once "were as brand new and as purely hypothetical as the latest theory to be found in the most recently published monograph of a German professor". [6])

---

[1]) We can see the process at work in Kings and Chronicles where "the Book of the Law of Moses" in 2 Kings 14:5, 6 becomes "the law in the Book of Moses" in 2 Chron. 25:3, 4.

[2]) And this on the lips of Jesus!

[3]) After all Moses had been bidden "write...plainly", argued a certain Heidegger. (F. W. Farrar, *History of Interpretation*, London (1886) p. 388).

[4]) J. L. McKenzie, "Moses", *Dictionary of the Bible*, Milwaukee (1965) pp. 589-90.

[5]) So J. L. McKenzie. McKenzie, a Catholic, agrees with his distinguished Catholic predecessor, Père Lagrange, whose work will occupy us in the sequel, that a difference must be made between the *historical* tradition of Moses as legislator and founder, which can be accepted, and the *literary* tradition of Moses, as author of the Pentateuch, which is not so certain.

[6]) W. H. Bennett, "The Old Testament" in *Faith and Criticism*, London (1893) p. 8.

Our Lord's "Did not Moses give you the law"? need be no more precise than His "Moses gave you circumcision" (Jn 7:22), which He proceeded to correct. [1]) The issue is not prejudged by such statements. The tradition is far from unimpeachable, and at the hands of the critical school of de Wette and his successors, became subject to

THE CHALLENGE

"The law came .. after." Gal. 3:17

Before de Wette came forward in 1805 with his theory of a late date for the Mosaic law, voices raised in question had been quite sporadic and were generally "off-beat" as far as Christian orthodoxy was concerned. From the Early Church, de Wette quoted *Ptolemaus* in his epistle to Flora, who had written:

> The entire law embraced in the Pentateuch of Moses, was not given by any one man... it was not given by the only God. It is, indeed, attributed to Moses not as if the very God enacted the law through him, but because Moses, incited by his own mind, enacted certain laws. It is also attributed to the elders of the people, for the principal men devised certain ordinances, and promulgated their own laws.[2])

The fact that this questioning was from the side of the Gnostics, who opposed sacrifice in principle, robbed it of any great impact.[3]) The same antithetical attitude to sacrifice may also have inspired certain *heretics of the seventh century* referred to by the Patriarch of Antioch, who objected that "when He had given order for the complicated Levitical meat-offering, God says afterward through Isaiah and Jeremiah that He had given no commandment unto Israel concerning sacrifices or concerning burnt offerings". [4]) Similarly, the Jewish proto-critic Hiwi, who flourished in Persia in the ninth century,

---

[1]) Cf. Gn. 17.

[2]) The translation is that of Parker in W. M. L. de Wette, *A Critical and Historical Introduction to the Canonical Scriptures of the Old Testament*, Vol. II, Boston (1859) p. 161.

[3]) For a discussion of the passage see R. M. Grant, "Historical Criticism in the Ancient Church," *JR* XXV (1945) pp. 183-96 and *A Short History of the Interpretation of the Bible*, Rev. ed., London (1965) pp. 50-51.

[4]) Anastasius the Sinaite, *Viae Dux*, Chap. XXII, Migne, *Patrologia*, LXXXIX (1865) p. 286. The translation is that of E. M. Gray, *Old Testament Criticism: Its Rise and Progress from the Second Century to the End of the Eighteenth*, New York (1923) p. 46.

may have derived his doubts from Gnostic or Zoroastrian sources. [1])

It was either *Hiwi* or a disciple that left us the medieval Geniza specimens edited by Schechter under the title "The Oldest Collection of Bible Difficulties, by a Jew" [2]) in which it is asked why later books of the Bible ignore laws important in the earlier. Elijah is commanded to eat what ravens brought, but the law had forbidden eating what had been torn by beasts. [3]) The laws of prohibited degrees in marriage in Deuteronomy differ from those in Leviticus. It was left to another Jew, the brilliant twentyseven year old, MANASSEH BEN ISRAEL of Amsterdam, to answer these and four hundred and seventy similar difficulties in his *Conciliator* of 1632. [4])

With the rise of rationalism in the seventeenth century repugnance to priesthood and sacrifice led to an even more vigorous questioning of the divine origin of the law. REIMARUS, as presented in Lessing's *Wolfenbüttel Fragments* in 1774, argued that the instructions and laws alleged to have been divinely communicated were so barbarous and destructive e.g. Moses' spoiling the Egyptians and the extirpation of the Canaanites claiming 'feigned commands of God', that to ascribe them to God was impossible. [5]) The morality of the law is defended by MICHAELIS in his massive, multi-volume work of 1770-1775, [6]) but the question of their dating does not come into his purview. [7]) More to the latter point was J. F. W. JERUSALEM's, *Briefe über die Mosai-schen Schriften und Philosophie*, Braunschweig (1762), which not only

---

[1]) See the discussion in I. Davidson, *Saadia's Polemic Against Hiwi Al-Balkai*, New York (1915) pp. 23-26.

[2]) *JQR* XIII (1901) pp. 354-74.

[3]) *Ibid* p. 348 and 366.

[4]) For "ravens", he said, some read "merchants". Sacrifice was said not to have been commanded, because it was a divine after-thought necessitated by the sin of the Golden Calf. (See the English translation in 2 volumes, 1842. Vol. I pp. 225-26, 218-23, and below). Calvin has another way with the latter difficulty viz. the Ten Commandments were the centre and all the other commandments mere appendages "therefore, God protests that he never enjoined anything with respect to the sacrifices" (Preface to *Harmony of the Four Last Books of the Pentateuch*, p. xvii). The same Calvin elsewhere so far forgets himself as to describe the notion of God making a throne of the Mercy Seat as "a crass figment", from which even a David and a Hezekiah were not free. (F. W. Farrar, *op. cit.*, p. 350).

[5]) Cf. D. F. Strauss, *Life of Jesus*, ET, London ([6]1913) p. 46.

[6]) J. D. Michaelis, *Commentaries on the Laws of Moses*, ET, 4 vols, London (1814).

[7]) His Articles 11 and 76 do, however, recognize that some laws never came into force e.g. sabbatical and jubilee year, or were not long continued. He notes that even a law described in Lev. 17:7 as "for all your generations for ever" is changed in Dt. 12:15, 20, 21, 22, and had thus been intended only for the wilderness period. (*Ibid*, Vol. I, p. 31).

answered the Deist criticism but also attempted to show inductively that Pentateuchal law went back to Moses. [1])

Outside these heretical circles it was the dating of the Mosaic literature rather than the Mosaic laws that was objected to by the critics who preceded de Wette. Typical was CARLSTADT at the time of the Reformation. He opposed a Mosaic Pentateuch, but allowed Mosaic laws. ANTHON VAN DALE, a Mennonite, distinguished between the legal and historical sections of the Pentateuch in 1696 and ascribed the latter to Ezra, but the former to Moses, with Ezra as the redactor who inserted the laws of Moses into their historical Pentateuchal framework [2])—a conclusion in exactly the reverse order to that which was reached by Graf. [3])

Understandably it was the ascription of the laws to Moses that inspired this hesitation. COLERIDGE, for example, was ready to question any mere tradition but felt that "where the writer ... relates that the *Word of the Lord came* unto priest, prophet, chieftain", the same was "to be received with full belief". [4]) GLADSTONE, also, who was far from inhospitable to the new knowledge, [5]) felt it to be the chief difficulty that "it is the legislation, for which in the sacred text itself the claim is constantly made of being due to direct communication from above, while no corresponding assertion in general accompanies

---

[1]) It was taken over by the Samaritans, and so must have antedated Ezra, it was known to the prophets in their writings, to Hezekiah in his reform, to Jehoshaphat in his appointment of teachers, to David in Psalms 78 and 104-07, to Joshua in his first chapter, to Deuteronomy in Ch. 17:18, which by speaking of a "second law" implies the first (pp. 15-24 of the 1783 edition). It is significant that most of his examples are drawn from Joshua and Chronicles.

[2]) "I make a distinction between the Books of the Law and the Pentateuch, for I believe the Books of the Law were before the Captivity in the custody of the priests and Levites,... to which class the sacred scribes belonged. As concerning the Pentateuch... it appears to me to have been compiled by Ezra the scribe, and this Ezra by Divine direction and inspiration composed it as the Book of the Law (which he inserted in its entirety) and the other historical and truly prophetic books". (A. van Dale, *Dissertationes de Origine ac Progressu Idolatriae*, Epist. ad Morin (1696) pp. 685-86 cited by Gray, *op. cit.*, p. 123).

[3]) When, in 1865, Graf produced the epoch-making work that was to give his name to the most influential of all schools of Pentateuchal criticism, it was the laws rather than the narrative that he ascribed to the time of Ezra. He continued to believe the narrative to be older until 1869.

[4]) S. T. Coleridge, *Confessions of an Inquiring Spirit*, London (1956 edition) p. 49.

[5]) Against the theory of inerrancy, he had argued that the divine method was "one of sufficiency, not perfection—sufficiency for the attainment of practical ends, not conformity to ideal standards", (W. E. Gladstone, *The Impregnable Rock of Holy Scripture*, Rev. ed, London (1890) pp. 11-12).

the historical recitals". [1]) He calculated that the claim was made thirty times in the twentyseven chapters of Leviticus.

To a Bible-believing generation only an answer from a Bible text could convince and such answers were sought. Briggs pointed out that the words "Moses said" could be paralleled by the reference to Samuel speaking in Acts 3: 24, where the words were those of the prophet Nathan in 2 Sam. 7 long after Samuel's death. [2]) They meant no more than that the words occurred in the book traditionally associated with the names of the men concerned. [3]) Could it not be that such ascriptions were merely literary devices like the ascription of all wisdom to Solomon (despite the clear reference several times in Proverbs to other authors), [4]) and all Psalms to David (despite Ps. 137's reference to Babylon). The name of Moses as the nation's founder and lawgiver, was appropriately prefixed to all laws, including those given much later. The "law of Moses" was thus a popular title like "Webster's Dictionary", "Davidson's Hebrew Grammar" and "Peake's Commentary" (which in the new edition contains not one word by Professor Peake), and was not a scientific description of origin. [5])

In support of this, attention was drawn to a number of phenomena within the Old Testament itself. In 1 Sam. 30:25 it is said that David was the first to make the statute that the spoils of war were to be equally divided between participants and civilians, but in Num. 31:27 this law is already ascribed to Moses. [6]) In the Pentateuch the laws of

---

[1]) *Ibid.*, p. 172.

[2]) Samuel had died in 1 Sam. 25.

[3]) C. A. Briggs, *General Introduction to the Study of Holy Scripture*, Edinburgh (1899) p. 271. Briggs writes: "In the passage, Moses and all the prophets from Samuel said (Acts 3:22-24) it is necessary to interpret 'Samuel' of the book of Samuel and think of the prophecy of Nathan; and if this be so; is it not most natural to interpret 'Moses' here as referring to the book of Deuteronomy rather than the person of Moses"?

[4]) E.g. Prov. 25:1, 30:1, 31:1.

[5]) This argument now finds complete vindication in the recent *Temple Scroll* from the Dead Sea area, where thirty pages of minute instructions about the temple are prefaced by the words "God said to Moses", and commands from the Pentateuch given there in the third person e.g. "if a woman vows to God" are rewritten in the first. This attests Jewish usage at the time the Talmud tradition arose. See Y. Yadin, "The Temple Scroll", *BA* XXX (1967) pp. 135-39.

[6]) It is antecedently more probable that the former derivation is correct. Precedents and case law will precede code law. Law codes arise out of life rather than precede life. The nineteenth century required traffic laws for railways, but not for motor cars, the early twentieth required them for private cars but not for private planes, the late twentieth requires them for all three. Cf. J. M. P. Smith, *The Origin and History of Hebrew Law*, Chicago (1931) p. 3.

sacrifice in Lev. 1-7 interrupt the connection between the instructions
to consecrate a priesthood for the tabernacle in Exodus, and the
account of their fulfilment in Lev. 8-9. Where Lev. 7:38 says the laws
of the preceding seven chapters were given to Moses on Sinai, Lev. 1:
1 speaks of them as given at the door of the tabernacle. It is not difficult to unwrap the ascription to Moses from the earlier stage of the
laws which lacked it.[1])

The recognition of "layers" within the laws does not mean that
there are contradictions, but rather accounts naturally for what would
otherwise be contradictions. The critics were not slow to draw
attention to this and other advantages accruing from the new knowledge. It was a relief to find some old difficulties removed. "The hare
is called unclean because it has not a cloven hoof, although it chews
the cud! The picture of Moses writing this unbiological sentence at
the dictation of the Lord is one at which the most devout mind is
startled", writes McKenzie.[2]) "The attribution of the mass of material
called the law of Moses to the dictation of God Himself has made it
extremely difficult for many to accept any idea of God speaking to
man in the Old Testament". [3])

While it might seem a difficulty that the law was no longer seen as
the foundation of the structure of Old Testament faith, it was recalled
that St Paul both in Romans and in Galatians had argued that the "Law
had come after". Although in the critical reconstruction this meant
"after the prophets", Paul's argument that it had come after the
prophetic-type religion of the patriarchs was not so different. In both
cases the emphasis was on the priority of the spiritual over the legal,
and so C.H. Dodd could write in his commentary on Romans 4:
"The Old Testament critic might put the point differently: the early-
prophetic stories of Abraham know nothing of circumcision, which
is mentioned only in the late priestly document". [4]) Where to Paul
promise preceded law, because Abraham lived four hundred years
before Moses, to the critic, it was because the JE document, which
described Abraham's faith, preceded the P document, which described
his circumcision, by four hundred years. Instead of the order "the
law and the prophets", the reversal to "the prophets and the law"

---

[1]) Cf. the double titles "This is the law of.." (6:9 etc) and "the Lord spake
unto Moses" (6:8). Similarly "if a man..." in 1:2, 2:1, 3:1 and "the Lord called
unto Moses" in 1:1.

[2]) J. L. McKenzie, *The Two-Edged Sword*, London (1959) p. 35.

[3]) *Ibid*, p. 36.

[4]) C. H. Dodd, *Romans*, Moffatt NT Commentary (1932) p. 69.

was necessary, [1]) and became the fundamental formula of the Higher Criticism following Wellhausen in 1880. [2])

One result of this reversal was what has been described as "the over-population of the post-exilic period" to which the bulk of the Old Testament was now ascribed. Schechter compared Kautzsch's time chart in his *Introduction* of 1894 with a chart of Bible chronology which appeared in 1866. Where the pre-critical writer had full details for before 1088 B.C. and had a blank after 450 B.C., the critical writer had the first thousand years blank and was full after 450 B.C. [3]) Where the question had been which if any of the Psalms were not Davidic, and which parts if any of the Pentateuch were not Mosaic, now the question was which if any at all were by these authors? [4])

That the reaction from tradition had gone too far has only slowly been perceived within the critical school, but enlightened Conservatives pointed it out from the beginning. Böhl and Bredenkamp protested at once against the "law-prophets" order being reversed to "prophets-law" and asked whether early Israel was in fact a people "not under the law"? Bredenkamp insisted that "law was the older sister of prophecy and its inspiration". [5]) Without questioning the critical analysis into four documents or the relative dating of the documents (p. 16), [6]) he nevertheless asserted the authenticity of

---

[1]) It is on record that at least one Old Testament theology in two volumes, which prior to Wellhausen had followed the order "law-prophets," appeared in a second edition with the volumes reversed! Cf. A. Duff, *History of Old Testament Criticism*, New York (1910) p. 139.

[2]) Although Wellhausen originated neither the hypothesis of the late date, nor that of sources, his name is usually associated with Graf's, because of the thorough-going way in which he buttressed Graf's theory by the source analysis. He took over Hupfeld's theory that there were four sources in the Pentateuch— the Jehovist (J), the Elohist (E), the Priestist (P) and the Deuteronomist (D). This "four source hypothesis" of Hupfeld in 1853 replaced the "two source hypothesis", based on the alternation of the divine names, Jahweh and Elohim, drawn up by Astruc just a century before in 1753.

[3]) S. Schechter, "The Study of the Bible" (1899) in *Studies in Judaism*, Series 2, London (1908) p. 41.

[4]) *Ibid*, p. 39.

[5]) C. J. Bredenkamp, *Gesetz und Propheten*, Erlangen (1881) pp. 202-03.

[6]) The critical school found a fixed date for one of the sources, Deuteronomy, in its connection with Josiah's Reform in 621 B.C., and used this as a pivot on which the whole traditional structure of the history and literature could be turned. The Jahwist-Elohist source (mainly the dual narrative of Genesis, Exodus and the second half of Numbers, omitting the ritual references but including the laws of Exod. 20-24 and 32-34) was shown to be older than 621 B.C., but the Priestist (comprising the ritual sections of the narrative and the laws between Exod. 25 and Num. 10, including the whole of Leviticus) to be later.

law-giving by Moses. The prophets knew the covenant (p. 54). The law was no more the product of Judaism than the Christian religion was the product of the Church (p. 202). Law had been the foundation.

Böhl saw both prophecy and law as predating Moses. [1] Pre-Mosaic prophecy is found in the prophetic-type patriarchal religion, and pre-Mosaic law in Exod. 5:1 and 1 Jn 2:7 ff (cf. 3:11ff) (p. 10). He drew attention to the Pauline insight of the law as a parenthesis ("*pareisēlthen*") and made

THE DEFENCE

"The law came in between .." Rom. 5:20

That the prophets were themselves heirs to tradition was recognized also by C.G. MONTEFIORE when he asked in 1891 why the prophets said they were harking back to old traditions (Amos 2:10-12; Hos. 13: 4, 12:14; Is. 1:21, 26; Hos. 4:6, 8:1, 12; Jer. 2:2,3) if they were innovating? [2] Kuenen's answer that where the idea of development is unknown "the new ideas were immediately regarded as old ones revived" [3] is judged as hardly satisfactory. Moses must have had a larger place than the critical school allowed him.

GLADSTONE was another who could not see how the law could be entirely detached from the name of Moses: "Supposing it to be granted that this or that portion of the Legislative Books may have been an addition in the way of development, of an appendage and supplement to a scheme already existing, how and why it came to be placed under the shelter of the great name of Moses, but because that name had already acquired and consolidated its authority, from its being inseparably attached to the original gift of the law?" [4] There were better reasons for believing in Moses as lawgiver than Lycurgus in Greece, where the main evidence is merely that a Code has been attached to his name. In the case of Moses, however, his role as national founder and leader in the Exodus strengthens the likelihood that he also gave laws. [5]

These testimonies from the first years of criticism find their echo today in the current recognition that Israel from the first was a

---

[1] E. Böhl, *Zum Gesetz und zum Zeugniss,* Wien (1883).
[2] C. G. Montefiore, "Recent Criticism Upon Moses and the Pentateuchal Narratives of the Decalogue," *JQR* III (1891) p. 257.
[3] A. Kuenen, *The Religion of Israel,* Vol. I, London (1874) p. 371.
[4] W. E. Gladstone, *op. cit.,* p. 191.
[5] *Ibid.,* pp. 180-81.

people under law. VON RAD writes his *Old Testament Theology*, perhaps the major one of our time, again in the older "law-prophets" order, and asserts that "Wellhausen's revolutionary hypothesis that the law came not before but after the prophets... is only valid for the literary collection into major theological works (Deuteronomy and the Priestly Document) of traditions which in themselves are very much older than their collection. It is beyond question that God's will as expressed in law was announced to Israel as early as the earliest stage of Jahwism". [1]

In quite similar fashion, ZIMMERLI takes up the old question of law and prophets in his book of that title [2] and shows how Wellhausen was both right and wrong. He was right in removing the cultic legislation of the Priestly Document from the time of Moses (p. 42) but "even after the subtraction from the Pentateuch of the Priestly Document, as Wellhausen proposed, and of Deuteronomy, as de Wette had previously proposed, there still remains an element of law, which is rooted in the older sources" (p. 30). Admittedly the law in the form given to it by the Priestly Document is later than the prophets, but the prophets themselves belonged to a people who traced their origin to the proclamation of the law (p. 42). The question is, how far does Moses, or at least the law which came to bear his name at a very early period, precede the prophets? (p. 30).

Gladstone's point is also made again, but in a different connection, by PÈRE DE VAUX in a discussion of aetiology. [3] Aetiology does not create the tradition, nor does worship create it. Aetiology presupposes *some* prior fact to account for traditional ascriptions. "If there had never been a conquest of Canaanite cities one would never have dreamed of explaining such and such a ruin by an account of conquest". [4] The same must surely be said of Moses and the law.

Full circle is reached in 1966, when EISSFELDT, one of the greatest of literary critics, again returns to St Paul's "*pareisēlthen*" and writes an article bearing the title of this section "the law came in between" [5]

---

[1] G. von Rad, *Old Testament Theology*, Vol. II, The Theology of Israel's Prophetic Traditions, ET, Edinburgh (1965) p. 390.

[2] W. Zimmerli, *The Law and the Prophets*, Oxford (1965).

[3] "Aetiology"—the telling of a story about a past happening to account for a present condition.

[4] R. de Vaux, "Method in the Study of Early Hebrew History", in J. P. Hyatt (ed.) *The Bible in Modern Scholarship*, Nashville (1965) p. 24.

[5] O. Eissfeldt, "Das Gesetz ist zwischeneingekommen", *ThLZ* XCI (1966) cols 1-6.

and argues that this best describes some of the relationships. [1])

The sequel seeks to tell the story of these three chapters in the history of the study of

Moses and the law.

The enquiry will deal with the "middle books" of the Pentateuch rather than Genesis and Deuteronomy, and will cover three periods of sixty years.

---

[1]) It was only when this work was nearing completion and the formulas with which Wellhausen begins Parts I and II of his *Prolegomena* were being checked (see below pp. 48, 73), that the author discovered that this New Testament verse, which he had decided on to describe the modern view of the development of the law, not after the Exile, but between the Exodus and the Exile, had in fact been used by Wellhausen himself, as the formula introducing his Part III, to express his late date view that the law came between Israel and Judaism—"which things are an allegory" of one's debt to Wellhausen, even when one has forgotten it!

PART ONE

THE LAW BY MOSES

THE PRE-GRAFIANS (1805-1865)

CHAPTER TWO

BEFORE 1805

Before 1805 Pentateuchal criticism had already had a long history, but the laws of the Pentateuch had not been singled out for particular critical attention, except in the isolated instances mentioned in the last chapter. Discussion centred rather around the difficulty of Moses being the author of the Pentateuch as a whole than of the laws in particular. Where the laws were noticed the verdict was generally positive. It was felt that here, if anywhere, lay the Mosaic core of the Pentateuch.

SIMON, for example, thought that the repetitions in the Pentateuch precluded full Mosaic authorship, but specifically excluded repetitions in the laws, which might have been occasioned by some new contingency. [1] This, however, failed to explain, why so unimportant a regulation as that against seething a kid in the mother's milk should occur three times, while the all-important *Shema* appeared only once. [2] Documents alone could account for this, and a beginning was made with the isolation of the Law of the Covenant, the Ritual Decalogue and the Code of Deuteronomy.

The analysis into Jahwistic and Elohistic documents undertaken by ASTRUC stopped short of the legal material, [3] but EICH-

---

[1] R. Simon, *A Critical History of the Old Testament*, ET, London (1682) pp. 38-39. "I do not pretend to speak here of repetitions of the same thing which are in the different chapters or different books of the Law, for there may be reasons for repeating the same thing in several places according to some new contingency, as we see in the Commandments or Ordinances of the Law... But there is another sort of repetition that makes the text obscure". On R. Simon see further J. Steinmann, *Richard Simon et les origines de l'exégèse bibliques*, Paris (1960).

[2] Conservative replies to the problems of doublets and anachronisms were often more ingenious than convincing. Of the former, Albert Schweitzer mentions Osiander's claim that the temple was cleansed twice, the devils twice sent into the swine (once from one demoniac and once from two) and Jairus' daughter raised several times (*The Quest of the Historical Jesus*, ET, London ([2]1911) p. 13). Of the latter, Carpenter gives Bishop Watson's solution to the difficulty of the anachronistic reference to Dan in Gn. 14:14, alleged by Tom Paine as implying a later date than Judges 18, that Dan here was neither the town, nor the tribe but a river, in fact one of the two rivers that go to make up the Jordan! (*The Bible in the Nineteenth Century*, London (1903) pp. 10-11).

[3] J. Astruc, *Conjectures*, Bruxelles (1753). Duff places Astruc's analysis alongside that favoured by modern critics and finds remarkable agreement down to Gn. 17,

HORN,[1]) handled this also, and distinguished the Priest's Codex of the middle books from the people's law-book in Deuteronomy. Both books were Mosaic, and the former must already have taken its form on Mount Sinai, or the laws of the fourth book would have been included in it (II, pp. 419-20). It was to be expected that the people's law-book would be more frequently quoted in the later literature than that of the priests (p. 428). GEDDES rejected the two-document theory in favour of a series of fragments, many of which were later than Moses. He regarded the law as Mosaic and defended it against its critics. The Hebrew legislator, by giving a central sanctuary and the multitude of sacrifices, united the people to one another and to God. [2])

Four Preparatory Steps

A. The Isolation of the P Document

While this seventeenth and eighteenth century criticism did not propound the Grafian solution, it contributed to the first of the four lines of investigation that were to make it possible—the isolating of the P document. EICHHORN worked only with the two-document

---

the very point where only the later clue of a second Elohist could produce a satisfactory result. (A. Duff, *A History of Old Testament Criticism*, New York (1910) pp. 123-24).

[1]) J. G. Eichhorn, *Einleitung ins Alte Testament*, 3 vols, Leipzig (1781-1783). Eichhorn claimed that the credibility of the Pentateuch gained by the use of plural documents: "The harmony of the two narratives at the same time with their slight deviations proves their independence and mutual reliability". (II, p. 329).

[2]) A. Geddes, *The Holy Bible*, Vol. I, London (1792) p. xiv. In view of the later attitude of the Catholic Church to criticism it is noteworthy that Geddes, Astruc and Simon were all Catholics. Simon even justified his criticism by an anti-Protestant polemic: "Catholics, who are convinced that their religion depends not only on the text of Scripture but also on Church Tradition, are not shocked at seeing that the ravages of time and the negligence of copyists have introduced changes into the sacred books as well as profane ones. Only biased or ignorant Protestants are shocked at it". (*Critical History*, p. 8 cited by J. R. Thrane, *The Rise of Higher Criticism in England 1800-1870*, Microfilm (1956)). However, the Church was also shocked and condemned his views! See *The Cambridge History of the Bible*, pp. 195, 218 ff, where the lines of fellow-Catholic, Dryden, are quoted:

"If Scripture, though derived from heavenly birth,
Has been but carelessly preserved on earth..."

Criticism was in fact to prove a double-edged weapon. "The criticism that affected what was accepted on the Church's authority affected still more the authority of the Church, and the inquiry that learned to doubt what tradition had sanctioned grew into doubt of tradition". (A. M. Fairbairn, *The Place of Christ in Modern Theology*, London ([6]1894) p. 501).

analysis, as Astruc had done, but almost all the passages in Genesis later assigned to P went into his Elohim document. [1]) His successor at Jena, ILGEN detected a second Elohist, in 1798, and came near to accelerating the course of Pentateuchal criticism by fifty years, but was not followed by other critics, and gave up criticism for schoolmastering without ever carrying his work beyond the first volume dealing with Genesis. [2]) Another suggestion that was not taken up at the time, but was to receive its meed of praise from Wellhausen, was that of BUTTMANN, who in discussing the Flood-Myth in 1812 argued that the exact figures and chronology of the Elohist branded him as a later rather than an earlier writer than the Jahwist. [3]) This was in reply to de Wette, who had taken the opposite position. It was a remarkable anticipation of the late dating of P which was to be the hallmark of the Graf-Wellhausen view.

Although P as a separate document was not yet recognized, this was less of an impediment to the progress of investigation than might be imagined. The middle books of the Pentateuch are in any case one block of material, and results very like those of Graf could be reached by scholars working without any further analysis. [4]) A great step forward was taken when Deuteronomy was divided off from the middle books as a separate document. It was now possible to compare the codes of Deuteronomy and Leviticus as VATER [5]) did, and to show how such differences as those concerning the priestly dues, the Levites' income, and the relation between priests and Levites required different authorship. Vater found traces of a long history of development in the laws, some not being known in the early history, part of Deuteronomy being Josiah's law-book (IV, p. 684), and the Pentateuch itself being first compiled from these many fragments in the Exile (p. 686). Leviticus also showed traces of compilation as in the closing formula of chapters 1-7, the repeated injunction against eating

---

[1]) T. K. Cheyne, *Founders of Old Testament Criticism*, London (1893) p. 25.
[2]) K. D. Ilgen, *Die Urkunden des Jerusalem. Tempelarchivs*, Vol. I, Halle (1798).
[3]) P. Buttmann, *Mythologus*, Vol. I, Berlin (1828) p. 183. "Das... Elohim-Fragment schildert das Kommen und die Dauer der Flut in lauter Wiederholungen, und dabei mit genauen chronologischen Angaben, die das sichere Gepräg späterer Ausführung alter poetischer Sagen sind". First published 1812.
[4]) Cf. Perlitt on Vatke: "Ohne schon die einzelnen Quellenschriften des Pentateuch präzise abzugrenzen, wird Vatke durch 'innere Kritik', also durch Vergleich und Kombination divergierender Elemente, zu seinen entscheidenden Beobachtungen geführt". (L. Perlitt, *Vatke und Wellhausen*, Berlin (1965) p. 105).
[5]) J. S. Vater, *Commentar über den Pentateuch*, 4 vols, Halle (1802-1805).

the blood in 3:17, 7:26 and 17:10, and the assimilation of chapters 4 and 5 to each other (pp. 451-52).

B. The Dating of the D Document

This second chief line of investigation into the origin of Deuteronomy and the other legal material received its most noteworthy results at the hands of de Wette in 1805. In his doctor's dissertation,[1]) and his *Beiträge zur Einleitung*, he adopted for the first time, on an extensive scale, the method of historical criticism, i.e. the placing of the law codes against the historical books of the Old Testament to determine their date of origin in relation to the *praxis* revealed at each period. Graf and Wellhausen were to popularize this method in their definitive works, but de Wette laid the foundations and much of the super-structure on which they were to build. De Wette's first result was that Deuteronomy belonged to Josiah's Reform, [2]) rather than the Mosaic era, and was the latest portion of the Pentateuch. Deuteronomy required the centralization of the cult, but Samuel, Saul, David and Solomon sacrificed apart from any central sanctuary. Only from Josiah was this law known. The same was the case with the other laws of Deuteronomy. Saul's choice as king was not governed by the Deuteronomic law of kingship or any other law. Samuel's hesitation would be incomprehensible if Deuteronomy had been known to him.[3]) Internal evidence shows that this law is post-Solomonic, while the prohibition of the worship of the host of heaven must be later than Manasseh.

C. The Dating of the Levitical Laws

It was not only on Deuteronomy that de Wette laid his hand. He began the third line of investigation—that of the dating of the laws of Leviticus. The Pentateuchal laws of unity of worship, sacrifice

---

[1]) W. M. L. de Wette, *Dissertatio Critico-Exegetica*, Jena (1805). Seldom can such great results have followed from so slight a work. De Wette's historic dissertation is a slender brochure of a few pages but is *sehr wissenschaftlich*.

[2]) Others before him had of course noted this, but had usually still held to Mosaic authorship. Cf. R. Smend, *Wilhelm Martin Leberecht de Wettes Arbeit am Alten und am Neuen Testament*, Basel (1958) p. 36. (Hereafter referred to as *de Wettes Arbeit*). Lessing's essay on Hilkiah (Göring edition XVIII, pp. 303 ff) is claimed by Hempel (*ZAW* LI (1933) p. 299) as possibly constituting Lessing rather than de Wette the father of Deuteronomic criticism. He connects 2 Kings 22 with the *core* of Deuteronomy by asking if Josiah's Scripture was not rather "nur diejenigen Hauptstücke des fünften Buches, welche das zweite Gesetz enthalten".

[3]) W. M. L. de Wette, *Beiträge zur Einleitung*, Vol. I, Halle (1806) p. 153.

and the distinction between priests and Levites are not kept in the later books (p. 226). He writes: "ohne Bedenken werden wir also die Opfergesetze des Levitikus als die Erfindung und Aufzeichnung späterer Priester verwerfen können". Aaron and his sons offered no more precisely than Abraham before them and Samuel after (p. 263). One may twist and turn as he will yet it is plain and clear that the prophet Jeremiah did not recognize the Sinaitic genuineness of Leviticus and other similar laws (p. 185). "The Book of Judges contains no direct reference, or even allusion to the Pentateuch and the Book of Joshua, ... none to the Law-book or Law of Moses, none to the peculiar institutions of the Jehovah cultus". The description of the tabernacle in Exod. 25-28 is modelled on the temple, and so the document that contains it must at least be as late as Solomon. The many unimportant things legislated for in such detail were impossible to Moses at the beginning, but belong to the developing policies of the state, and were the product, not of Sinai, but of the later priests, and the pedantry of Judaism (II, pp. 274-75, 279). The laws regarding the *Gottesdienst* in the Pentateuch are subject to *successiver Ausbildung* —gradual development (I, p. 265). In this de Wette stated the basic principle of Grafianism. [1])

D. The Attack on the Cultic History

One other obstacle stood in the way of the new theories—that of the cultic history given in the Old Testament itself in such books as Chronicles and Joshua,—and de Wette did not hesitate to face it. The first section of his *Beiträge* was devoted to a consideration of the value of the Chronicler as a witness to the early existence of Mosaic institutions and law. [2]) Eichhorn had claimed that the reliability of I and II Chronicles was attested by the author's careful use of historical sources. De Wette replied that whatever sources were used was unimportant, as one author's mind alone was reflected throughout (p. 61). In the Chronicler's use of Samuel and Kings, where he can be checked, he is slovenly and tendentious. His work is marked by a preference for the Levites, a love of marvels, a partiality towards Judah and a hatred of Israel—making it completely unreliable. [3])

---

[1]) A. T. Chapman, *Introduction to the Pentateuch*, Cambridge (1911) pp. 30 and 37.
[2]) W. M. L. de Wette, *Beiträge zur Einleitung*, Vol. I, Chap. I.
[3]) E. L. Curtis and A. A. Madsen, *Chronicles*, *ICC*, Edinburgh (1910) p. 46, summarizing de Wette.

This verdict on Chronicles was to be echoed by Graf, who like de Wette was to devote one part of his major work to this book alone. Until Chronicles is disposed of there can be no Grafianism. Almost every advocate of the new theories between de Wette and Graf had to take up this study, so that we may well describe it as a fourth line of investigation in this period. De Wette was answered by Dahler in 1819, [1]) and he, in immoderate terms, by Gramberg in 1823. [2]) In 1834 Movers, in a work that was to be influential until Graf, largely rehabilitated the Chronicler's reputation. [3]) Of all this investigation de Wette was the true originator, and in Wellhausen's view was not improved on by any later critic including Graf himself. "The difficulty ... is not to collect the details of evidence, but so to shape the superabundant material as to convey a right total impression". This de Wette did. [4])

Along with the rejection of Chronicles went excisions from the Book of Joshua of the passages referring to a written law of Moses and the fully developed priestly institutions of the latest parts of the Pentateuch. Geddes had already perceived that Joshua had been compiled by the same author as the Pentateuch and was its necessary appendix. [5]) De Wette now argued that it was not an old book, and its witness to Mosaic law was therefore useless. [6]) Once the principle of cultically flavoured interpolations in the historical books was admitted, the way was open for the removal of all the evidence contrary to the new hypothesis.

---

[1]) J. G. Dahler, *De Librorum Paralipomenōn*, Lipsiae (1819).
[2]) C. P. W. Gramberg, *Die Chronik nach ihrem geschichtlichen Charakter und ihrer Glaubwürdigkeit neu geprüft*, Halle (1823).
[3]) F. C. Movers, *Kritische Untersuchungen über die biblische Chronik*, Bonn (1834).
[4]) J. Wellhausen, *Prolegomena*, Edinburgh ([2]1885) p. 172.
[5]) A. Geddes, *op. cit.*, p. xxi.
[6]) W. M. L. de Wette, *Beiträge zur Einleitung*, Vol. I, pp. 150-51.

CHAPTER THREE

THE YEARS 1805-1865

A. Grafians before Graf

In the group of critics that followed de Wette, several came near to the Grafian position.

In addition to his work on Chronicles, Gramberg in 1829 wrote on the cultus. [1]) Over seven periods of Old Testament history he traced the development of the sanctuary, the offerings, the priesthood, the festivals and other usages—institutions which were to be so often discussed in Grafianism. The tabernacle he found to be a poetic fiction (I, p. 20), and Leviticus post-Josianic, although some of its laws may have been Mosaic (p. 40). Josiah's law-book was part of Exodus (p. 305), Leviticus and Numbers were from the beginning of the Exile (possibly after Ezekiel), and Deuteronomy from the end (p. xxv). Sacrifice in the earlier time lacked sin and guilt offerings, but these came in with Leviticus (pp. 96, 123-24). In reaching these results, Gramberg worked without source analysis and took the evidence of Genesis as one. This had little adverse affect on his results because of the silence of P on cultic institutions in Genesis and because of the nearness of J and E to each other in time.

In similar fashion, George dealt with the feasts in 1835. [2]) In his preliminary section on source criticism, he claimed that the first trace of a law-book in the Old Testament was that of Deuteronomy in Jeremiah. A comparison of the laws of Leviticus and Numbers with those of Deuteronomy clearly showed them to be later. The Sabbath year of the latter was earlier than the Levitical Jubilee Year (pp. 28-37), the demand for centralization in Deuteronomy than its presupposition in Leviticus (pp. 38-44), and the unpropertied and undifferentiated Levitical priests of this book than the Levitical cities and threefold order of Levites, priests and high priests of the Levitical law (pp. 45-69). Deuteronomy was therefore prior to Leviticus and Numbers, and Ezekiel was the middle term between them. In the feasts proper, the Levitical dating to specific days of the month was a late character-

---

[1]) C. P. W. Gramberg, *Kritische Geschichte der Religionsideen des alten Testaments*, 2 vols, Berlin (1829-1830).

[2]) J. F. L. George, *Die älteren jüdischen Feste*, Berlin (1835).

istic, as was also the idea of sinfulness and the need of atonement. This came in only after the Exile (p. 293), when "the people had reached a consciousness of their sin and declension from God, and through outward gifts and cleanliness now wanted to avert the fearful wrath of God, and with it to bring about atonement, and that for this the priesthood should act as mediators" (pp. 73-74).

The year 1835 was fruitful in criticism, for in it appeared not only the above volume, but two New Testament works—Strauss' *Life of Jesus*, and Baur's *Pastoral Epistles*, and two further Old Testament works of the Grafian type—Vatke's *Biblische Theologie* and von Bohlen's *Genesis*.

VATKE followed the by now familiar negative method of arguing from the silence of the historical books of the Old Testament as to Mosaic institutions, to their non-existence, but took a step forward in attempting a positive reconstruction of what the religion of Israel really was in each period. [1]) The resultant picture, couched in terms of Hegelian developmentalism, [2]) was not a reassuring one. Mosaic religion rose no higher than the star worship of Kaiwan and other nature deities. [3]) The antithetic principle of prophetic individualism struggled in vain with this older worship until after the eighth century. It was only after the Exile that the synthesis of the fixed ritual of the Pentateuch became possible (p. 216). [4]) So full a system at the beginning was incredible. Israelite religion had a much more lowly origin. Moses was a beginner, not a completer. [5]) If he had given a law at all, it was no more than the Ten Commandments. [6]) The prophets

---

[1]) Perlitt speaks of him as sharing de Wette's passion for both history and systematic theology, and so using his literary criticism to build a Biblical theology (*Vatke und Wellhausen*, p. 93).

[2]) Hegel's dialectic of an antithesis of protest challenging the thesis of the *status quo* and emerging as a synthesis at a higher level, allied itself to the age-long speculation of the Third Reich. Augustine had written of an age before the law (childhood), an age under the law (manhood) and an age beyond law (old age). This "Greisenalter des Geistes", Hegel found in Christianity, the first absolute religion. Vatke saw the three stages of the Old Testament as the nature religion of the pre-history, the Mosaism and prophecy of the eighth century B.C. ff reacting from the nature religion, and the writings of Jeremiah, Ezekiel and the Exile as the final stage.

[3]) W. Vatke, *Die Biblische Theologie*, Vol. I, Berlin (1835) pp. 184-245.

[4]) Ezekiel could not have written Chaps 40-48 if Leviticus and Numbers had been in existence. Instead he had said that the law in the desert was not good. (So H. P. Smith on Vatke in *Essays in Biblical Interpretation*, London (1921) p. 138).

[5]) Vatke, *op. cit*, pp. 200 ff. Cf. Perlitt, *op. cit*, p. 106.

[6]) Priests and Levites are not distinguished by the older prophets (Vatke, p. 348).

were the true "originals" in Israel (p. 481). Not until the legal period
after the Exile was Moses exalted as a lawgiver, the tabernacle as the
central sanctuary, and the idea of atonement as basic in sacrifice
(p. 535). [1])

A similar beginning of Israelite religion in polytheism was posited
by VON BOHLEN in the long introduction to his Genesis commentary. [2])
The argument from non-use—neglect of the one sanctuary (ET,
p. 171), no sacerdotal caste (p. 187)—is again used to date the
Pentateuch after the Exile.

> "After having been neglected in its most weighty enactments, from
> the death of Moses downwards, it is only after a thousand years have
> passed away that we find its laws observed even to their minutest
> particular; whereas in every other instance upon record, legislative
> systems have been observed with the greatest strictness at the period
> of their first introduction, and have only fallen by slow degrees into
> neglect" (pp. 132-33).

The counter argument that the Middle Ages show a similar neglect
of the Justinian Code provides no parallel in that the whole system
of religion was not then founded on the code as the Mosaic was
(p. 133).

Furthermore the circumstances of the code's alleged origin tell
against it.

> "The Levitical institutions of the Pentateuch are... of such a nature
> that they could not possibly have been enacted by any single individual;
> no man could have founded so complete a hierarchy, and least of all
> could the leader of a wandering tribe done so, who in truth was little
> likely, on an expedition in itself so adventurous, to have thought
> of encumbering himself with 'all the heavy baggage' as Goethe terms
> it, 'of petty religious observances' " (p. 284).[3])

---

[1]) Sin offerings and guilt offerings were lacking of necessity in the earlier
time, for "wozu auch die Satzungen von Sünd- und Schuldopfern, wenn das
Bewusstsein der menschlichen Sündhaftigkeit nicht lebendig erweckt... wird".
(pp. 218-19). The period of the Judges was a time of development not apostacy,
and did not require to be grieved over. The sense of sin arose late.

[2]) P. von Bohlen, *Die Genesis historisch-kritisch erläutert*, Königsberg (1835)
ET (1855). The introduction comprises Vol. I of the English translation.

[3]) Von Bohlen thought Leviticus only paralleled by the Brahmin ritual of his
beloved India about which he had written a major work (*Ancient India*) and to
which he planned to travel

"aber Gott und der König und mein Weibchen sprechen 'Nein,'
Und der Pilger nach Indien fror in Königsberg ein".
The last line was to prove only too true. He succumbed to the German frosts
in 1840, when only fortyfour. (*Ibid*, pp. xviii, xxiiii).

Von Bohlen's work was dedicated to de Wette and is interesting for the reaction it called forth from that scholar. After reading the volume DE WETTE wrote to the author:

> I always remained uncertain how far I ought to carry my view that the Levitical system was established in a later age, for I could not deny that Moses had a share in it, and even now cannot come to any determination upon this point. You have carried out this view securely and firmly. I will not shun the investigation and the results shall hereafter be made known to you.[1])

B. THE ANSWER OF DE WETTE

De Wette had concluded his letter by expressing the hope that he would be able to offer a critique in due course. This appeared two years later in *Theologische Studien und Kritiken*, and was a fullscale review, not only of von Bohlen, but of the three works of 1835—von Bohlen's, Vatke's and George's. [2]) De Wette's considered estimate is unfavourable to these negative critics, who have "suspended the beginnings of Hebrew history, not upon the grand creations of Moses, but upon airy nothings".

> His criticism is as follows. If Deuteronomy was the first law as they now say, why is it called the second law and placed in this position in the order of books? (p. 969). The dry style of the middle books is as certainly older than the mystical-allegorical handling of history in Deuteronomy, as this is younger than the epic handling of the other books (p. 970). Is it probable that for eight hundred years, while Israel had the sagas of Moses, the Judges and Samuel, she had no law? Mosaic law and saga must have gone hand in hand, and their development was as unlikely in the post-exilic period as in the Mosaic Age (p. 971). The laws were the product of the priests who sat in Moses' seat in the period between Moses and David, and some must have been from Moses himself as the founder of the theocracy (p. 973).[3])
> It is not at all certain that we can infer that there was no sacrifice in the time of the Judges, because we cannot detect traces of sacrificial laws then. Our knowledge of the religious usages of that dark period

---

[1]) W. M. L. de Wette, letter of 11th Oct. 1835 quoted in Translator's Preface, ET, von Bohlen, *Introduction to the Book of Genesis*, Vol. I, London (1855) p. xxvi.

[2]) *Ibid*, Rec. "Vatke, 'Relig. A.T.,' George, 'Die älteren Jüdischen Feste,' von Bohlen, 'Die Genesis,'" in *ThStKr* X (1837) pp. 947-1003.

[3]) De Wette wrote: "Ich glaube, es muss eine feste Voraussetzung der Kritik des Pentateuchs bleiben, dass Mose nicht nur die Zwei-Tafelgesetze, sondern auch noch andere Gesetze gegeben und die wichtigsten Einrichtungen des theokratischen Staates, wenn auch nicht geradezu gegründet, doch befohlen und angeordnet habe".

is not sufficiently accurate for any such inference. David had priests, and made Levites temple servants. The exaggerations of Chronicles have this much historical foundation (p. 975). The division of the Kingdom required new laws of centralization because of the end of the local sanctuaries (p. 978). Different local sanctuaries account for such different usages as the sin offering and trespass offering (p. 974). Some laws were ideal and never brought into practice, e.g. that of the Levitical cities (p. 976). Some lived on in private priestly circles and not in the open (p. 976). Some were only summarily given, not completely, and nothing can be built on their omissions (p. 977). The Day of Atonement with its Azazel demonology is certainly not late (p. 971).

It may be thought that by this attitude de Wette went back on the work of his youth thirty years earlier, but this was not really so. Certainly his emphasis had veered around, but the same set of facts were patent of both interpretations. In youthful irresponsibility he had delighted to tear down, and could argue from the silences to the non-existence of some Mosaic laws. A universal negative is, however, notoriously difficult to prove, and silence certainly could not prove that no Mosaic law existed.

As the writer of an *Introduction* in 1817, [1]) and in its successive re-editings, he had been compelled to build up, where once it had sufficed to tear down. His view had always been that the priestly laws and narrative were earlier than the Deuteronomic. As we have seen

---

[1]) W. M. L. de Wette, *Lehrbuch der historisch-kritischen Einleitung*, 6th ed., Berlin (1845), first published 1817, ET from the 5th ed., (1840) by Theodore Parker, Boston (1843). That de Wette had not changed his essential position is clear from the retention, in the successive editions of his *Introduction*, of the following statements. "Though it may be admitted that among the Mosaic laws, some may be old and genuine, yet at least the proof of their originality, which has been sought for in their relation to the state of the nation while in the wilderness is uncertain" (pp. 72-73 of ET, Vol. 2, Boston 1859). "The observance or non-observance of particular laws, the appearance or non-appearance of particular legal institutions, in a certain period, can prove nothing either for or against the existence of a written law book. But the internal reasons which tend to show the date of the different legal fragments of the Pentateuch, may be confirmed by the circumstance, that we can find in the history a gradual progress in the observance of the Law. Thus, in the state and development of the formal worship of Jehovah at the time of David and Solomon, we see the result of the influence of the Elohistic document. In the Reformation effected by Josiah, (624 BC) we find men forbidden to worship Jehovah freely, in various sacred places, as had previously been the practice. This is the result of the book of Deuteronomy, which was written about that time" (p. 158). The Chronicles problem still looms large and receives sixtythree pages to only twentythree for Kings.

Buttmann, [1]) and later Wellhausen, [2]) criticized him for this. His final view of the documents as stated in the fifth and sixth editions of his *Introduction* placed the composition of the Elohist in the period of the early kings (p. 218), the Jahwist in that of the prophets (p. 219), and Deuteronomy in the Assyrian Age (p. 220). If a name was to be given to the change in de Wette, it could be said that he had passed from the negative and agnostic criticism of the Fragment Hypothesis to the positive source criticism of the Supplementary Hypothesis. He remains a salutary warning of the danger of hasty generalizations built upon only part of the evidence. This logical fallacy of the undistributed middle was to be the major pitfall of Grafianism.

It was necessary to return to de Wette at this point, because it was his position, rather than that of Vatke, George, and von Bohlen that was to dominate Old Testament study. By concentrating on the latter the impression may have been given that they were an influential school, but this was not so. Their work attracted little attention, and what there was, was unfavourable, even contemptuous as when de Wette said that "the coming to the surface of this hypothesis was necessary only to complete the entire round of possible assumptions", and that "the only thing lacking to make it attractive was truth". [3]) Hupfeld characterized it as "a monstrous error that turned everything topsy-turvy and perverted and entangled the questions at issue and did not solve them". [4]) The influential schools of Old Testament thought at this time were two—Conservative apologists, Hengstenberg, Hävernick, Keil, and Ranke and the adherents of the Supplementary Hypothesis, Stähelin, Bleek, Tuch and Ewald.

C. THE CONSERVATIVE SCHOOL

Of the Conservative writings, those of HENGSTENBERG were the most considerable. Writing the second and third volumes of his *Beiträge zur Einleitung* [5]) in 1836 and 1839, he devoted much attention

---

[1]) P. Buttmann, *op. cit.*, pp. 208-14.

[2]) J. Wellhausen, *Geschichte Israels*, Berlin (1878) p. 173, where he ridicules those who hold fast to a hypothesis a few decenniums old, "for such is de Wette's discovery that Deuteronomy is more recent than the Priest's Code"—a statement dropped in the 2nd ed, *Prolegomena* (1883).

[3]) Cited W. H. Green, "Professor Robertson Smith on the Pentateuch", *Presbyterian Review*, III (1882) p. 110.

[4]) Green, *loc. cit.*

[5]) E. W. Hengstenberg, *Dissertations on the Genuineness of the Pentateuch*, ET, 2 vols, Edinburgh (1847), first published 1836-1839.

to Vatke, von Bohlen, and George, as well as to de Wette, who in his opinion remained unanswered in his time (II, pp. 2-4). In the first section of his work (I, pp. 69-212), he lists traces of the Pentateuch in early Old Testament books such as Amos and Hosea, and in the fourth section (II, pp. 1-121), similar traces in the debated book of Judges. In the seventh section (II, pp. 283-364), he answered in detail the alleged differences in the laws of the various codes. His arguments are not always convincing, but they were influential in preventing the spread of Grafianism in his day and still remain almost all that can be said for the Conservative side.

HÄVERNICK's work [1]) was also weighty, but less well arranged. KEIL's, being but a section of his general *Introduction*,[2]) was slighter, but his views found frequent expression in his elaborate commentaries on the books of the Pentateuch. RANKE's two volumes, published respectively in 1834 and 1840,[3]) illustrate the significance of 1835, and the critical writings which appeared then, in the history of criticism. Where the 1834 volume is concerned with the "fragmentary" hypothesis of Vater, which is answered by an appeal to the unitary structure and theme of the Pentateuch,[4]) the 1840 volume answers the new "development" hypothesis in such matters as the differences between Deuteronomy and the other law books in the matter of the priests and Levites (Vater), the unity of worship (de Wette) and the festal calendar (George). The preoccupation of the critical school with the former of these concerns in the shape of the Supplementary Hypothesis prevented the latter from re-emerging for a quarter of a century.

D. THE SUPPLEMENTARY HYPOTHESIS

The Supplementary Hypothesis was perhaps first represented in STÄHELIN in 1830, [5]) although he acknowledges the earlier work of de Wette in showing the connectedness of Vater's Elohim fragments, and of Ewald, in showing the unity of the "genealogies" docu-

---

[1]) H. A. C. Hävernick, *A Historico-Critical Introduction to the Pentateuch*, ET, Edinburgh (1840), first published 1837.

[2]) K. F. Keil, *Manual of Historico-Critical Introduction*, ET, Edinburgh (1869), from the 2nd ed. First published 1853.

[3]) F. H. Ranke, *Untersuchungen über den Pentateuch aus dem Gebiete der höheren Kritik*, 2 vols, Erlangen (1834 and 1840).

[4]) For unity of structure, appeal is made to the *toledoth* series and the chronology, which were later to be isolated as the hallmarks, not of the Pentateuch as a whole, but of the P document, the final editorial redaction into which the other sources were fitted.

[5]) J. J. Stähelin, *Kritische Untersuchungen über die Genesis*, Basel (1830).

ment. [1]) The former had been at fault in not allowing for a similar unity in the Jahwist, and the latter by resolving Jahwist and Elohist into one. The use of the divine names and the differences in style show plainly that there are two documents, not one, in Genesis, of which the Elohist was the *"Grundschrift"* and the Jahwist the *"Ergänzer"*.

In a second work, [2]) Stähelin carried his investigation to the middle books of the Pentateuch. He showed that there was a corresponding first and second legislation, of which the first recorded five feasts and the second three, together with other differences, e.g. in naming the months and preparing the Passover (p. 26). This first legislation has the style and vocabulary of Gn. 1—2:3 and must belong with the *Grundschrift* (pp. 55-60). It was probably Mosaic. The second legislation found in the two Books of the Covenant in Exod. 19-24 and 34 had the style of the Jahwist *Ergänzer* and agreed in the form of the laws with Deuteronomy, with which it must belong. It represented a much later modification of the five feast legislation into three, by the dropping of trumpets and atonement to suit conditions in Canaan, which did not allow so many absences from home (pp. 60-65, 72ff and 164). This *Ergänzer* may have been the Deuteronomist. This linking of the Books of the Covenant (JE) with Deuteronomy (D) anticipates Graf, but the placing of the combined work after P is the reverse order to that which Graf was to adopt.

The view that came to prevail in the Supplementary School, however, was different again. As stated by EWALD in his *History of Israel* (1843-1852), [3]) P or the Book of Origins, was to be placed between the Book of the Covenants and the Prophetic Narratives (JE). Deuteronomy retained its position at the end of the series. The Original

---

[1]) H. Ewald, *Die Komposition der Genesis*, Braunschweig (1823). As epitaph to the Fragment Hypothesis the words of Addis are apt: "It was right in its affirmation of various origin: it was wrong in its denial of unity. Real unity of plan may consist with diversity of origin". (W. E. Addis, *The Documents of the Hexateuch*, Vol. I, London (1892) p. xxvi).

[2]) Stähelin, *Kritische Untersuchungen über den Pentateuch*, Berlin (1843).

[3]) H. Ewald, *History of Israel*, ET, Vol. I, London (1869) pp. 68-132, first published 1843. Ewald, who in 1827 became Eichhorn's colleague and later successor at Göttingen, had been only nineteen when he produced the work on the unity of Genesis mentioned above, which gave him his doctor's degree. (Cf. A. R. Gordon, "Ewald", *ExpT* XXV (1913-1914) pp. 511-16 and W. Zimmerli, *The Law and the Prophets*, p. 20 where fascinating personal details of his stormy career are given—three dismissals from professorial posts for political insubordination and three charges of insulting the king—illustrating Wellhausen's inscription on his copy of his teacher's portrait "his hand against every man and every man's hand against him" (Gn. 16:12)).

Document or *Urschrift* P was to be dated from Solomon, and E and J were mere supplements to it from the tenth to the eighth centuries. By thus recognizing two Elohist sources, combined and supplemented by the Jahwist, Ewald to some extent "disassociated himself from the supplement hypothesis" and "produced a sort of combination documentary and supplement hypothesis". [1])

TUCH in his Genesis commentary,[2]) specifically took issue with the argument from silence as stated by de Wette and von Bohlen. Offerings are naturally not yet Levitical in the *Grundschrift* in Genesis (p. xlviii), but have become so by the time of the *Ergänzer* (p. lii). Institutions out of the law everywhere push themselves through in the Historical Books (p. lxix). There are eight hundred traces of the Pentateuch in the Prophets (p. lxxi). The prophetic rejection of sacrifice relied on by von Bohlen, is in opposition only to the dead spirit of it, as Micah 6:8 makes clear, and presupposes the existence rather than the non-existence of the law (p. lxix). The *Grundschrift* has no trace of a central sanctuary, and is to be placed before David (p. lxxii), the Jahwist Supplementer between Solomon and Uzziah, and nearer the former than the latter (p. lxxvii).

BLEEK'S *Introduction* also followed the Supplementary Theory of an E *Grundschrift* worked over by J and finally redacted by D in the Age of Manasseh. The bulk of Leviticus is shown to be Mosaic by the use of such phrases as "outside the camp" in Lev. 1-7, 13-14 and 16, "the door of the tabernacle" in Lev. 17 and the omission of the king from the sacrificial list in Lev. 4.[3]) Other laws and the rest of the Pentateuch are post-Mosaic. It was substantially this position which SAMUEL DAVIDSON introduced to English readers in his *Introduction* in 1862-1863.[4]) This work was noteworthy for its wide acquaintance with German criticism, which had not before had a favourable hearing in England.[5]) Although it had been represented before 1850 by the

---

[1]) G. Fohrer, *Introduction to the Old Testament*, ET, New York (1968) pp. 108-09.

[2]) F. Tuch, *Commentar über die Genesis*, 2nd ed, Halle (1871), first published 1838.

[3]) F. Bleek, *Einleitung in das Alte Testament*, Berlin (1860) p. 184. ET, London (1869), from 2nd ed. 1865.

[4]) S. Davidson, *Introduction to the Old Testament*, 3 vols, London (1862-1863).

[5]) It was said that, when Pusey began to learn German in 1825, in order to study German Old Testament works, there were only two persons at Oxford who understood it (J. E. Carpenter, *The Bible in the Nineteenth Century*, p. 17). John Henry Newman decided that Pusey's early writings were unsettling and did not learn German (H. Chadwick, "Der Einfluss der deutschen protestantischen Theologie auf die englische Kirche im 19. Jahrhundert", *EvTh* XVI (1956) pp. 565, 561). Cambridge University had no book by F. C. Baur before 1877 (*ibid*, p. 565). The notorious collection of essays, in the main by university professors, *Essays and Reviews*, which in 1861 had an impact like *Honest to God* a century

great preacher, F. W. Robertson,[1]) it was mainly associated with rationalists like F. W. Newman.[2])

In a work on the *History of the Hebrew Monarchy*,[3]) Newman insisted that Leviticus and Numbers were also piece-meal works like Genesis, and had been a growth rather than a composition. Samuel had not known Deuteronomy on kingship or he would scarcely have hesitated (p. 297), nor was "the idea admitted either by the nation or by any king of Judah earlier than Hezekiah, that 'in Jerusalem alone men ought to worship'. The most pious prior to this used the High Places without any suspicion of offending" (p. 122). Deuteronomy was from the time of Josiah (pp. 295-300). Thus far his was an almost solitary English voice.

later—fifth edition sold out in two weeks, the sixth to ninth in four more, so that lending libraries had to be formed to make it available at twopence a day (Thrane, *op. cit*, p. 493), praised by agnostics like F. Harrison, blamed for making agnostics of men contemplating holy orders like Morley, Lecky, Pater and Sidgwick (L. Elliott-Binns, *English Thought 1860-1900*, London (1956) pp. 21-22), protested by petition from ten thousand clergy (A. O. J. Cockshut, *Anglican Attitudes*, London (1959) p. 72), its seven authors characterized as "the seven extinguishers of the seven lamps of the Apocalypse" and "the seven against Christ"—is antique in its Pentateuchal criticism. Its most daring statements are the disharmony of Genesis and geology, and Bunsen's views on the non-Mosaicity of the Pentateuch (p. 60) and the laws (p. 62). (Page references to the eighth edition of 1861). Editor, F. Temple's opening essay on "the world's coming of age" is modern enough, a century later, although it goes back to Lessing almost a century before! An English translation of Lessing's *Education of the Human Race* by F. W. Robertson had appeared in 1858 but the main purveyor of Lessing's writings in England, and of "Germanism" in general was perhaps S. T. Coleridge (See Chadwick, *op. cit*, pp. 566 ff and his *Lessing's Theological Writings*, London (1956) p. 48). The question of dependence is discussed at length in the 1956 edition of Coleridge's *Confessions, op. cit,* pp. 17-33.

[1]) His biographer writes of his 1850 Genesis sermons: "Neither did he shrink from putting his congregation in possession of the results of German criticism upon Genesis. He made them acquainted with the discussion on the Jehovah and Elohim documents, but he did not deny the Mosaic compilation of these documents.. While declaring that the Mosaic Cosmogony could not be reconciled with geological facts, [he] still succeeded in showing its inner harmony". (Quoted in the editor's preface to F. W. Robertson, *Notes on Genesis*, London (1877) p. viii). Robertson had been converted to criticism in an intellectual crisis, while touring Austria and Germany in 1846. (Cf. J. Tulloch, *Movements of Religious Thought during the Nineteenth Century*, London (1885) pp. 303-07 and Stopford Brooke's biography, *Life and Letters of Frederick W. Robertson*, Vol. I, London ([2]1880) pp. 103 ff. Cf. pp. 233, 319).

[2]) Newman, brother of the later Catholic cardinal, married to a Plymouth Brethren wife, himself an erstwhile convert of J. N. Darby, had also been a preacher and for a brief period a missionary in Persia.

[3]) F. W. Newman, *A History of the Hebrew Monarchy*, London ([2]1853), first dublished 1847. This work was described as "a combination of kissing and smiting under the fifth rib", because it politely preferred de Wette to Hengstenberg, and insisted on following German guides (pp. ix-xi).

E. THE RETURN TO SOURCE ANALYSIS

The downfall of the Supplementary Hypothesis and the coming of Grafianism was accelerated by the return to source analysis by HUPFELD in 1853. [1]) He complained that critics had concerned themselves with the supplements to the *Urschrift* rather than with the *Urschrift* itself (p. 5), and proposed a re-investigation of Ilgen's theory. When the Jahwist was removed from Genesis there still remained re-duplications such as those concerning the name Israel, the departure of Jacob, and the naming of Bethel. These were within the Elohist document itself and suggested the need of further division. When analysis was applied a second Elohist was readily separable from the first, although strangely enough, not so clearly demarked from the Jahwist, except for the use of the different divine name. The remaining *Urschrift* was a homogeneous document.

> It began in Gn. 1, continued through one half of the separated double narratives of Genesis, included the *toledoth* sections, and ran on into Exodus and the legal section of the middle books of the Pentateuch. In this section there was covenant and promise in Genesis, but no cult, offering, or altar, and no distinction of clean and unclean (p. 88). Quite different, and later in time, was the Jahwist with his patriarchal offerings and early difference of clean and unclean. Of a similar point of view to the Jahwist, but still later in time was the Second Elohist. No one of these sources supplemented another, but all three were put together by a redactor—J and E first, P and D afterwards. [2])
>
> BÖHMER, a pupil of Hupfeld, printed the text of the three sources in 1862 [3]) and essayed a dating—the P *Grundschrift* from the South in the time of David (p. 23), the Jahwist from the North in the time of Elisha (pp. 90-92), the Second Elohist from the North in the time of Jeroboam II (pp. 119-20) and the redactor from the time of Josiah (pp. 123-304).

---

[1]) H. Hupfeld, *Die Quellen der Genesis*, Berlin (1853). Lichtenberger describes Hupfeld as a pious Christian, hostile to allegorization and ingenious hypotheses! (F. Lichtenberger, *History of German Theology in the Nineteenth Century*, ET, Edinburgh (1889) p. 414). He saw his task as being that of "restoring the gospels of the Old Testament" which had become lost in a synopsis. After all the Syriac church had reacted from Tatian's *Diatessaron* back to "the gospels of the separated ones"! (But presumably because the Gospel four were already well established as canonical in a way which the Pentateuchal four were not).

[2]) Synoptic criticism was to provide a close parallel with the recognition that Matthew, the "second law" like D was late and not by the writer whose name it bore, Mark, the vigorous narrative writer was early like J, Luke supplementary like E, and John like P of a different order, ideological and the last to be written.

[3]) E. Böhmer, *Das erste Buch der Thora*, Halle (1862).

While this dating is still far from that of Graf, two steps forward had been taken. On the one hand, a part of the Elohist had been detached and could remain in the early history, when the remainder was made late (although, albeit, it was the last that was to become the first and the first last!) On the other hand, the combination of the new source with J before being attached to P and D, prepared the way for the dating of P after D. [1]) Graf's theory would never have won its way without these two discoveries, although Graf himself did not use them but worked on lines that ignored source analysis.

F. The First Grafians

Graf's [2]) method was again that of historical criticism. Addis says "like de Wette he began with a comparison of History and Law, but where de Wette argued from the sanctuary to the date of Deuteronomy, he argued chiefly from the priests and Levites to the date of P". [3]) There is a good deal more than this in Graf. In fact there was scarcely a detail advanced by the negative critics of the previous half century that was not incorporated into his system.

> In an early work, *Commentatio de Temple Silonensi* in 1855, he argued that the tabernacle was an idealization based on Solomon's temple, and had been projected into the Wilderness period by a post-exilic interpolator. In 1862 in a letter to his old teacher Reuss, he stated that the whole middle portion of the Pentateuch was post-exilic,[4]) and wrote in his Jeremiah commentary (on 7:22-23):
>> aus denselben geht vielmehr auf das unzweifelhafteste hervor, was sich ausserdem auch noch aus vielen innern Beweisen ergibt, dass die Ceremonialgesetze in der Mitte des Pentateuchs, und was damit zusammenhängt, wie die Beschreibung der Stiftshütte, den spätesten Bestandtheil des Pentateuchs bilden und erst in die Zeit nach dem Exil gehören.[5])
> These "viele innere Beweise" were offered in his *magnum opus* in 1865.[6])

---

[1]) J. B. Harford, "Since Wellhausen," *Expositor*, 9th series, IV (1925) p. 13.

[2]) Karl Heinrich Graf, 1815-1869. From 1849 to 1868 Graf taught languages as a school-master at Meissen, but was passed by for theological posts. (See G. Beer in *PRE* XXIII, pp. 588-92 and K. Budde and H. J. Holtzmann (ed.), *Ed. Reuss' Briefwechsel mit seinem Schüler und Freunde K. H. Graf*, Giessen (1904) for Graf's disappointment at missing preferment, constant ill-health (he died at 54), early doubts through Reuss' teaching and renewed confidence from 1840 ff. Cf. "The Reuss-Graf Correspondence", *ExpT* XVI (1904-1905) pp. 265-66).

[3]) W. E. Addis, *The Documents of the Hexateuch*, Vol. I, London (1892) p. xxxviii.

[4]) K. Budde and H. J. Holtzmann (ed.) *op. cit*, p. 501.

[5]) K. H. Graf, *Der Prophet Jeremia*, Leipzig (1862) p. 123.

[6]) Graf, *Die geschichtlichen Bücher des Alten Testaments*, Leipzig (1866). Actually published in 1865, vide Kuenen, *Hexateuch*, p. xix.

With de Wette's dating of Deuteronomy to Josiah as a pivot, he ranges over the laws showing how this one is pre-Deuteronomic and that post-Deuteronomic, and it is always JE and D that have the priority and P that is latest.

The three feasts of Deuteronomy are later than Elkanah's one, but not so late as P's five (p. 25). The eight day Feast of Tabernacles, and the fortynine year Jubilee are later than the seven day and seven year celebrations (p. 38). The Day of Atonement of P is unknown to Deuteronomy and the pre-exilic books and so is very late (p. 41). Priest and Levite are not distinguished until after the Exile, and P which knows this distinction is later than D which does not (pp. 42-47). Also late were P's tithe legislation (pp. 47-50), priestly dues from the offerings (pp. 50-51), tabernacle (pp. 52-65),[1]) cities of refuge (pp. 66 ff), offerings (pp. 69 ff) etc.

In a second section, Graf attacked the credibility of the Chronicler as a historical source, and while not going as far as de Wette, roundly rejected the view of Movers that the Chronicler was a mere copyist of sources. His was a tendency writing of little real value as history.

Graf was not alone in coming to these conclusions. He begins his work by a reference to his own teacher REUSS, who in 1850, had confidently predicted that the view that Leviticus was younger than Deuteronomy would soon be an integral part of Old Testament science.[2]) In the article in which these words occurred, Reuss argued that the *cultus* was not a creation of the Mosaic period (p. 332), Samuel did not know a priestly caste (p. 331), Israel had no central sanctuary until eight hundred years after Moses (p. 329) and the laws of the middle books of the Pentateuch were given for a concentrated community, not a great scattered nation. They were therefore impossible in the time of Moses or David and must date from after the Exile (p. 337). Reuss had taught these views to his pupils, Graf and Kayser, in Strassburg in 1833, but hesitated to come into print, except in this one article, until his own pupils shamed him into speaking out in his *L'histoire sainte et la loi* in 1879.[3]) He tells the story in the "Foreword" to his *Introduction* in 1881.[4])

---

[1]) If the tabernacle had been existing at Kiriath-Jearim, the ark would have been brought into it, or if elsewhere it could have been brought to the ark at Kiriath-Jearim to house it. (*ibid.* p. 52).

[2]) E. Reuss, "Judenthum", *Ersch und Gruber's Encyklopädie*, Leipzig (1850) p. 334. "... den Beweis, dass die andern Mosäischen Bücher jünger sind, was für mich nur ein einfacher Folgesatz des ersten ist, muss ich, um Weitläufigkeiten zu vermeiden, auf einen andern Ort versparen. Es wird, lange ehe diese Encyklopädie vollendet sein wird, ein integrirender Theil der kritischen Wissenschaft Vieler sein".

[3]) Reuss, *L'histoire sainte et la loi*, Paris (1879) especially pp. 23-24.

[4]) Reuss, *Die Geschichte der Heiligen Schriften Alten Testaments*, Braunschweig (1881) pp. vii and viii.

> My intuition [in 1833] was that the prophets preceded the law
> and the Psalms were younger than both.... . The Books of Kings
> blamed what the prophets by their example encouraged.

His student days had been passed in an atmosphere concerned with
belief in miracles, but "this greatest miracle of all, that Israel should
begin with a complete and finished cult, no one explained".

Another disciple of Reuss was ORTH, who in 1859 wrote articles on
the *Tribe of Levi* [1]) and the *Centralization of the Cult* [2]) which anticipated
Graf both in method and in result. The historical method is used in
detail to show the gradual development into the post-exilic period
of the Levites, the priestly dues and the sanctuary—three of the five
pillars on which Wellhausen built. Only the feasts and sacrifices
were omitted. Wellhausen and Duhm acknowledge their dependence
on this work of Orth.[3])

A work to which Graf refers is that of POPPER on the *Biblical Account
of the Tabernacle*.[4]) Popper sought to show, partly with the help of
the Septuagint, that there were in Exodus and Leviticus two accounts
of the tabernacle—that in Exod. 35-40 and Lev. 8 being later than
that in Exod. 25-30:18. It could not have received its present form
until long after the Babylonian Captivity.[5]) This book called forth a
review from Merx in which the post-exilic origin of the laws was
acknowledged.[6]) This was in 1865 and before Graf wrote. To Graf,
however, remains the achievement of giving the theory the complete
form that was to compel attention, even if not command assent.

---

[1]) J. Orth, "La tribu de Levi et la loi", *Revue de Theologie*, III, Paris (1859)
pp. 384-400.

[2]) Orth, "La centralisation du culte du Jéhovah", *ibid*, IV (1859) pp. 350-60.

[3]) J. Wellhausen, *Prolegomena*, p. 4; B. Duhm, *Die Theologie der Propheten*,
Bonn (1875) p. 17.

[4]) J. Popper, *Der biblische Bericht über die Stiftshütte*, Leipzig (1862).

[5]) But cf. now D. W. Gooding, *The Account of the Tabernacle*, Cambridge
(1959). Also A. H. Finn, "The Tabernacle Chapters", *JTS* XVI (1915) pp. 449-82.

[6]) A. Merx, "Aphoristische Bemerkungen über die Pentateuchkritik nebst
einer Besprechung von Popper, Dr. Julius, 'Der biblische Bericht über die Stiftshütte' (1862)", *Protestantische Kirchenzeitung für das evang. Deutschland* (1865),
No. 17, pp. 376-87.

CHAPTER FOUR

MOTIVES FOR GRAFIANISM

A vantage point has now been reached from which it is possible to look back over the first period to see if anything of the moods and motives that led to the rise of Grafianism can be traced.

A. Evolutionism

It is often asserted today that Grafianism was a child of Darwinism or Hegelianism, [1]) and is no longer cogent to an age not dominated by these philosophies. The longer view that has been taken of the history in this work prevents such a judgment being made. [2])

It is true that Graf wrote only six years after the appearance of Darwin's *Origin of Species* and in some of his phraseology reflected the evolutionary mood, as when he asked whether the law was to be regarded:

> following nature and analogy, as a fruitful seed of organic development, or as something from the first complete and giving the foundation of that future development.[3])

---

[1]) Delitzsch made the charge already in his *ZKWL* articles in 1882, when he spoke of the new system as "nach dem Schema der Darwinischen Anschauung von der thierischen Ahnenreihe des Menschen" (F. Delitzsch, "Urmosaisches im Pentateuch", *ZKWL* III (1882) p. 299). Cf. also his letter to Orelli of 20th December 1877: "Die Theologie der Gegenwart geht mit dem Darwinismus, welcher die Negation des Supernaturalen ist" and Orelli's comment of 1884 "charakteristisch ist aber bei Vatke wie bei Baur, dass von eigentlicher Offenbarung nicht die Rede ist, sondern mit einer Art theologischen Darwinismus das Höhere aus dem Niedrigen..abgeleitet wird". In his view both Baur and Vatke derived from Hegel. (E. Kappeler, *Conrad von Orelli*, Zürich (1916) pp. 331 and 371).

[2]) De Wette in 1805 could obviously have been neither Darwinian nor Hegelian! (Cf. Perlitt, *op. cit* (p. 190)). Herderian vitalism was, however, in the air—see below.

[3]) K. H. Graf, *Die geschichtlichen Bücher des Alten Testaments*, Leipzig (1866) p. 1. J. D. Smart, *Interpretation of Scripture*, Philadelphia (1961) p. 249 quotes S. R. Driver as saying "Progress: gradual advance from lower to higher, from the less perfect to the more perfect, is the law which is stamped upon the entire range of organic nature, as well as upon the history of the civilization and education of the human race". (Cf. also J. Wedgwood, *The Message of Israel*, London (1894) p. 302. "We have to take up the same changed view of the scriptures as... we have already been led to take up with regard to the outward world; as we have expanded the week of Creation into the milleniums of a still incomplete evolution, so we have to expand the one primeval giving of the Law on Sinai for a development of the Law prolonged through the whole history of [sic] the race").

But no one with the history before him can seriously maintain that Darwinism played any part in Graf's thought.

Moreover, as Wellhausen pointed out in reply to the charge that Graf's defenders taught the sudden entry into the world of the Israelite *cultus*, both this charge and that of Delitzsch and Zöckler that they taught Darwinism could not be true. [1]) The later the emergence of the law, the less cf real evolution there was, for as a one-sided critic of Wellhausen put it "out of a thousand years of history, only twenty really evolved—from Josiah to 586 B.C." [2]) In all the rest of this period not even Solomon, Elijah or Hezekiah made any difference. "What evolution there was, was really devolution, for it was a backward movement from the life of the green tree to the dead wood of legalism" (p. 102). It should be added in fairness that this is a gross caricature. Wellhausen repudiated the suggestion that he posited an abrupt appearance of the laws, [3]) and it was undoubtedly the smoothness of his system in its exhibition of the unfolding of Israelite religion that commended it, as e.g. Pfleiderer has testified. [4]) Whether this is rightly called "evolutionism" is best postponed until the debt to Hegel and Herder has been discussed. Perlitt writes:

> "Wie Herder dem optimistischen Fortschritts- und Aufstiegsglauben der Aufklärer widersprach, wie er 'vegetative Entwicklung von unten und göttliche Leitung von oben sanft' verknüpfte, so jagte auch Wellhausen keinem Fortschritt in der Geschichte nach, sehnte sich nach keiner Evolution (am wenigsten nach einer Evolutions-'Theorie') und verwarf die Vorstellung einer kausalmechanischen Bestimmtheit". [5])

---

[1]) J. Wellhausen, *Prolegomena*, p. 366. For Zöckler's charge cf. O. Zöckler, *Geschichte der Beziehung zwischen Theologie und Naturwissenschaft* Vol. II, Gütersloh (1879) p. 497.

[2]) W. L. Baxter, *Sanctuary and Sacrifice*, London (1895) pp. 37-41.

[3]) J. Wellhausen, *loc. cit*. Cf. F. W. Newman, (*op. cit*, p. xiii) "*The British Quarterly.*. announces that I represent 'the ceremonialism and sacerdotalism of the books of Moses to have been invented at a stroke, and its main features suddenly imposed'. . . On the contrary, I trace the ceremonial and the priesthood from Eli and Hophni and Phineas and Abimelech. I show it repressed under Saul, magnified under Solomon, growing socially influential under Asa and Jehoshaphat.. re-establishing itself.. under Josiah *after 500 years of growth* .. . Not the system only, but the books, I represent to have been a gradual product".

[4]) O. Pfleiderer, *The Development of Theology in Germany since Kant*, London (1890) p. 274.

[5]) L. Perlitt, *op. cit*, p. 185.

B. HEGELIANISM

Many writers have worked out in detail the connection between Hegel, Vatke, Graf, and Wellhausen. Wellhausen testified prominently at the end of his Introduction to the *Prolegomena* that it was from Vatke that he had learnt best and most [1] Vatke was certainly a Hegelian. He studied at Berlin while Hegel was there, quotes Hegel in his writings and gives a view of Israelite history in the schematic Hegelian framework. König pointed out from the first the similarity of Wellhausen's treatment, and was followed by Robinson, Kegel, Pedersen, Albright, and Kraus.

Robinson believed that this Old Testament form of Hegelianism would have the same fate as the New Testament form of it elaborated in the same year as Vatke by Baur. [2] KEGEL showed how Vatke himself outgrew this system, and in his latest writings, after forty years of working at Pentateuchal problems, came to another mind. Kegel, in the two parts of his book, [3] opposes Vatke, the opponent of the Graf-Wellhausen Hypothesis of 1882, [4] with Vatke, the founder of the hypothesis in 1835. He criticizes the Grafians for believing, that "what the Hegelian Vatke found *a priori*, was what the history of the Old Testament religion gives *a posteriori*" (p. 39). Vatke's latest view, that P was after all earlier than D, was more satisfactory. He admitted however, that Vatke still held to the principle of development.

In a second work, inspired by Friedrich Delitzsch's *Great Delusion*, Kegel returned to the attack with more violence. [5] The Hegelian Grafians were to blame for this final stage of Higher Criticism that made the Old Testament the devil's delusion. Delitzsch's anti-Semitism and Wellhausen's scorn of Judaism had a common basis in

[1] Wellhausen, *op. cit*, p. 13. Cf. also "Vatke's Buch ist der bedeutendste Beitrag, welcher überhaupt je zur Geschichte des alten Israel geleistet worden ist" from p. 4, which according to Perlitt *op. cit*, p. 167, was deleted from subsequent editions of the *Prolegomena* because of heavy attacks. But see Perlitt, p. 149 for Wellhausen's appreciative letter to the old Vatke in 1880.

[2] G. L. Robinson, "The Genesis of Deuteronomy," *Expositor*, 5th series, IX (1899) pp. 369-70. Cf. Orelli already in 1884 "Ich habe die Uberzeugung, dass wie die Baursche Bewegung so auch diese Vatkesche mit der Zeit wird überwunden werden". (E. Kappeler, *op. cit*, p. 372). Baur made no secret of his philosophical bent. He wrote: "Ohne Philosophie bleibt mir die Geschichte ewig tod und stumm" (cited from L. Elliott-Binns, *op. cit*, p. 90).

[3] M. Kegel, *Wilhelm Vatke und die Graf-Wellhausensche Hypothese*, Gütersloh (1911).

[4] W. Vatke, *Historisch-kritische Einleitung*, Bonn (1886), posthumously published. Vatke died in 1882.

[5] Kegel, *Away from Wellhausen*, ET, Nashville (1924).

Hegel's preference of Greek religion to Jewish (pp. 25, 76). [1]) Hegel's dislike of a transcendent God and his intervention in history reappears in Wellhausen's immanence and naturalism (p. 26). The criterion by which Wellhausen judged D to be older than P, viz. "that the idea, as an idea is older than the idea, as history" was pure Hegelianism (p. 38). The sooner scholars abandoned this philosophically and historically unsound theory the better. [2])

In 1931 PEDERSEN [3]) subjected the Hegel-Vatke-Wellhausen question to a searching examination and came to similar results, which have been repeated by ALBRIGHT, [4]) and in part by Kraus. [5]) KRAUS appeals to the three periods—of JE, of D and of P, through which Wellhausen traces his processes of centralizing, ritualizing and denaturizing—particularly the last—as Hegelian (pp. 243-44), [6]) but this is not the

---

[1]) A different reason is given by Delitzsch's own pupil, the Conservative Jewish scholar Hoschander, who ascribes Delitzsch's remarkable change to a "turning of his mind" resulting from the bitter disappointment of his ardent nationalistic hopes through the German defeat in World War I. (*JQR* XVI (1925-1926) p. 450). Friedrich Delitzsch should not be confused with his father Franz Delitzsch discussed earlier, and again below.

[2]) Kegel's work was not confined to these generalizing treatments. He had attempted to come to terms with crucial points of the Wellhausen system in his studies of Josiah's Reform (1919) and Ezra's Reform (1921). The latter work, together with a study of the Israelite priesthood, was translated into English, and appeared along with an abridgement of *Away from Wellhausen* in the composite American volume *The Aftermath Series* edited by H. M. Du Bose in 1923 and 1924.

[3]) J. Pedersen, "Die Auffassung vom Alten Testament", *ZAW* XLIX (1931) pp. 161-81.

[4]) W. F. Albright, "The Ancient Near East and the Religion of Israel", *JBL* LIX (1940) pp. 85-112; *From the Stone Age to Christianity*, Baltimore ([2]1946) Chap. II. Albright writes: "To the nationalistic Wellhausen there was something inspiring in the progress of biblical institutions from early Israelite anarchy to national unity and from alleged primitive fetishism to abstract monotheism, which foreshadowed the reign of the Hegelian *Geist*". ("The War and Biblical Studies" in H. R. Willoughby (ed.) *The Study of the Bible Today and Tomorrow*, Chicago (1947) p. 172). For a different estimate of Wellhausen's nationalism see Perlitt, *op. cit*, p. 179. Eissfeldt remarks that his work span exactly coincided with the Kaiserreich—1870-1918 ("Julius Wellhausen", *KS* I Tübingen (1962) p. 56).

[5]) H.-J. Kraus, *Geschichte der historisch-kritischen Erforschung des Alten Testaments*, Neukirchen (1956).

[6]) The process of denaturization, for example, is seen in the history of the Feast of Tabernacles, which in its earliest appearance in Judges 9:27 and 21:21 is a nature festival of wine-drinking, dancing and bride-capture, but by the time of the Deuteronomist in 621 B.C. has become connected with the Exodus and wilderness wanderings (e.g. living in tents—Dt. 16), and by the time of the Priestist and later Judaism is transformed into the *Simḥat Torah*, the rejoicing over the giving of the law. Hegel's three stages are thought to be illustrated here. (Kraus, *Worship in Israel*, ET, Oxford (1966) pp. 5-6).

impression left on every reader's mind. [1]) Wellhausen's one reference to Hegel in the *Prolegomena* is in connection with the rhythmic monotony of the Deuteronomic framework of Judges. When he says "one is reminded of the "*Satz*", "*Gegensatz*" and "*Vermittelung*" of the Hegelian philosophy, when one's ear has once been caught by the monotonous beat", [2]) it does not sound as if he is a Hegelian.

BENTZEN in his review of Pedersen, [3]) and COOK in a review of Kegel, [4]) thought that these scholars had not made out their case. The true originator of Grafianism was Reuss, who came to his view before Vatke, was not a Hegelian, and was put off from reading Vatke when he found Vatke was. [5]) George Adam SMITH says:

> It is indeed striking that the attempt to prove the late date of the Levitical legislation from principles of the Hegelian philosophy, which Vatke made in 1833 [*sic* ?1835] should have been ignored in the history of criticism; and that that late date should not have been accepted till Graf and others proved it by *inductive evidence* in 1866 and following years.[6])

With this verdict agrees R. SMEND in his careful investigation of 1958 into the relation of these Bible critics to the philosophical

---

[1]) Kraus agrees, however, that the end result is different in the two systems for it is really the first not the last period that Wellhausen prefers (p. 248), and this is drawn out further by *Hahn* in his illuminating article "Wellhausen's Interpretation of Israel's Religious History", (J. L. Blau (ed.) *Essays in Jewish Life and Thought* (Baron Festschrift), New York (1959) pp. 299-308) where it is shown that whereas for Vatke the three Hegelian periods were the thesis of simple patriarchal worship, the antithesis of prophetic criticism and the synthesis of purified post-exilic ceremonial, for Wellhausen the real antithesis is between the natural, early religion in which worship grew out of life, and the artificial legalistic ritual of the post-exilic period. The latter was a decline, not a higher synthesis, a de-naturing, a degeneration—devolution not evolution (pp. 300-301). *S. R. Külling* seeks to minimize these differences by drawing attention to the tragic element in Hegel's "owl of Minerva" passage, and by insisting that Wellhausen's end result was only *apparently* a backward step (he twice uses *scheint*), as law was necessary to preserve religion and to be a *Panzer* of supernatural monotheism (*Prolegomena* last three pages). (*Zur Datierung der "Genesis-P-Stücke"*, Kampen (1964) pp. 153-56.)

[2]) J. Wellhausen, *Prolegomena*, p. 231.

[3]) A. Bentzen, "Skandinavische Literatur zum Alten Testament", *ThR* [N.F.] XVII (1948-1949) p. 286.

[4]) S. A. Cook, "Some Tendencies in O.T. Criticism", *JTS* XXVI (1925) pp. 156 ff.

[5]) E. Reuss, *Die Geschichte der Heiligen Schriften*, p. ix.

[6]) G. A. Smith, *Modern Criticism and the Preaching of the Old Testament*, London (1901) p. 46.

systems of the nineteenth century. [1]) In reply to the allegation that
de Wette was under the influence of the philosopher Fries, [2]) Smend
shows that his influence dated only from 1811, whereas de Wette's
critical work dates from 1805. In fact 1811 marks a decade's *caesura*
in his critical studies, so that it is more true to say that the philosophical system retarded rather than advanced his criticism (p. 110). Vatke,
unlike de Wette, did build within a philosophical framework, and
without this framework could not have built, yet even here the building
stones were independent of the framework, and were seen to better
advantage when the scaffolding was torn down by Wellhausen
(p. 113). Wellhausen did not read Vatke until 1874, but had accepted
Graf's theory in 1867 (p. 114), and maintained that all that was best
in Vatke did not come from Hegel (p. 115). He denied that Simon,
Astruc or de Wette had been controlled by philosophic presuppositions, and deplored the tendency to categorize writers instead of
answering their arguments. [3])

Finally to be noted is the recent major work of PERLITT (op. cit)
which should now at last give pause to "dependence on philosophy"
theories. [4]) Perlitt contrasts the great German secular historians
Niebuhr, Ranke and Mommsen, with the historical philosophers
from Herder to Hegel, and concludes that it is with the former rather
than the latter that Wellhausen stands. Vatke was a Hegelian but it
was something other than his Hegelianism that Wellhausen appreciated "ein treues Gefühl für die Individualität der Sachen" (p. 152).
Wellhausen came to his historical reconstruction in 1878 only after
a solid base had been laid in his literary criticism of 1876-1877 (p. 168).
He criticised Duhm for his too-rigid application of the "development"
measuring stick (p. 188), and Strauss and Baur for their Hegelian
schematism (p. 205). The influence of Tübingen he regarded as des-

---

[1]) R. Smend "De Wette und das Verhältnis zwischen historischer Bibelkritik
und philosophischem System im 19. Jahrhundert", *ThZ* XIV (1958) pp. 107-
119.

[2]) Cf. J. D. Smart, *op. cit*, p. 241, Karl Barth and others.

[3]) Smend (p. 111) quotes an article to this effect by Wellhausen in *Beilage
zur Allgemeinen Zeitung* (1908) p. 353. Cf. now J. Barr, *Old and New in Interpretation*,
London (1966) p. 180: "The diagnosis of presuppositions as evolutionary may
be historically false; and so may be the attempt to depict such scholarship as
Wellhausen's as if it was related deterministically to the given cultural environ-
ment".

[4]) These are still repeated in the Albright Festschrift (*The Bible and the Ancient
Near East*, New York (1961)) on p. 15 (J. Bright) and pp. 36-37 (G. Mendenhall)
and in other writings by the editor, G. E. Wright and Albright himself.

tructive (*loc. cit.*) He had his presuppositions—who has not? [1] —but they were rather those of Herder's primitivism, than Hegel (pp. 211, 206). [2]

By proleptically including Wellhausen, as well as Graf in this discussion, we have taken the negative case at its strongest point but must conclude that at most it is in forms of expression rather than in basic principles that Hegelianism influenced Grafianism. The central Grafian position on the dating is independent of this alleged dress. [3]

C. RATIONALISM

A third origin for Grafianism has been sought by Orr [4] and others in a mood of anti-supernaturalism stemming directly from rationalistic Deism. It was certainly true that some of the Deists anticipated de Wette, e.g. Parvish with the dating of Deuteronomy to Josiah, as Cheyne conceded, [5] and that Eichhorn, [6] de Wette, [7] and their

---

[1] "Man muss einen Vorbegriff haben von der Wahrheit, um sie zu finden" p. 187.

[2] So also Kraus, *Geschichte, op. cit*, p. 248 "Klingen hier nicht wieder die romantischen Ideen Herders an . . . ?"

[3] So also the Albright scholars mentioned on p. 40 fn. 4 who do not want to disturb the Grafian dating. Mendenhall, in fact, asks if the canonization, if not the collection of the old legal traditions, was not connected with the Persian Empire's conceptions of law, and instances their similar concern to codify Egypt's religious and customary law (*op. cit*, p. 53).

[4] J. Orr, *The Problem of the Old Testament*, London (1905) Chap. I; *The Bible Under Trial*, London (1907). Numerous articles in *Interpreter, Contemporary Review* etc.

[5] T. K. Cheyne, *Founders of Old Testament Criticism*, London (1893) p. 2. See above on Lessing, p. 18.

[6] J. M. Robinson, *A History of Free Thought in the Nineteenth Century*, Vol. I, London (1929) pp. 130, 132 quotes Reuss "The rationalistic Eichhorn maintained the Mosaic authorship of the Pentateuch long after the supernaturalist Vater had disproved it" (he did so only down to his third edition), but notes that he reduced all the Old Testament miracle stories to natural events misunderstood. Moses was not an imposter, but he was not above kindling a fire on Mt Sinai to give the impression of a theophany in fire and smoke, the shining of his countenance being the natural effect of being overheated. (So Strauss, *op. cit*, pp. 47-48). These verdicts, like those on Eichhorn's master, Semler, by Barth and Kraus, may need revision if the "rehabilitating" movement going on now in Europe extends from Wellhausen (Perlitt), Vatke (Perlitt), de Wette (Smend) and Semler (Hornig) to Eichhorn. On Semler see G. Hornig, *Die Anfänge der historisch-kritischen Theologie*—Johann Salomo Semlers Schriftverständnis und seine Stellung zu Luther, Göttingen (1961).

[7] Perlitt (*op. cit*, p. 134) disagrees with this characterization of de Wette from Hengstenberg. Lichtenberger (*op. cit*, pp. 34 ff.) speaks of the excellence of de Wette's translation of the Bible, and the purity of his character, and calls

successors were in the main rationalists. [1]) Kuenen, also was frankly
so, as he is at pains to make clear in the opening chapter of his *Religion
of Israel*. [2]) Israel is one of the religions of the world, "nothing less,
nothing more" (p. 5). He did not believe any miracles had taken
place in the Old Testament: "the probability that such may be placed
to the account of the tradition is infinitely greater than the probability
that they really occurred" (pp. 20-21). It has been claimed by Peake
that Kuenen never allowed his view to be imposed on the evidence
or to dictate his results. His assumption was that miracles could have
occurred, although he did not believe any had. [3]) A similar claim was
made for Wellhausen by Irwin. [4])

What then is to be made of the fact that Wellhausen resigned from
the Theological Faculty in Greifswald, and gave as his reason in his
letter of resignation, that instead of preparing his students for service
in the Church, he was incapacitating them for their office, and that
this weighed heavily on his conscience? [5]) Although a Conservative

---

him "the Nathanael of the modern theology". His acceptance of Fries' psychology
enabled him to be critical without disturbing his faith. Smart (*op. cit*, p. 241)
speaks of him as hoping to avoid the weakness of both rationalism and orthodoxy
and "as a consequence, he was regarded as a pietist by the rationalists and as a
rationalist by the pietists, an almost sure sign that he was breaking through
traditional attitudes with courage". Smend is prepared to accept the term "rationalist" for de Wette, and believes that it was his rationalism that kept him from
going all the way with Herder, for whom Balaam's ass really spoke (for de
Wette it did not!) but prefers "rationalist in a higher style", as he differed even
more markedly from Eichhorn, and went his own way ("myth") between them
(*de Wettes Arbeit*, p. 29).

[1]) When H. J. Rose made this accusation in his *State of Protestantism in Germany*
in 1828, Pusey, who had studied in Germany under Eichhorn and with Ewald,
came to the defence of the German scholars. (See *Edinburgh Review* CVII (August
1831) pp. 238-55). This, Pusey's earliest publication, was later withdrawn when
its author became the champion of orthodoxy. (W. B. Boyce, *The Higher Criticism
and the Bible*, London (1881) p. 73; J. H. Rigg *The Character and Life-Work of
Dr Pusey*, London (1883) pp. 28 ff).

[2]) A. Kuenen, *The Religion of Israel*, ET, Vol. I, London (1874).

[3]) A. S. Peake, *The Bible, its Origin, its Significance and its Abiding Worth*, London
([6]1920) p. 96. Similarly McFadyen quotes Kuenen: "Without for a moment
concealing my own conviction that there is not one single miracle on record
which we can accept as a fact, I would nevertheless place in the forefront of
historical criticism the principle that miracles are possible. To this principle
I have never been consciously untrue, while pursuing the very path which has
led me to the conviction I have just avowed". (J. E. McFadyen, *The Approach
to the Old Testament*, London (1926) p. 156).

[4]) W. A. Irwin, "The Significance of Julius Wellhausen", *JBR* XII (1944)
pp. 160-73.

[5]) The text, except for the last phrase, which comes from Zimmerli's quotation
of Jepsen's original article, is found in the chapter by Jepsen in C. Westermann

like Orelli felt that this was the only honourable thing for a radical critic to do, [1]) this opinion is not shared by Jepsen, who recalls that "Wellhausen's predecessors from de Wette, through Vatke, down to Graf and Kuenen, were theologians; his pupils—and that would be the vast majority of theologians—remained theologians". [2]) While it is true that Wellhausen diverted his attention to Arabic studies, this was not through any loss of faith in the Old Testament [3]) but was rather in connection with it, [4]) and was in fact followed by intensive work on the Gospels. Perlitt insists that he remained a theologian (p. 207), and like Herder, rejected the rationalist view of automatic progress and mechanistic evolution, because for him it was "God who stood behind the mechanism" (p. 185).

While the recent rehabilitation of the great critics as "theologians" may have gone too far, it remains true that the difficulties of the Old Testament are difficulties for believers as well as for doubters. The critics did not introduce them into the Old Testament, but found them there and sought to explain them. Merx reminded his readers [5]) that although it was the Deist, Reimarus, who began the critical school, it was an untutored Kaffir, posing a real problem about the Flood story, who set Colenso off on the path of criticism. Not rationalism, but the exigencies of a busy missionary's life brought him into the field. [6]) Colenso's biographer records that when the Zulu asked

---

(ed.) *Essays On Old Testament Interpretation*, London (1963) p. 247. "I became a theologian because I was interested in the scientific treatment of the Bible; it has only gradually dawned upon me that a professor of theology likewise has the practical task of preparing students for service in the Evangelical Church, and that I was not fulfilling this practical task, but rather, in spite of all reserve on my part, was incapacitating my hearers for their office". Cf. Zimmerli, *op. cit*, p. 22.

[1]) See Orelli's letter of 7th July 1882 in Kappeler *op. cit.* (p. 354). Was he then aware that three weeks later he would be invited to take Wellhausen's place? (see the letter of 27th July (p. 358)).

[2]) Jepsen, *loc. cit.*

[3]) Zimmerli notes that when he moved to Marburg to the chair of Semitic languages, after holding a similar post at Halle, he was expressly forbidden to teach Old Testament because of his awesome reputation as a literary critic, but at Göttingen from 1892 until 1918 was under no such restriction (*op. cit*, p. 23).

[4]) Wellhausen's own words introducing his *Vakidi* are quoted by Eissfeldt (*KS* I, p. 70) "Dem Übergang vom Alten Testament zu dem Arabern habe ich gemacht in der Absicht, den Wildling zu lernen, auf den von Priestern und Propheten das Reis der Thora Jahves gepropft ist".

[5]) A. Merx, "Nachwort", Tuch's *Genesis*, Halle (²1871) pp. cii and cxix.

[6]) Thrane, *op. cit*, quotes the following contemporary limerick:

in addition how the Mosaic laws on slavery could really emanate
from "the merciful Father of mankind", he realized that to explain
these passages as written by Moses under the misapprehension that
they had been put in his mind by divine inspiration, was to place "a
very great strain on the cord which bound me to the ordinary belief
in the historical veracity of the Pentateuch". [1]) This was in 1861, and
by 1862 Colenso had written the first part of his Pentateuchal studies.
When *Essays and Reviews* reached Africa in 1863 he read both it and
its critics without being satisfied, and then ordered the works of
the German critics of both shades of opinion. Neither Ewald nor
Hengstenberg pleased him, but with de Wette and Bleek and Kuenen
he found what he had been seeking. [2])

Additional proof that the difficulties of the Old Testament are
really there, and are not just imagined by the critics, has recently
been adduced by Brownlee, from the rewriting of Genesis that was
thought necessary by the writer of the Book of Jubilees. [3])

> "Jubilees answers practically every question any sceptic has put
> to the Book of Genesis,... [thus]... showing that the inconsistencies
> pointed out by reverent (and irreverent) literary critics... are really
> there. If there is no problem, why does Jubilees seek to integrate
> the two stories of creation?... and omit the Abimelech affair...?
> Here is another demonstration, therefore, that the recognition of the
> two accounts of Genesis as really variant forms of the same episode
> is not a cunningly devised theory of modern higher critics, with an
> alleged hostility toward the truth of the Bible". [4])

Believing scholars then, as well as doubters, must make up their
minds about these matters. [5]) While the critical solution may in its

---

A bishop there was of Natal
Who had a Zulu for his pal;
Said the Zulu, 'My dear,
Don't you think Genesis queer?'
Which converted my lord of Natal.

[1]) P. B. Hinchliff, *John William Colenso*, London (1964) pp. 88-89.

[2]) Hinchliff, *op. cit*, p. 89 and see further next chapter.

[3]) W. H. Brownlee, *The Meaning of the Qumrân Scrolls for the Bible*, New York
(1964) pp. 72-76.

[4]) Brownlee continues, "We moderns may think the ancient Jews were naïve;
but the way they rewrote Genesis shows that they recognized most of the problems
of modern literary criticism and undertook a reinterpretation with a freedom
which is shocking to the present-day Fundamentalist". (*loc. cit*).

[5]) Duff thinks there is significance in the fact that from 1804 the British and
Foreign Bible Society was disseminating Bibles as never before: "This was the
first really Bible-reading age in the history of the world.. The fairly general
reading throughout the century since then has had a powerful influence in promo-

long history have been propounded by rationalists, it has often enough been checked by those who were not. Bleek and König in Germany, and Robertson Smith and Driver in England come to mind. Of H. L. Strack the Schaff-Herzog Encyclopedia says "While acknowledging the full right of critical investigation, he is convinced that such investigation can be and ought to be combined with reverence for the Holy Scriptures and an earnest Christian faith". [1]

D. ROMANTICISM

This does not say, however, all that needs to be said on the problem. There are other currents of thought than those mentioned. BOSCHWITZ mentions some of these in his enquiry into the motives of Wellhausen's history writing. [2] Herder's aestheticism was in the air when criticism began.[3] There is something of the Romantics in Wellhausen's preference for the unspoiled primitive. This idealizing of Israel's earlier condition as "natural" and a "blossoming of life" in contrast to the strait jacket of later legalism is reminiscent of Rousseau and his immediate disciples. [4] HAHN draws attention to Wellhausen's preference for the "early" in the three areas in which he worked—Arabia, the Gospels and the Old Testament. What impressed him about the "early" was its freshness and naturalness, its spontaneous free initiative instead of obedience to norms. [5] Similarly PERLITT sees behind Wellhausen, Herder's preference for patriarchal times, for the youth of nations, for natural growth. [6] SMEND, in seeking to distinguish

---

ting strictly scientific criticism; for it is impossible now for any teacher to ignore in public the difficulties in the Scriptures, since most people have seen these with their own eyes". (*History of Old Testament Criticism*, p. 115).

[1] Article, "Strack", S. M. Jackson (ed.) *The New Schaff-Herzog Encyclopedia*, Vol. 11, New York (1911) p. 109, but see below p. 74.

[2] F. Boschwitz, *Julius Wellhausen, Motive und Massstäbe seiner Geschichtsschreibung*, Marburg (1938).

[3] Johann Gottfried Herder, who was born in 1744 and died in 1803, served throughout his life as a Lutheran clergyman, but from 1767 achieved greater fame as a leader in German letters. He it was who inspired the youthful Goethe in 1770 to give rein to feeling, and with him shared the leadership of the brilliant *Sturm und Drang* movement, which was to be the precursor of Romanticism proper.

[4] "Romanticism" is used here, not in the technical sense of the Schlegels and their successors, but in its more popular sense of the primitive idyll, with its concern for the simple past, love of wild nature, stress on individuality, self-expression and original innocence, and impatience with the teaching of original sin.

[5] Hahn, *op. cit*, pp. 303 ff.

[6] Perlitt, *op. cit*, p. 211. On p. 212, however, he warns us against seeing Wellhausen as a Romantic like Renan, and reminds us that it was just this romanticizing of early Israel that Wellhausen condemned in his review of Renan's *History*.

the new criticism from rationalism, speaks of both being concerned to
bridge the gap between modern man and the Bible, but that where
rationalism did so by bringing the Bible into the present by "modernizing", Herder did so by carrying man back into the past by
"archaizing". [1])

The "archaizing" of Herder took the form of an aesthetic appreciation of the Bible as literature. Where to Michaelis, Moses had been
a statesman and to Voltaire, a priestly deceiver, to Herder he was a
poet. [2]) The higher critical questions as such did not concern him. [3])
His works on the Old Testament in one way or another focused
attention of the beauty of its poetry and attributed this to the dew of
culture's early youth. They were on Genesis 1 (1774), [4]) Solomon's
Song (1778), [5]) on the study of theology (still largely poetry) 1780), [6])
and on the spirit of Hebrew poetry (1782-1783)[7])—a work which Herder
said had been in his heart since childhood. This is not the place to
discuss these fragrant works, but only to record their influence,
which like the author's description of the book of Job, is

> "ein Weihrauch der manche Ohnmacht erquicken wird bis zum Ende
> der Zeiten".

It is surely no accident that each of the modern investigators—
Kraus, Hahn, Perlitt and Smend—have taken us back to one name,
and that each of our lines of investigation—whether of evolution, or
philosophy, or rationalism—has also pointed to the same name—
that of Herder. [8]) The critical succession from Wellhausen back to
Herder can be established along two lines of parentage. In the one
line are Wellhausen, Ewald, Eichhorn and Herder, in the other,
Wellhausen, Vatke, de Wette and Herder.

Wellhausen's debt to *Ewald* is indicated by his dedication of the

---

[1]) R. Smend, *De Wettes Arbeit*, p. 26.

[2]) Dr Rippner, "Herder's Bibelexegese", *MGWJ* XXI (1872) p. 20.

[3]) "Herder, so könnte man sagen, hat die Bibelkritik nicht wesentlich gefördert;
aber seine Verehrer nennen gerade das sein wesentliches Verdienst, dass er die
Bibel den Kritikern entrissen hat, dass er sie von den Fesseln und Schrauben
und Zangen erlöst hat, mit welchen man den schlichten einfachen Text gebunden
hielt". (*Ibid*).

[4]) *Aelteste Urkunde des Menschengeschlechts*, 3 vols, Riga (1774-1776). The last
volume dealt with Genesis 2-6.

[5]) *Salomons Lieder der Liebe* (1778).

[6]) *Briefe, das Studium der Theologie betreffend*, 3 vols (1780).

[7]) *Vom Geist der ebräischen Poesie*, 3 vols (1782-1783).

[8]) The writer has developed this point at length in an unpublished M. A. thesis,
Herder and Wellhausen, Typescript, University of Auckland (1968).

Prolegomena "to my unforgotten teacher, Ewald". [1]) Ewald's study wall was adorned by the portraits of Eichhorn, who had been his teacher, and Herder. [2]) From Herder he had learnt to see the Hebrew poets "as bringing us nearer the spiritual forces at work amidst the people of Israel". [3]) *Eichhorn* himself breathes the very spirit of Herder, [4]) when he bids the readers of Genesis:

> "Read it as two historical works of the old world [J, E,] breathe therein the air of its age and country. Forget the age you live in and the knowledge it affords you.. The youth of the world demands a spirit that has descended to the deeps. The first rays of the glimmering light of reason do not harmonize with the clear light of broad noon. The shepherd only speaks in the soul of the shepherd; and the primitive Oriental in another Oriental.. This book is like the world in its childhood.. it is like a painting.. it is like the language of poetry".[5])

In the other line of ancestry, Wellhausen's debt to *Vatke* has already been discussed. Perlitt speaks also of Vatke's debt to both Ewald and de Wette, and behind them to Herder. [6]) Smend's first pages are devoted to de Wette's debt to Herder, under whose preaching and instruction he grew up at Weimar. [7]) *De Wette* describes Herder as

> "der Mann der.. auf meine allgemeine und theologische Bildung durch seine Schriften so viel Einfluss gehabt, der mir auf der dürren Steppe des theologischen Kriticismus und Rationalismus als ein begeisterter Seher erschien und mich auf die ewig grüne, vom Wasser des Lebens getränkte Weide hinweis, den ich immer als den Vorläufer einer verjüngten begeisterten und begeisternden Theologie betrachtet habe". [8])

Hahn has spoken of Wellhausen's preference for free initiative to obedience to norms, and it remains for us now to trace this impatience

---

[1]) Cf. also his tribute reprinted in R. Smend (ed.) *J. Wellhausen, Grundrisse zum Alten Testament*, Münich (1965) pp. 120-38.

[2]) T. K. Cheyne, *Founders of Old Testament Criticism*, London (1893) p. 72.

[3]) Cheyne, *ibid*, p. 87, who remarks the coincidence that the first book treated by the mature Ewald was also the Song of Solomon (p. 80).

[4]) Cheyne, *ibid*, pp. 17-18 thinks Westphal exaggerated Eichhorn's debt to Herder—certainly it was more the cross-fertilization of contemporaries—but admits the common "rhetorical style".

[5]) Translation by T. Parker in de Wette *op. cit*, pp. 31-32. From Eichhorn Vol. II, Leipzig (¹1781) pp. 405-406.

[6]) L. Perlitt, *op. cit*, pp. 88 ff. Vatke studied under Ewald, followed de Wette at Berlin, gave de Wette's portrait the honoured place on his wall (p. 87), and exclaimed in a youthful letter "Herder ist ebenfalls mein Mann".

[7]) Cf. Cheyne, *op. cit*, p. 31.

[8]) Smend, *De Wettes Arbeit*, p. 11.

with law back beyond even Herder to its probable origins in the
Deists' aversion to "priestcraft". Reventlow has shown that Lessing,
and Reimarus were agreed in their rejection of cult ceremonies, and
that Eichhorn, who was influenced by Lessing's theory of the education of the race, also "teilt das aufklärerische Ideal der rein moralischen
Lehrreligionen, die frei von „Ceremonien" ist". [1]) Herder does not
go as far as this, but does stress that law is a yoke to be out-grown:

> "What, then, would have been the conduct of that god-like man
> [Moses], had he appeared in those times, when his commands were
> made a snare to catch the souls of men and hold them in a state of
> perpetual childhood... in times, when his system of laws, once living
> in all its members, had become a lifeless mass, when the least of his
> precepts had been converted into a golden calf, round which men
> danced and revelled in the extravagance of hypocritical idolatry?
> With thousand-fold reasons might he have ground it to powder,
> and given it, as a cup of abomination, to his sacrilegious and idolatrous
> people".[2])

Wellhausen's own attitude to institutional religion is perhaps indicated by the quotation from Hesiod prefixed to Part II of the *Prolegomena*, which comes to deal with Chronicles and the overwritten
sources—
Πλέον ἥμισυ παντος, "the half is more than the whole".[3])

For him religion could well do without this institutional half. The
inadequacy of this German Protestant spiritualism and individualism has often been pointed out, [4]) but is perhaps put too strongly
by Sandmel:

> "The nineteenth-century German scholarship, which was preeminently
> Protestant, was largely conducted by exponents of individualism
> in religion. Hence there was little or no sympathy for institutional
> religion in general, and since Roman Catholicism is priestly, little
> for the biblical priestly system. As a result many Wellhausians
> described the P Code as if they were describing the Catholic Church
> to which they felt superior and condescending".[5])

---

[1]) H. G. Reventlow, "Die Auffassung vom Alten Testament bei Hermann
Samuel Reimarus und Gotthold Ephraim Lessing", *EvTh* XXV (1965) pp. 440,
441, 448.
[2]) J. G. Herder, *The Spirit of Hebrew Poetry*, Vol. I, ET, Burlington (1833)
p. 272. Cf. "bond-service" (pp. 21, 169).
[3]) Quoted from Boschwitz, *op. cit*, p. 28.
[4]) As e.g. by F. C. N. Hicks, *The Fullness of Sacrifice*, London (³1953) pp. 57-59.
[5]) S. Sandmel, *The Hebrew Scriptures*, New York (1963) p. 355. The difficulty
about this kind of statement is illustrated by the ambivalence which emerges in

Be that as it may, one must reiterate that the problem faced by Graf and Wellhausen was a real one and the means sought to answer it legitimate. Whether they were correct is another matter which must be dealt with in the sequel. [1])

SUMMARY — DESCRIPTIONS OF P

Before passing from the first period, which has isolated and sought to date the P document, the nature of the document and much of the investigation may be summarized by noting the names given to it throughout the period.

To the first investigators it was the *Elohim Document* from its preference for the divine name Elohim. [2]) This was more narrowly defined by Ilgen, and later, Hupfeld, as the *First Elohist*, when two Elohists were uncovered. [3]) Ewald noted two other characteristics — the ten genealogies or *toledoth*, [4]) and the "origins" (e.g. sabbath, circumcision, bloodless meat) and emphasised the latter in his title

---

Romanticism, as it continues into the nineteenth century, when leading Romantics themselves become Catholics or near-Catholics (e.g. Novalis and the Schlegels), and when its influence favours the medieval Christendom, which Herder had spurned as stifling native creativeness by its uniformity. Cf. O. Chadwick, *The Victorian Church*, Part I, London (1966) p. 174. "The Romantics altered popular attitudes to the Reformation by deepening popular sympathy for the middle ages.... A sentiment for monastic ruins generates no love for a Reformation which ruined monasteries... A world of common sense yielded to a world which saw common sense as shallow and reached after beauty and truth beyond the easy fetters of prose".

[1]) The oft repeated allegation that criticism was based on the belief that Moses could not write, despite the evidence cited by M. G. Kyle, *The Deciding Voice of the Monuments*, Oberlin (1912) pp. 80 ff and S. R. Külling, *op. cit*, p. 158 is too trivial to mention here. Eichhorn and many other critics argued the contrary. Külling cites Vater, Hartmann and von Bohlen, but with von Bohlen, as with Reuss and Dillmann, what seems to be meant is "unable to write this kind of historiography", which perhaps still needs to be said (see below). Steinmann's suggestion that Renan advised the Louvre not to purchase the Amarna tablets, because they contradicted his view that Moses could not write (J. Steinmann, *Biblical Criticism*, New York (1958) p. 59) seems unlikely in view of his persuading the Academy of Inscriptions to undertake the Corpus of Semitic Inscriptions as related by G. P. Gooch, *History and Historians in the Nineteenth Century*, London ([2]1952) p. 484.

[2]) This distinguished it from the sections using the divine name Jahweh, which went into the Jahwist document (J) beginning with Gn. 2: 4 and continuing to the end of Numbers.

[3]) The second Elohist is that which is now called the Elohist (E), and is usually thought to begin in Gn. 15.

[4]) The heading *toledoth* "these are the generations of" occurs ten times in Genesis.

Book of Origins. Stähelin and Tuch, from the fact that the document began in Genesis 1 and formed the framework of the Pentateuch, preferred the title *Grundschrift.* Schrader drew attention to a further factor by describing it as *The Annalistic Writer.*

Yet other titles were soon to come. Wellhausen's Q standing for *Quattoir* or "The Four Covenants" attests the interest of the document in the covenants with Adam, Noah, Abraham and Moses, as ushering in dispensations marked by a new stage of the ritual—sabbath, bloodless meat, circumcision and the full cult—and a new divine name—Elohim, El Shaddai and Jahweh. However, it was Kuenen's name P for *Priestly Code* that was to take on, despite the protests of Merx that Deuteronomy had more right to be called Priestly, and Bentzen, that A for *Aaronite* would better distinguish the particular priestly doctrine of the document from that of Deuteronomy. Merx's own suggestion of *Tabernacle Writing* reflects yet a further interest of P.

Putting together these characteristics, the contents of the document were defined as Gn. 1:1-2:4, Gn. 5, 9, 10, 17, 23, and one half of most of the other narrative units in Genesis and Exodus from the Flood to Exod. 16; the whole of the laws in Exod. 25 - Num. 10, except Exod. 32-34; and about one half of the remaining material in Num. 10-36. The laws were further divided into Tabernacle and Priesthood (Exod. 25-31, 35-40; Lev. 8-10), Offerings (Lev. 1-7), Clean and Unclean (Lev. 11-15), Atonement (Lev. 16), Holiness Code (Lev. 17-26) and Camp Order (Num. 1-10). A distinctive vocabulary of some fifty words; a lawyer-like style, which is precise and pedantic; and a high theology, stressing divine transcendence and avoiding anthropomorphisms, were thought to be characteristic of P.

PART TWO

THE LAW CAME AFTER

THE GRAFIANS (1865-1925)

CHAPTER FIVE

THE FIRST DECADE

The sixty years from 1865-1925 saw both the ascendancy of Grafianism, and the beginning of the movements away from it. [1]

The decade following 1865 may be described as one of uncertainty. The first prospects of Graf's hypothesis looked no rosier than those of Vatke's. English and German opinion was almost solidly against it. Wellhausen had not yet come into the fray, and the brunt of the battle was borne by the Dutchman, Kuenen [2] and some others in Holland and France. Antagonists there were many but advocates few. Among the former must be mentioned Riehm, Nöldeke and Schrader, and among the latter Colenso, Kuenen, Merx, Lagarde, Kalisch, Kayser and Duhm.

A. THE EARLY ANTAGONISTS

RIEHM had already devoted himself to the same problems as Graf in his work on Deuteronomy in 1854. [3] He had asked all the right questions concerning the relation of the Code of Leviticus to that of Deuteronomy, but had concluded that the differences were better explained by the lateness of D than of P. His demonstration of the seventh century dating of D was widely acclaimed, as was his critique of Graf which appeared in 1868. [4]

> Much of it followed the familiar line of seeking to establish the priority of P to D from the traces of P in D (pp. 358 ff), from the later organization of the *edah* with judges in D (pp. 364-65), and the inappropriateness of P's silence as to Levitical singers in the post-exilic period (pp. 365 ff).

---

[1] It is difficult to say, when these became really significant. They may be said to have begun about 1905, and to have gathered sufficient force to disturb critical complacency by 1925. This year was in no sense a landmark like 1805 and 1865, but it is a useful stopping place because of several review articles on the progress of criticism published about this time.

[2] Kuenen's own account in his *Hexateuch*, ET, London ([2]1886) pp. xi-xl is invaluable for these years, and was utilized by Wellhausen in his edition of Bleek's *Introduction*, Berlin (1878) pp. 152 ff to bring up to date the history of criticism since Bleek's death.

[3] E. Riehm, *Die Gesetzgebung Mosis im Lande Moab*, Gotha (1854).

[4] Riehm, Rec. " 'Die geschichtlichen Bücher des Alten Testaments', von Karl Heinrich Graf," *ThStKr* XLI (1868) pp. 350-79.

Riehm's most telling point against Graf, was that the latter's separation of the late P laws from the much earlier P *Grundschrift* narrative was quite impossible, [1]) because of the unity of language throughout.

> The narrative of the institution of circumcision in Genesis 17 was in the language of Leviticus, and must be by the same hand (p. 357). From this he argued that since the narratives were early the laws must be early also. A further article added the consideration that P was matter of fact and not tendentious, and was therefore older than the epic and prophetic interpretations of J.[2])
> This dating was also maintained by SCHRADER,[3]) who issued his edition of de Wette's *Introduction* in the Supplementary Hypothesis framework, with Hupfeldian modifications in 1869. He made only the barest mention of Graf—an omission for which Wellhausen was not slow to castigate him.[4])

NÖLDEKE's discussion, [5]) moved on somewhat similar lines to those of Riehm. The limits of P were now defined in detail, and the document dated from not long after the time of Solomon, when the building of the temple must have given a strong impulse to the unity of the cult and to the decline of the local sanctuaries (p. 127).

> Centralization was established under Hezekiah, as even the Assyrian testified (p. 126). Narratives and laws must belong together (p. 130), and no period so lacking in creativity as that of Ezra could have produced the latter (p. 127). On the other hand P as Mosaic was equally impossible. The unhistorical nature of much of P, particularly the numbers (p. 117), the tabernacle (pp. 120 ff) and Genesis 14 (Chap. III), is apparent. As Buttmann had so acutely perceived in 1812 the verisimilitude of P which had convinced most scholars of its age and reliability was its least reliable feature.

B. THE EARLY ADVOCATES

In 1862 COLENSO had attacked the historicity of the Pentateuch, from a mathematical point of view. [6]) It now appeared that nineteen

---

[1]) Graf held this much of the Supplementary Hypothesis, that the P *Grundschrift*, in its narratives was the oldest part of the Pentateuch. The priestly legislation was a great interpolation made after the Exile.

[2]) Riehm, "Die sogenannte Grundschrift des Pentateuchs", *ThStKr* XLV (1872) pp. 283-307.

[3]) E. Schrader, (ed.) de Wette's *Lehrbuch*, 8th ed, Berlin (1869).

[4]) J. Wellhausen, *Prolegomena*, p. 368.

[5]) T. Nöldeke, *Untersuchungen zur kritik des Alten Testaments*, Kiel (1869).

[6]) J. W. Colenso, *The Pentateuch and the Book of Joshua critically examined*, Vol. I, London (1862). By 1881 no less than three hundred replies to this work had issued from the press (so Boyce, *op. cit*, p. 129). The most famous—and fatuous—was

out of his twenty examples of historical improbabilities were from the
P document. KUENEN, for one, was convinced that P's pretentious
history was the least sound, rather than the most sound of the Pentateuchal sources, and was ready to accept the view that P's narratives
as well as P's laws were late. This view he communicated to Graf by
letter in 1866, as the one answer to the criticisms of Riehm. It was
also incorporated in his *Religion of Israel* (1869-1870). [1]) He had the
satisfaction of seeing Graf come over to his opinion in the last
article he wrote before his early death in 1869. [2]) Graf now conceded
the unity of the laws and narratives of P [3]) and admitted that what
had led him and other critics astray for so long was the difficulty of
recognizing that the first chapter of Genesis was not really the first
but secondary and late (p. 468). He held now to an inverted Supplementary Hypothesis. P had supplemented J, and was not an independent work.

This revised position of Graf was immediately felt to be of greater
cogency, and won the support of most of the radical critics, [4]) except
Colenso who held to the first Grafian position against Kuenen. [5])

> MERX who had argued for the post-exilic origin of the laws before
> the appearance of Graf's book (see above p. 34) now in a *"Nachwort"*
> to Tuch's Genesis, [6]) which he edited in 1871, signified his adherence.
> LAGARDE also in 1870,[7]) in connection with another matter, stated
> that this had been his view since 1864:

that of Bishop Wilberforce, who said that Colenso, as a mathematician,
could not forgive Moses for having written a book of Numbers! (Elliott-Binns,
op. cit, pp. 136-37).

[1]) A. Kuenen, *The Religion of Israel*, ET, 3 vols, London (1874-1875), first
published 1869-1870.

[2]) K. H. Graf, "Die sogenannte Grundschrift des Pentateuchs", A. Merx (ed.),
Archiv für wissenschaftliche Erforschung des Alten Testaments, I (1869) pp. 466-77.
In an excellent article on Kuenen, de Vries claims that the "Grafian" hypothesis
is misnamed, and that the honour should go to Kuenen (S. J. de Vries, "The
Hexateuchal Criticism of Abraham Kuenen", *JBL* LXXXII (1963) pp. 31-57),
but this is to forget that Kuenen himself admitted that it was Colenso and Graf,
who put him on the right track.

[3]) De Vries mentions also the importance of the work of W. H. Kosters,
Kuenen's pupil, who in a dissertation in 1868 analysed all the narratives from
Genesis to Numbers into those which were known to D and those which were
not, and found that the former proved to be the J and E stories and the latter
consistently belonged to the *Grundschrift* (*op. cit*, p. 44).

[4]) S. R. Külling, *op. cit*, therefore thinks the crucial date to have been 1869,
when both narrative and laws of P were together assigned to the Exilic date.

[5]) J. W. Colenso, *op. cit*, Vol. VI (1872) pp. 116-44, 576-89.

[6]) A. Merx, "Nachwort", Tuch's *Genesis*, 2nd ed. (1871).

[7]) P. Lagarde, *Symmicta*, Göttingen (1877) pp. 50-57, first published *Göttingische
Gelehrte Anzeigen* (1870), Stück 39, pp. 1549-60.

> I hold, as my pupils have known since 1864, the Elohist to be identical with the redactor of the Pentateuch, and to be either Ezra himself or one of the priests of the second Temple.

He supported this dating by his studies in the name Elohim, which he claimed must be later than Jahweh, as the abstraction is later than the concrete. Its origin, along with the Elohistic Psalms, was in the post-exilic period.

In England, KALISCH in his considerable commentaries on Leviticus (1867-1872) [1]) went the whole way with the new teaching and argued it out in excurses on the history of sacrifice (I, pp. 1-469) and the priesthood (I, pp. 559-659).[2])

To KAYSER, another of Reuss' pupils, it became obvious, that only within a more adequate source analysis could Graf's position be established. He therefore devoted himself to the literary critical side omitted by Graf. [3])

> Was the Elohist document the *Grundschrift?* Who supplemented whom? His answer was that J and E were originally independent documents (p. 111). The Elohist law and narratives belong together (pp. 3, 114), and had left no literary traces in Deuteronomy (pp. 122-35) or anywhere else before the Exile (p. 171), although constantly echoed in the Psalms and Nehemiah's prayer after the Exile (p. 172).

The Jahwist was the oldest, then Deuteronomy and finally the Elohist narrative and legislation.

Similar results were reached by Kuenen, but it was a German, working away at source analysis in these years, who was to establish the definitive dating of the documents in the order JEDP. This was Wellhausen, whose articles appeared in the *Jahrbücher für Deutsche Theologie* in 1876 and 1877. [4]) The honour of being the first German apologist for Grafianism must go, however, to DUHM whose *Theology of the Prophets* appeared a year earlier. [5])

> The connection to Grafianism is shown by the sub-title "als Grundlage für die innere Entwicklungsgeschichte der israelitischen Religion". Duhm showed just what a reconstruction of the religion of Israel

---

[1]) M. M. Kalisch, *Leviticus*, 2 vols, London (1867-1872).

[2]) Kalisch had still been "orthodox" when he wrote his *Exodus* in 1855, but had begun on the path of criticism with his *Genesis* in 1858. An elaborate critique of his position, and that of Davidson, Colenso and much else in criticism, was published by W. Smith in 1868 ff. (*The Books of Moses or the Pentateuch*, Vol. I, London (1868)).

[3]) A. Kayser, *Das vorexilische Buch der Urgeschichte Israels*, Strassbourg (1874).

[4]) J. Wellhausen, "Die Composition des Hexateuchs", *Jahrbücher für Deutsche Theologie*, XXI (1876) pp. 392-450, 531-602; XXII (1877) pp. 407-79.

[5]) B. Duhm, *Die Theologie der Propheten*, Bonn (1875).

Grafianism required. The prophets assumed gigantic proportions as the real founders of Israelite faith, while the Mosaic law was reduced to a less significant position in the post-exilic period. The Levitical system which gave the death-blow to prophecy in the post-exilic age could never have been its nursing mother in earlier times.[1]

It was this reconstruction that Wellhausen was to work out with so great brilliance in the epoch-making work, which well begins the next chapter.

---

[1] R. SMEND, who had written *Moses apud prophetas* in 1875, now enquired into "the stage in the development of Israelite religion presupposed by the prophets of the eighth century" ("Ueber die von den Propheten des achten Jahrhunderts vorausgesetzte Entwicklungsstufe der israelitischen Religion", *ThStKr* XLIX (1876) pp. 599-664) and "saw no reason why the Levitical legislation could not be older than Amos and Hosea, or that an organic relation could not have existed between the teaching of the prophets and the earlier faith of the nation" (W. Robertson Smith, "Old Testament Study in 1876", *Lectures and Essays*, London (1912) p. 396). This Smend, who is not to be confused with his grandson quoted earlier, was to become a distinguished higher critic (see below p. 114). The turning point came with his Ezekiel commentary, which he entered on expecting to prove Ezekiel's use of P, but found the opposite the case (*Ezechiel*, Leipzig (²1880) pp. vii, 313).

CHAPTER SIX

THE VICTORY OF GRAFIANISM

A. WELLHAUSEN

What would have been the fate of Grafianism if WELLHAUSEN had not written, no one can really say. [1]) We only know that it was Wellhausen's *Prolegomena* [2]) that fairly routed the opposition from the field. It is impossible to describe the effect of this great work: it was at once so massive, all-embracing and logically compelling. All that preceding critics had said was taken into its wide sweep, but how much more! The ordering of the material, the scintillating style so full of memorable sayings, the sledge hammer effect of the logic, the truculent dealing with opponents, the daring irreverence, and finally the broad vista of an Israel newly created, and so different, which rose before the reader's eyes, were overwhelming. It was no ordinary book that caused Kuenen to rhapsodize:

> I can hardly describe the delight with which I first read it—a delight such as seldom meets one in the path of learning. It was the crowning fight in the long campaign.[3])

Wellhausen said of Graf, that he had "brought forward his arguments somewhat unconnectedly, not seeking to change the general view, which prevailed of the history of Israel" (p. 368), and that "he laboured under the disadvantage of not knowing what success had been achieved in the separating of the sources" (p. 10). Neither of these things could be said of Wellhausen. In Part I of his work he marshalled his arguments with the precision of the regiments of an army taking the field. The five great areas which had been the subject of investigation for so long, formed his chapter headings—the

---

[1]) For a succinct summary of Wellhausen's writings down to 1897 see L. Meinhold, *Wellhausen*, Leipzig (1897), and for his full career, including his outstanding contribution to Arabic studies, see O. Eissfeldt, "Julius Wellhausen," *op. cit.* Early critiques, which at the same time give ample summaries of his works, are those of Roos, *Die Geschichtlichkeit des Pentateuches ins besondere seiner Gesetzgebung*, Stuttgart (1883) and O. Naumann, *Wellhausen's Methode kritisch beleuchtet*, Leipzig (1886).

[2]) J. Wellhausen, *Prolegomena to the History of Israel*, ET, Edinburgh (1885) from 2nd ed. 1883. First published as *Geschichte Israels*, Vol. I, Berlin (1878).

[3]) A. Kuenen, *Hexateuch*, p. xxxix.

sanctuary, the sacrifices, the feasts, the priests and Levites and the endowments of the clergy. Each chapter was a logical unit in itself capable of standing alone and bearing the whole weight of Grafianism if the others should be overthrown. On each subject he first set out the history in strict chronological order, then the laws in the order established by analysis, and then his conclusions as to which law prevailed at each period, and what the consequent life of Israel must have been.

These one hundred and sixtyseven pages were undoubtedly Wellhausen's master-piece, but the book continued for a further three hundred pages of additional discussion, in which the tone of the careful, scientific investigator gives place to that of a propagandist, who will use every trick of his trade to make good his case. Under the general heading of "The History of the Tradition" Wellhausen discusses in turn the sources of Old Testament history, and seeks to show that the original form of the history has been perverted at almost every point by priestly overwriting. He weights the scales by beginning with Chronicles and has no difficulty in making out his case here. He proceeds to Samuel, Judges and Kings and finally to the Hexateuch, as if all this literature came under the same condemnation. The third part of his book makes it plain that it is the post-exilic hierocracy, that has been the arch-distorter of the Old Testament.

Typical of Wellhausen's judgments are the following: "the nearer history stands to its origin, the more profane it is" (p. 245), "the ancient Israelites did not build a church first of all: what they built first was a house to live in" (p. 255). The theocracy could only have arisen "when the Chaldeans or Persians had relieved them of all care for worldly concerns", so that they were at liberty to concentrate themselves on "worship and religiousness" (p. 255). The sense of sin and atonement are even more remarkably ascribed to the atrocities of Manasseh's reign:

the rise into prominence of the cultus in the seventh century, . . . [was] rather helped than hindered by the long reign of Manasseh, evil as is the reputation of that reign. (p. 421)

This is about equivalent to the implication that the highest religion of Israel was that of the local sanctuaries—a euphemism for the high places—and that when these were put down "life and worship fell apart" (p. 77). One could hardly imagine a more blatant denial of a divine revelation in the religion of Israel than these quotations.

The relation of P to Ezekiel as well as to the Code of Holiness in Lev. 17-26 had come to loom larger and larger in the discussion. Wellhausen's conclusion was that P showed no trace of a Deuteronomic revision, and so was later than Deuteronomy. P had added the sin offering and trespass offering to the Holiness Code, and so was later than H, which in turn was later than D and Ezekiel. P's language has no parallels in Amos, Isaiah and Micah, few in Jeremiah and Deuteronomy, more in Ezekiel and most in the post-exilic period (pp. 377-87). The completed Pentateuch was the work of Ezra in 444 B.C. (p. 407).

B. GERMANY

The decade following the publication of the *Prolegomena* saw the capitulation of almost every influential Old Testament scholar in Germany to the new teaching, with the exception of the powerful triumvirate Delitzsch, Dillmann and Kittel. Even these, however, went a long way towards it.

DELITZSCH, who up to 1873 had thought Hengstenberg and Keil to have had the better of the exchange, came to another mind after reading Graf and Kayser in 1876. [1]) In a series of twelve articles in 1880, [2]) he carefully went over the problems associated with the tabernacle, incense altar, Day of Atonement, high priest, Levites, Passover etc., and refuted the Grafian views. Some laws, such as that on leprosy reflected an Egyptian or Wilderness background and were from Moses, but others were later. The document P was also late, although earlier than Ezekiel. Wellhausen regarded it as a great concession [3]) that Delitzsch should say:

> "the processes which resulted in the final form of the Torah, as we now possess it continued into the post-exilian period". (p. 620)

In the 1887 edition of his Genesis commentary Delitzsch repeats this, but adds:

---

[1]) So S. I. Curtiss, "Delitzsch on the Origin and Composition of the Pentateuch", *Presbyterian Review*, III (1882) pp. 553-88. One who became Delitzsch's pupil in the significant year, 1866, had this to say of him: "So hat er auch die radikale Umgestaltung der Pentateuchkritik durch Wellhausen nicht einfach ablehnend von der Hand gewiesen, sondern seine eigene mühsam erworbene Auffassung unverdrossen neu gestaltet... Er war einer der ersten unter den Konservativen Theologen, der einer freiern Stellung zur Tradition über den Kanon innerhalb der gläubigen Theologie die Anerkennung errungen hat". (C. von Orelli in Kappeler, *op. cit*, p. 73).

[2]) F. Delitzsch, "Pentateuchkritische Studien I-XII", Luthardt (ed.) *ZKWL* I (1880). The same journal carried a further series in 1882, in which it was shown that the Decalogue and five passages in Numbers, which some were assigning to P, were among the most primitive Mosaic materials ("Urmosaisches im Pentateuch", *ZKWL* III (1882) pp. 113 ff etc.).

[3]) J. Wellhausen, "Israel", *Encyclopaedia Britannica*, 9th ed. (1880) p. 418.

"nevertheless my conception of this process is profoundly different from the modern conception". [1])

In 1888, in a review of a Conservative American volume, he wrote:

I am certain... that the *Grundstock* of P is before Deuteronomy, and... that Deuteronomy as it lies before us was not first produced under Manasseh and Josiah, but... earlier.[2])

DILLMANN, who was one of the very greatest of critics, steadily held to the early origin of P. [3]) Deuteronomy presupposed the laws of leprosy, and clean and unclean from P. The references to the Ark and Urim and Thummim, which no longer existed after the Exile, ruled out a post-exilian origin (p. 669). A date of around 800 B.C. was probable, but as a priestly book, circulating only in priestly circles, it need not have entered life as a written law until Ezra (p. 655). This suggestion, made by de Wette also (see above p. 25), was to receive further currency from Kittel and Baudissin, but was unacceptable to Würster, who argued that one of the aims of P was to establish his idea of a theocracy, and for this a private circulation would not do. [4])

KITTEL was early on the scene with a criticism of the *Prolegomena* in 1881. [5]) P and D, being for different communities, could be contemporary. P in Lev. 17:3 demands centralization and must be pre-Hezekianic. Incense and the incense altar were not late, nor was the sin offering. Neither the festival nor the Levitical history required Wellhausen's conclusions. These arguments were included also in the first edition of Kittel's *History of the Hebrews,* [6]) but somewhat

---

[1]) Delitzsch, *Neuer Commentar über Genesis*, Leipzig (1887) p. 17.

[2]) Delitzsch, "Die nordamerikanischen Pentateuch-kritischen Essays", *ZKWL* IX (1888) p. 232. Another pupil of Delitzsch—one of several who must occupy us in the sequel—regretted this change in his old master. Where in his *Introduction* of 1857 he had argued that Moses had written Deuteronomy and the sections ascribed to him in Exodus and Numbers, and Joshua and Eleazar had written J and P from Mosaic materials soon after his death, Delitzsch's final position of Deuteronomy after Solomon, and the others before the Exile, was an unnecessary retreat before criticism. (So E. Rupprecht, *Die Anschauung der kritischen Schule Wellhausens vom Pentateuch*, Erlangen (1893) p. 27).

[3]) A. Dillmann, *Die Bücher Numeri, Deuteronomium und Josua*, Leipzig (²1886) pp. 593-690.

[4]) P. Würster, "Zur Charakteristik und Geschichte des Priestercodex", *ZAW* IV (1884) pp. 112-33.

[5]) R. Kittel, "Die neueste Wendung der pentateuchischen Frage", *Theologische Studien aus Württemberg* (1881) pp. 29-62, 147-69.

[6]) Kittel, *A History of the Hebrews*, ET, 2 vols, Oxford (1895-1896) first published 1888.

modified in later editions. Kittel accepted the Wellhausen framework
and was content to argue for the early origin of some laws. [1]) His
position, along with those of Delitzsch and Dillmann, was subjected
to criticism by Kayser in 1881. [2])

> Particular points of Pentateuchal criticism were dealt with by CURTISS
> and BAUDISSIN in their histories of the priesthood. The former attempt-
> ed an answer to a number of the Grafian arguments.[3]) The latter [4]) con-
> centrated on a particular point—the pre-exilic origin of P. He sought
> to show that P was prior to Zerubbabel and Ezra, because of the silence
> about singers and doorkeepers, and to Ezekiel, because the Zadokites
> were a subdivision of the Aaronites and not *vice versa*. His further
> assumption that P was earlier than Deuteronomy and circulated as a
> *Privatschrift* was not so happy (p. 280).
> Among the many early popular critiques were those of Bredenkamp
> (1881) and Böhl (1883) noted in the first chapter, and Roos (1883)
> and Naumann (1886) noted above in this (p. 58). BÖHL, in particular,
> took issue with the deductions drawn from the silence of the later
> books concerning the law. It was only accidental that the Book of
> Kings had omitted the Levites from the enthronement of Joash,
> where they appear in Chronicles.[5]) It could no more be deduced
> from "no such passover since the days of Joshua" in 2 Kings 23:22
> that the Passover had been in abeyance, than from the same formula
> in Neh. 8:17 that the Feast of Tabernacles had not been held and no
> critic wanted to argue this (p. 21). Jeremiah could say that sacrifice
> and covenant had not been given in the Wilderness, because the former
> existed before Exod. 5: 1 and the latter from the time of the patriarchs
> (p. 30). Despite the silence, the Pentateuch had been in existence
> in the days of Elijah and Samuel, and from it they had drawn their
> strength (pp. 62, 67).[6])

---

[1]) Kittel, *The Scientific Study of the Old Testament*, ET, New York (1910) pp. 86-87.

[2]) A. Kayser, "Der gegenwärtige Stand der Pentateuchfrage", *Jahrbücher für Protestantische Theologie* VII (1881) pp. 326-65, 520-64, 630-65.

[3]) S. I. Curtiss, *The Levitical Priests*, Edinburgh (1877). Curtiss, although an American, is included here because his work was done under Delitzsch. Baudissin was also a pupil of Delitzsch in 1866 as the correspondence published by Eissfeldt indicates (see Eissfeldt, *KS* I pp. 234-38 and his fuller chapter "Vom Lebenswerk eines Religionshistorikers (Wolf Wilhelm Graf Baudissin)", *KS* I pp. 115-42). In 1884 Baudissin wrote *Der heutige Stand der Alttestamentlichen Wissenschaft*, Giessen (1884) with the same viewpoint, but his later writings show a retreat from the early date for P to the Grafian one, as Eissfeldt notes (pp. 121-22).

[4]) W. W. Baudissin, *Die Geschichte des alttestamentlichen Priesterthums*, Leipzig (1889), also "Priests and Levites", *HDB* Vol. IV (1902) pp. 67-97.

[5]) E. Böhl, *op. cit*, p. 20.

[6]) In any case church history had similar silences. "Kingdom of God" in the sense used by its Founder disappears from history until the Reformation, as does the Pauline understanding of "justification", and the Decalogue prohibition of images *ibid*. (pp. 24-26),

Most scholars in Germany, however, preferred Wellhausen's way of putting things, e.g. KAUTZSCH, who confessed that the *Prolegomena* had convinced him, where the earlier works of Wellhausen and Graf had not, [1]) and SCHULTZ who laboriously rewrote his *Theology* to bring it into line with Grafianism in the second edition. [2])

C. SWITZERLAND

In Switzerland neither Orelli at Basel nor Oettli at Berne was hospitable to the new criticism. [3]) ORELLI's correspondence has a revealing reply to a query from F. Godet in which he states that the source analysis is not certain, and the date of P in the Exile impossible in the light of the priority of Gn. 1 and 6-8 to the Babylonian versions from the time of Nebuchadnezzar. D cannot be as late as Jeremiah. [4])

Another critic of Wellhausen was FINSLER, who in 1887 wrote a reply to the *Prolegomena* which was of no great significance, [5]) except for the reply which it called forth from MARTI. In 1880 Marti had opposed Grafianism by seeking to demonstrate the pre-exilic origin of P from traces in the prophets. [6]) In his review of Finsler [7]) he relates his change-over to Wellhausen's side, and expresses the hope that Finsler through a study of the *Composition* as well as the *Pro-*

---

[1]) E. Kautzsch, Rec. "Wellhausen, J., 'Geschichte Israels' ", *ThLZ* (1879), No. 2, pp, 26-30. Cf. also his vindication of the critical method in his *An Outline of the History of the Literature of the Old Testament*, ET, London (1898) p. vii and pp. 164-66.

[2]) H. Schultz, *Old Testament Theology*, ET, 2 vols, Edinburgh ([2]1909) from 2nd ed. (1878), first published 1869.

[3]) The careers of these two Swiss, who had been born in the same year (1846) and had studied at Zürich, were strangely parallel. Both were called to Greifswald. Orelli declined to be Wellhausen's successor in 1882 pleading the needs of Switzerland. Oettli did become professor in Greifswald but only in 1895. (Bredenkamp had served there from 1883 but in theology). Both published pamphlets against the Wellhausen school in 1895-1896 (Orelli's was *Wider unberechtigte Machtsprüche heutiger Kritiker*, Düsseldorf (1895), and Oettli's *Der gegenwärtige Kampf um das Alte Testament*, Gütersloh (1896)). They died in 1910 and 1911 within a year of each other.

[4]) C. von Orelli in Kappeler, *op. cit*, pp. 340-42 (letter of 19.9.1879). Cf. also p. 325 (1877) for the view that Assyriology will be a corrective to criticism, and above on pp. 35, 60. Despite their differences, Orelli remained on excellent terms with his colleague, Kautzsch (p. 8). Oettli's publications are later—see below.

[5]) R. Finsler, *Darstellung und Kritik der Ansicht Wellhausens*, Zürich (1887).

[6]) K. Marti, "Die Spuren der sogenannten Grundschrift", *Jahrbücher für Protestantische Theologie*, VI (1880) pp. 127-61, 308-54.

[7]) Marti, "Wellhausen's Ansicht von Geschichte und Religion des A.T.", *Kirchenblatt für die reformierte Schweiz* (1887) pp. 65-67, 69-72, 93-96.

legomena will do the same. He concludes with some lines that were true of so many of his contemporaries:

> Lange hab' ich mich gesträubt
> Endlich gab ich nach.
> Wenn die Tradition zerstäubt,
> Wird Wellhausen wach.

D. FRANCE

The archaeologist HALÉVY argued against a post-exilic origin of the laws, because of the use of P by Psalm 51 and Ezekiel 20. [1]) The traces left by an earlier P on many parts of the Old Testament—Prophets, Deuteronomy etc—were the subject of detailed investigation in his large work on Genesis (Vol. II, pp. 183-548). [2]) Another comprehensive two-volume work, but favourable to criticism, was that of WESTPHAL, in which one volume was devoted to a history of criticism, and the second volume to an exposition of orthodox Wellhausenianism. [3]) Unorthodox criticism found expression in the extravagance of the school of Vernes, Havet and d'Eichtal, who made the Pentateuch a unity of the time of Alexander the Great. [4])

E. BRITAIN

The leader of the critical movement in Britain, ROBERTSON SMITH, has been described as the only original critic Britain has produced. [5])

---

[1]) J. Halévy, "Esdras et le Code Sacerdotal", *Revue de l'Histoire des Religions*, IV (1881) pp. 22-45; "Esdras a-t-il promulgué une loi nouvelle?" *ibid*, XII (1885) pp. 26-38; "Le Code Sacerdotal pendant l'Exil", *ibid*, XIV (1886) pp. 189-202.

[2]) Halévy, *Recherches Bibliques*, 2 Vols, Paris (1895, 1901). See further under "Jewish Opposition".

[3]) A. Westphal, *Les Sources du Pentateuque*, 2 vols, Paris (1888-1892). Westphal preferred to connect Deuteronomy with Hezekiah's Reform rather than Josiah's. See his *The Law and the Prophets*, ET, London (1910) p. 304.

[4]) It is strange to find this radical school being welcomed by a Conservative like R. Sinker, who writes: "There is vastly greater logical justice in the views of M. Vernes than in those of the Wellhausen school", and "you will learn more from a Frenchman when he is wrong, than from a German when he is right!" (*"Higher Criticism"*: *What is it and Where does it lead us?* London (1899) pp. 131, 137).

[5]) H. W. Robinson, ("The Contribution of Great Britain to Old Testament Study", *ExpT* XLI (1929-1930) pp. 246-50). He was also somewhat of an all-round genius, being called to or considered for chairs in mathematics, logic and church history, in addition to those in his chosen fields of Hebrew and Arabic. Before his early death at 48, he had edited the ninth edition of the *Encyclopaedia Britannica*, and served as Librarian at Cambridge University. He humorously attributed his wide knowledge to the fact that he was one of the few men, who had read every word in the *Encyclopaedia Britannica*. See the *Life* by J. S. Black and G. Chrystal, London (1912).

In his contributions to the *Encyclopaedia Britannica*, of which he became editor, he popularized the new views both through his own articles and those of Wellhausen. In 1875 his article *Bible* [1]) set out a mild criticism including the statement that Deuteronomy was not referred to before Jeremiah and was rightly to be dated to Josiah's reign (p. 637), and that there was no conclusive reference to the Elohistic record in the prophets before the Exile, or in Deuteronomy itself (p. 638).

For these statements he was arraigned before the high courts of his church. He defended himself and the cause of free enquiry with spirit and skill.[2]) The main point at issue was whether the late date of Deuteronomy was consistent with its inspiration. Robertson Smith maintained that it was.[3]) Law-books were revised every day, yet still retained the original author's name. He refused Kuenen's description of it as a fraud perpetrated by Hilkiah, and claimed for it an earlier origin under Manasseh.[4]) He repudiated the charge that his enquiries had ever been dictated by rationalistic assumptions (p. 37),[5]) and affirmed that he held to the inspiration of Scripture with all the Fathers of the Protestant church:

> because the Bible is the only record of the redeeming love of God; because in the Bible alone I find God drawing nigh to man in Jesus Christ and declaring His will for our salvation. And the record I know to be true by the witness of His Spirit in my heart, whereof I am assured that none other than God himself is able to speak such words to my soul (p. 21).

---

[1]) W. Robertson Smith, "Bible", *EBrit*, 9th ed. Vol. III, Edinburgh (1875) pp. 634-48.

[2]) Robertson Smith, *Answer to the Form of Libel* (1878); *Additional Answer to the Libel* (1878); *Answer to the Amended Libel* (1879); *Open Letter to Principal Rainy* (1880). On the occasion of his first condemnation (on 20th May 1878) a German friend recalled that it was two hundred years, all but a day, since Richard Simon's similar pioneer work had been condemned (*Life*, p. 287).

[3]) The Book of Deuteronomy was, he wrote, "beyond doubt a prophetic legislative programme; and if the author put his work in the mouth of Moses instead of giving it, with Ezekiel, a directly prophetic form, he did so not in pious fraud, but simply because his object was not to give a new law, but to expound and develop Mosaic principles in relation to new needs". ("Bible", *op. cit*, pp. 637-38). Cf. *The Old Testament in the Jewish Church*, (1881) p. 431, where it is shown that Deuteronomy is an expansion of the Mosaic Book of the Covenant.

[4]) Robertson Smith, *Answer to the Form of Libel* (1878) p. 54.

[5]) The justice of this claim may be checked by those who follow the chronological sequence of the *Lectures and Essays* (1912) from "Christianity and the Supernatural", pp. 109-36 esp. p. 134 (1869), through the critiques of Kuenen, pp. 191 ff (1870), pp. 251-52 (1871), pp. 349-66 (1876), to the review of Renan's *History*, pp. 608-22 (1887). In early life he studied at Bonn and Göttingen, but avoided Heidelberg as "too rationalistic": in late life he rejected a contributor to the *Britannica* as "too sceptical and devoid of reverence". (*Life* p. 488).

Robertson Smith was condemned [1]) and ejected from his professorial chair, but his pen was not silent. In his major work on criticism, [2]) which remains perhaps the best introduction to the subject in English,[3]) he claimed that the new views were more consistent with divine inspiration than the old. They presented a divine law achieving its object in the life of Israel at the time of its institution, where the old view had the contradictory picture of a divine law given but totally ineffective and unnoticed for a thousand years (p. 315).

> To so complete a theory of the religious life as presented in the middle books of the Pentateuch nothing could be added (p. 212). Religious history thereafter could be only obedience or disobedience (p. 213), prophecy could be only an exposition of an authoritative law (p. 215), and new revelation was impossible without a change of dispensation. This, however, was not the picture of the religion of Israel as presented in the rest of the Old Testament. If the Pentateuch was by one writer, the silence of the pre-exilic books as to so much of its contents would brand the whole as post-exilic. On the critical view of a composite document at least some were saved for Moses (p. 308).

Despite the condemnation of its propounder, it was this reverent and moderate criticism, as represented in DRIVER, rather than the more radical Continental position represented in Cheyne that won its way in Britain. [4])

[1]) The trial dragged on for five years, and finally it was his views on the Levitical legislation rather than Deuteronomy which became the point at issue. Although they had made up one of the eight counts against the article "Bible" in 1877, they had been dropped in favour of the Deuteronomy charge by 1880 when the author came to final trial. He was acquitted on this latter charge on 27th May 1880, but three weeks later a further volume of the *Britannica* carrying his article "Hebrew Language and Literature" appeared, and started off a further process in which the centre of interest moved to the date of the Levitical law (*Life*, pp. 372, 428). It was ironical—and unjust—that his final condemnation was virtually for "contempt of court" in publishing the second article, when in point of fact it had been written prior to the first acquittal and would have appeared long before had not a late contributor held up publication! (*Life*, p. 371).

[2]) Robertson Smith, *The Old Testament in the Jewish Church*, Edinburgh (1881). These lectures, addressed first to public audiences, attracted many hundreds of hearers, and when published, sold six and a half thousand copies in fifteen months.

[3]) So J. B. Harford 1925. The present writer can add that it was this book that first made him aware that the real issues of criticism were not matters of documents and the divine names.

[4]) For Cheyne's estimate of Driver's moderateness see his *Founders of O.T. Criticism*, Chaps XI-XIII, and for the impact of "moderate" criticism—Riehm rather than Wellhausen—see C. Gore's introduction to *Lux Mundi*, an essay volume, which like its predecessor *Essays and Reviews*, sold out ten editions in its first year (*Lux Mundi* ([10]1890) p. xx). On pp. 353-54 Gore had argued that the Old Testament was historical, but that this did not preclude "the attribution

Driver was regarded as a safe man when Gladstone favoured him for the Hebrew chair at Oxford in preference to Sayce.[1]) In 1882 he wrote an article reviewing the linguistic arguments for the dating of P which was a model of caution.[2]) In the same year in a review [3]) of Wellhausen's *Britannica* article *Israel* he regretted that this article had not been entrusted to Robertson Smith "who from first to last has struck a note which may be listened for in vain in all that Wellhausen has ever written".[4])

When Driver's own great *Introduction* [5]) appeared in 1891, it satisfied neither the radical critics, nor the Conservatives, but it speedily commended itself to the majority of English students as a satisfying compromise. [6]) While the results were not unlike those of Wellhausen, the tone was quite different. Greater allowance was made for older elements in the laws. On Dt. 14:4-20, which is almost verbally identical with a passage in Leviticus, Driver wrote:

---

to the first founders of what is really the remoter results of their institutions... Moses himself established a certain germ of ceremonial enactment... and this developed always as 'the law of Moses', the whole result being constantly attributed, probably unconsciously and certainly not from any intention to deceive to the original founder.. What we are asked to admit is not conscious perversion, but unconscious idealizing.. the reading back into past records of a ritual development which was really later.... . Inspiration excludes conscious deception or pious fraud, but it appears to be quite consistent with this sort of idealizing".

[1]) Time was to reverse this estimate. See A. H. Sayce, *Reminiscences*, London (1923) pp. 213-14 and below.

[2]) S. R. Driver, "On Some Alleged Linguistic Affinities of the Elohist", *Journal of Philology* XI (1882) pp. 201-36, reviewing Giesebrecht.

[3]) Driver, Review "J. Wellhausen, 'Israel' Encyclopaedia Britannica," *The Academy* XXI (1882) pp. 131-32.

[4]) The thesis of W. B. Glover in *Evangelical Nonconformists and Higher Criticism in the Nineteenth Century*, London (1954), that it was the reverent and believing nature of Old Testament criticism in Britain that secured its victory, while perhaps over-stated, does draw attention to an important factor. There were also some curious side-lights, mentioned by Glover, such as John Skinner's being preferred to George Adam Smith for the Old Testament post in the English Presbyterian College in 1890, because he had been converted in a revival (p. 202), and A. S. Peake as late as 1920 refraining from going to the theatre lest it be used to discredit Higher Criticism (p. 218). In the Robertson Smith trial, while some Evangelicals like Horatius Bonar were in the van of the opposition, Alexander Whyte came to his defence with the plea that "the world of the mind does not stand still: and the theological mind will stand still at its peril" (*Life* p. 430). Similar sentiments were expressed by A. B. Davidson and A. B. Bruce. Smith himself had no difficulty in reconciling the new views with his evangelical faith, and was amazed at the reaction to his first article (See A. Vidler, *The Church in an Age of Revolution*, Harmondsworth (1961) p. 171). See further below on pp. 70, 76.

[5]) Driver, *Introduction to the Literature of the Old Testament*, 7th ed, Edinburgh (1898), first published 1891.

[6]) Four editions were sold out in the first year.

it is thus apparent that at least one collection of Priestly *toroth*, which now forms part of P was in existence when Deuteronomy was written, and a presumption at once arises that others were (p. 145).

An orthodox Wellhausenian would have simply denied that Chap. 14 was in the original Deuteronomy. Driver also regarded H as early, where Cheyne put it in the Exile.

Despite its slow beginning, and possibly for the reason suggested by Glover, criticism in Britain won an almost total victory. Where in 1880 A. Cave had said that ninetynine per cent of British and United States scholarship accepted the Mosaic authorship of the Pentateuch, [1]) in 1887 Briggs could write:

> There are no Hebrew Professors on the Continent of Europe, so far as I know, who would deny the literary analysis of the Pentateuch into the four great documents... The Professors of Hebrew in the Universities of Oxford, Cambridge and Edinburgh, and tutors in a large number of theological colleges hold to the same opinion. A very considerable number of the Hebrew Professors in America are in accord with them... I doubt whether there is any question of scholarship whatever in which there is greater agreement among scholars than in this question of the literary analysis of the Hexateuch. [2])

Oxford under Driver and Cheyne became as famous in Old Testament studies as Cambridge under Lightfoot, Westcott and Hort in New Testament studies. [3])

F. America

The course of criticism in America was similar to that in England, [4]) and involved the condemnation of its first propounder, BRIGGS. [5])

---

[1]) So Glover, *op. cit*, p. 36.

[2]) C. A. Briggs, Review "Dillmann's 'Numeri...' etc", *Presbyterian Review* VIII (1887) p. 340.

[3]) So Glover, *op. cit.*

[4]) Americans like the geographer Edward Robinson of Union Seminary had studied in Germany from 1826 and German essays had been translated in New York in 1829. Theodore Parker had translated Astruc in 1835 and de Wette in 1843, with so many additions of his own that he questioned whether his own name should not stand with de Wette's as author. Andrews Norton before 1845 had contrasted the cult negation of Amos with cultic Malachi and had accepted the late date for the laws. (See the first of G. F. Moore's two articles "Alttestamentliche Studien in Amerika", *ZAW* VIII (1888), esp. pp. 36-37).

[5]) The first to suffer for Higher Criticism in America was the Baptist, C. H. Toy, who was dismissed from the Southern Baptist Seminary in 1879. Briggs retained his chair, but was suspended from the Presbyterian ministry in 1893. Details are given in his *General Introduction to the Study of Holy Scripture*, Edinburgh (1899) pp. 286-89 and 615 ff. See also H. P. Smith, "Charles Augustus Briggs",

As editor of *The Presbyterian Review* Briggs from 1881-1883 presented essays from both sides by a wide range of scholars, including A. Hodge and B. Warfield, T.W. Chambers and W. H. Green, S. I. Curtiss and H. P. Smith. [1]) Answers to the *Prolegomena* were attempted by Bissell in 1885, Vos in 1886 and above all by Green in many writings. [2]) BISSELL dealt thoroughly with the laws both within the codes, and in the traces they had left in the Prophets, Psalms and Historical Books. [3]) Vos took up Wellhausen's five areas one by one, [4]) while GREEN dealt at length with the feasts [5]) The journal *Hebraica*, in successive issues between 1888 and 1892, carried a debate between Green and Harper which served to present the *pros* and *cons* of criticism to American readers. [6]) Only the narrative portions of the Pentateuch appear to have been dealt with, but when for the legal

---

ExpT XXV (1913-1914) pp. 294-98. Interesting comment on the progress of criticism among Southern Baptists is contained in the article by S. S. Hill, "The Southern Baptists: Need for Reformulation, Redirection", *Christian Century* LXXX (1963) pp. 39-42, where the outcry that greeted the dismissal of Ralph Elliott in 1962 is compared with the very different response to that of Toy for the same views: "When C. H. Toy... was asked to resign from the Faculty of the Louisville Seminary in 1879 because he had accepted the documentary hypothesis of Pentateuchal authorship there was hardly a stir: Toy was so obviously 'wrong' that his firing provoked no serious demurrers. Critical biblical scholarship was simply not a live option for the constituents of the convention in 1879" (p. 39). For Toy's early views see his article, "The Babylonian Element in Ezekiel", *JBL* (1881-1882) pp. 59-66 esp. p. 65, where he traces the P codification of law to Babylonian influence in the Exile; and also the 1966 Southern Baptist dissertation on Toy by B. G. Hurt noticed in *ZAW* LXXIX (1967) p. 95.

[1]) Moore's second article dealing with the decade down to 1889 summarizes these articles. (*ZAW* IX (1889) pp. 274 ff).

[2]) W. H. Green wrote against Colenso in 1863, and against Robertson Smith and Kuenen in *Moses and the Prophets* in 1882. His *The Higher Criticism of the Pentateuch* and his *Unity of the Pentateuch* appeared in 1895. Moore *ZAW* IX (1899) p. 280 quotes him as saying the following: "The critics have veiled Mt Blanc with fog, and then said it has disappeared. But, see the fog is blown away and the eternal mountains are still in their place", and notes the characterization of criticism as a "fog", but doubts if Green's writings are a "lauter Wind" to dispel it. When he enumerates the fifteen exceptions to centralization listed by Robertson Smith, and succeeds in justifying them all (*Moses and the Prophets*, pp. 159-69) the conservative fog seems thicker than the critical one!

[3]) E. C. Bissell, *The Pentateuch, its Origin and Structure*, New York (1885).

[4]) G. Vos, *The Mosaic Origin of the Pentateuchal Codes*, London (1886).

[5]) Green, *The Hebrew Feasts*, New York (1886). Essays by these and other American writers are contained in the symposium *Moses and his Recent Critics* edited by T. W. Chambers in 1887, and reviewed by Delitzsch in the article cited on p. 61. Another Delitzsch pupil among the anti-critics was A. P. Bissell.

[6]) Green and W. R. Harper, "The Pentateuchal Question", *Hebraica* V-VIII (1888-1892).

portions are added Green's *Hebrew Feasts* and his book on Robertson Smith, and Harper's *Priestly Element in the Old Testament*, [1]) a fairly complete picture of the viewpoints is obtained. It was Harper's that was to prevail, as is evidenced by the large number of American scholars so soon to be engaged on the *International Critical Commentary*. [2])

G. 1890-1900

The last decade of the nineteenth century saw the complete triumph of Grafianism. [3]) The great introductions of Driver, [4]) Holzinger, [5]) Addis, [6]) and Carpenter and Harford, [7]) the great histories of Stade [8]) and Kittel, [9]) and theologies of Marti [10]) and Kautzsch, [11]) the great dictionaries edited by Hastings [12]) and Cheyne and Black, [13]) and the

---

[1]) W. R. Harper, *The Priestly Element in the Old Testament*, Rev. ed, Chicago (1902).

[2]) J. M. P. Smith, "The Contribution of the United States to Old Testament Scholarship", *ExpT* XLI (1929-1930) pp. 169-71. The suddenness with which America capitulated to radical criticism is noted by Moore, *op. cit*, p. 288 and by J. D. Smart, *op. cit*, p. 282. Smart writes: "In America at the close of the nineteenth century the transition was made in many instances directly from an uncritical orthodoxy to a pure historicism such as characterized German scholarship at the time, the result being a radical antithesis, between uncritical evangelicals and critical liberals". He contrasts the position in Britain discussed above, and mentions the long succession of books appearing in Britain between 1890 and 1920—by George Adam Smith, McFadyen, Sanday, Gore, Burney—which aimed to show that Higher Criticism need not have a destructive effect on the preaching of the Old Testament.

[3]) That this was the decade of Old Testament criticism is made plain by an index of periodical articles from 1890 to 1899, which lists five times as many articles on Old Testament criticism as on New Testament criticism (so Glover, *op. cit*, p. 25).

[4]) S. R. Driver, *op. cit*.

[5]) H. Holzinger, *Einleitung in den Hexateuch*, Freiburg (1893).

[6]) W. E. Addis, *The Documents of the Hexateuch*, 2 vols, London (1892-1898).

[7]) J. E. Carpenter and G. B. Harford, *The Composition of the Hexateuch*, 2 vols, London (1902).

[8]) B. Stade, *Geschichte des Volkes Israel*, 2 vols, Berlin (1887-1888).

[9]) R. Kittel, *op. cit*.

[10]) K. Marti, *Religion of Old Testament*, ET, London (1907), first published 1897.

[11]) E. Kautzsch, *Biblische Theologie des Alten Testaments*, Tübingen (1911), first published as "Religion of Israel", *HDB* Extra Vol. (1904) pp. 612-735.

[12]) J. Hastings (ed.) *A Dictionary of the Bible*, 5 vols, Edinburgh (1898-1904).

[13]) T. K. Cheyne and J. S. Black (ed.) *Encyclopaedia Biblica* 4 vols, London (1899-1903). Of these two dictionaries a Conservative reviewer wrote: "The one represents the Bible as error and romance, mingled with truth, and the other as truth mingled with romance and error. For certain purposes the distinction is a real one, but here it is immaterial... In either case the Bible is like a lottery bag, from which blanks and prizes must be drawn at random. If the one section

commentaries of the *International Critical Commentary* series could only have come about after criticism itself had come of age as the new orthodoxy. This is not to say that opposition had been silenced. Rather the converse as will be seen in the next chapter, but the anti-Grafians were now in as small a minority, as the Grafians had been before Wellhausen. In 1912 Steuernagel could say that the conclusions of Pentateuchal criticism were as certain as human science could make them, [1]) and this was the dominant mood for more than a generation around the turn of the century.

---

of the critics may be trusted, the prizes abound; if the other section be right, the blanks predominate. But in either case... faith is impossible, and therefore Christianity is destroyed". (R. Anderson, *The Bible and Modern Criticism*, London (²1903) pp. 14-15).

[1]) C. Steuernagel, *Lehrbuch der Einleitung in das Alte Testament*, Tübingen (1912) p. 6.

CHAPTER SEVEN

OPPOSITION TO GRAFIANISM

Having traced the Grafian Hypothesis to its establishment as the new orthodoxy, and thus reached the mid-point of this survey, it is necessary now to make a change in method. Up to this point contributions towards Grafianism, however meagre, have been recorded, while the much more numerous works representative of traditional opinion have been left unnoticed. From this point on it is the restatements of typical Grafianism that must be omitted so that attention can be paid to divergent views put forward in opposition to the dominant hypothesis. Only thus can one explain the situation of the present day.

It is convenient to make a five-fold division of the opponents of Grafianism—Conservative, Jewish, Catholic, archaeological and critical. [1])

A. Conservative Opposition

Our survey appropriately begins with the work of the Orientalist James ROBERTSON of Glasgow, who cites Robertson Smith on the conservatism of the Orientals and then says "one poor orientalist here and there may be pardoned for having so much in common with them when so many scholars are of another mind". [2]) His concern is mainly with the religious reconstruction proposed by Wellhausen— the growth of monotheism, the localization of deity, image worship (Chaps VII-XII)—which he finds to be inconsistent with the developed stage of faith and literary tradition in the eighth century prophets (Chaps III-V). When he comes to the question of the laws (Chaps XIII-XVIII), he seeks to show that Israel was under authoritative

---

[1]) While in general agreement with J. B. Pritchard's criticism of this kind of division in another work on the grounds that "results of research should stand quite independent of any racial, national or religious background" of the scholars involved (*JQR* XXXIX (1948-1949) p. 103), a history, like that attempted here, must take them into account. All the scholars to be reviewed were "conservative" but this word meant something different to Jew, Catholic and evangelical Protestant, and it is to the last-named that the term is specifically applied here.

[2]) J. Robertson, *The Early Religion of Israel*, Edinburgh ([2]1892) pp. viii-ix.

institutions from the first, [1]) that non-mention does not mean non-existence,[2]) and that the theory of plural sanctuaries is not established.[3]) While refraining from drawing conclusions on the dates of the Old Testament books, it is clear that Robertson has profound misgivings about the new school.

> These misgivings are shared by a small group of Continental scholars, among whom Robertson's book immediately becomes popular. Orelli becomes his translator, and OETTLI follows his method of using Amos and Hosea as a pivot in an examination of their priestly terminology, [4]) and religious ideas. His conclusion is that Amos and Hosea know a Pentateuch, which has both priestly narrative and priestly institutions and law.[5]) The analysis of the Pentateuch into sources is not denied, and this is true also of GASSER, who mounts a full-scale attack on the evolutionary theory in a work dedicated to Orelli.[6]) For him the issue is that of the idea of God, rather than just that of the history of the cultus.[7])

More thorough-going in his rejection of the new school is RUP-PRECHT, who between 1893 and 1897 wrote almost a thousand and a half pages in criticism. One of his works is dedicated to W. H. Green, constant quotations are made from him, and it is to this writer, rather than to Robertson, that there is the closest resemblance.

> Although extended to inordinate length by later expansions,[8]) his essential position is already contained in the short work of 1893,[9])

---

[1]) He finds Wellhausen's application of his formula in Part I of the *Prolegomena* "these having not the law, do by nature the works of the law" illogical. He cannot at the same time argue from the non-observance of the laws to their non-existence and yet concede that although the codes are late, the *praxis* is early (p. 394).

[2]) Else there would be no circumcision in Islam, because the Koran does not mention it (p. 396).

[3]) For the prophets there is only one legitimate sanctuary, and for the Book of the Covenant very few (pp. 403-13).

[4]) S. Oettli, "Der Kultus bei Amos und Hosea," *Greifswalder Studien*, Gütersloh (1895) pp. 1-34.

[5]) Oettli, *Amos und Hosea*. Zwei Zeugen gegen die Anwendung der Evolutionstheorie auf die Religion Israels, Gütersloh (1901).

[6]) C. Gasser, *Das Alte Testament und die Kritik*, Stuttgart (1906).

[7]) He notes that while König agrees with Wellhausen on the date of P, and de Wette and Nöldeke differ, and Vatke differs with Wellhausen on the identification of D with Josiah's law-book where Dillmann, Driver and Baudissin agree, in matters of faith the radical critics are on one side, and the moderate critics on another (p. 95).

[8]) E. Rupprecht, *Das Rätsel des Fünfbuches Mose und seine falsche Lösung*, Gütersloh (1894); *Des Rätsels Lösung*, 2 vols, Gütersloh (1896-1897).

[9]) Rupprecht, *Die Anschauung der kritischen Schule Wellhausens vom Pentateuch*, Erlangen (1893).

with its "defensive" and "offensive" parts—his answer to specific points (pp. 17-44) and his appeal to the testimonies to Old Testament authorship found in New Testament writers (pp. 44-77). The moderate criticism of Strack is no more acceptable [1]) than the radical criticism of Cornill [2])—in fact analysis is unnecessary—[3]) critical views are *a priori* ruled out by theological considerations.

Combining the view-points of both Robertson and Rupprecht was Möller, who sought to use critical methods to overthrow critical theories. He showed that the new datings for the laws did not fit the history any better than the old. Deuteronomy is concerned with centralization, but Josiah's Reform was not. [4]) In the Book of Kings the latter was directed against idolatry. Deuteronomy's "holy war" against Canaanites and Amalekites is hopelessly anachronistic in the time of Josiah (Chap. I). Similarly it is not P, but the whole Pentateuch, that is needed to explain the reform of Ezra-Nehemiah, especially concerning mixed marriages. P's emphasis on tabernacle, Ark and Urim and Thummim is an anachronism after the loss of these things in the Exile (Chap. II). Nor is the dating of the Book of the Covenant any happier. By the arguments of the critics it would have to be later than the prophets, Deuteronomy and Ezra, because it commands sacrifice and forbids idolatry and foreign wives (pp. 162-66). P belongs to the Wilderness period and is shown to be earlier than D in its laws for the Passover and profane slaughter. It is incredible that Israel three times over should have accepted a falsification of her early history—in the ninth and eighth centuries at the hands of JE, in the sixth at the hands of D and in the fifth at the hands of P.

Many further works were to flow from Möller's pen on Pentateuchal analysis,[5]) the religion of Israel, and Old Testament theology and Introduction. Quite modern sounding are Möller's assertions in reply to Marti,[6]) that pre-Mosaic religion was not the polydaemonism

---

[1]) A view obviously held also by Strack's translator in the Schaff-Herzog Encyclopaedia, who follows the article from the *PRE* ("Pentateuch" *PRE* Vol. 15, pp. 113-124) with an appendage that is virtually a denial ("Hexateuch" *Schaff-Herzog* Vol. V, pp. 260-265 and 265-271).

[2]) The former occupies him in *Das Rätsel* and the latter in *Die Anschauung*.

[3]) Even his old master Delitzsch comes in for criticism (see above p. 61) as past his best, when he made concessions. It could be just as well retorted, however, that it is Delitzsch, who remained younger in mind, while his critic failed to adjust with the years.

[4]) W. Möller, *Are the Critics Right?* ET, London ([2]1903), first published 1899.

[5]) W. Möller, "Genesis," *The International Standard Bible Encyclopaedia*, Vol. II, Grand Rapids (1947) pp. 1199-1214, first published 1929; "Exodus", *ibid*, pp. 1056-67.

[6]) Möller, *Die Entwicklung der alttestamentlichen Gottesidee*, Gütersloh (1903).

of holy stones, wells, trees and animals (pp. 19-50). Henotheism and monotheism were not stages of Israel's religion but artificial modern constructions arising from a literalizing of symbolic language which occurs equally in late documents as in early (pp. 51-134). Ethical monotheism was not first introduced by the prophets but Jahweh was ethical from the beginning (pp. 135-83).

Turning back from the Continent to Robertson's successors in Britain, Conservative works included *Lex Mosaica* and those of Baxter and Orr.

> LEX MOSAICA appeared in 1894 under the editorship of Richard Valpy French.[1]) It contained essays by a large number of writers, among whom Rawlinson and Sayce were perhaps the best known. The traditional date of the law of Moses was accepted and the fortunes of this law in the succeeding periods of the Old Testament were traced in opposition to the Graf-Wellhausen view.
>
> Of a different kind was the volume of BAXTER, *Sanctuary and Sacrifice* (1895), which subjected Wellhausen's fifty pages on these two themes to five hundred pages of acute and bitter criticism. Imitating Wellhausen's method and eschewing the use of tradition or authorities, he relied on logic, sophistry and sarcasm to make his points. Many of these were well made, as subsequent enquiry has proved. It was inevitable that Wellhausen's methods should have called forth this kind of reply, but it is doubtful if scholarly investigation was advanced by it. The volume deserves to be placed alongside of the *Prolegomena* if only as an example of the fact that the new orthodoxy was no better fitted to stand against such weapons as Wellhausen had employed than the old.[2])

It could be objected against these works that to show the difficulties of the Grafian theory, did not go any way towards re-establishing the traditional view, and this was even more true of the major work of ORR which followed in 1905. [3]) It is true that Orr attempted a harmonization of each problem raised by Graf, but only after massing at the head of each chapter "the difficulties and perplexities of the

---

[1]) R. V. French, (ed.) *Lex Mosaica*, London (1894).

[2]) The following examples from Baxter's first chapter illustrate his method. Wellhausen is illogical in accepting the record of Josiah's Reformation, but denying that of Hezekiah; in quoting Jer. 7 against sacrifice in the Wilderness, but not on the significance of Shiloh; and in positing a redactor stupid enough to overwrite Kings with centralization, and yet to leave the references to the high places. See further A. S. Peake, "Wellhausen and Dr Baxter", *ExpT* VII (1895-1896) pp. 400-05; W. L. Baxter, "Professor Peake on the Reply to Wellhausen", *ibid*, pp. 505-12; A. S. Peake, "A Reply to Dr Baxter", *ibid*, pp. 559-64. Baxter's temper does not improve throughout the exchange!

[3]) J. Orr, *The Problem of the Old Testament*, London (1905).

critical hypothesis", so that although the arguments of his opponents are fairly stated in detail, the strength of their case as a whole is never allowed to emerge. That Orr should choose his own ground for the contest, and decline to fight on that favoured by his opponents is not in itself reprehensible, but he must accept with it the consequence of leaving the enemy entrenched in some parts of the field.

> Peake [1]) pointed out such faults in method, as beginning with general-
> izations and moving to the text; putting critic against critic as if
> their disagreements established again the traditional position, when
> in fact they were agreed in denying it; and in adding harmonization
> to harmonization as if that strengthened the traditional view, whereas
> each additional harmonization made it less probable.[2])

On the other side it must be said that Orr made out an impressive case. Conservative, without being obscurantist, he acknowledged the existence of a P style but did not believe that this necessitated a separate document later than Moses. [3]) He was even more sceptical, as others have been since, of E's separate existence.[4]) Deuteronomy as a pseudonymous work was not incompatible with just views of Scripture

---

[1]) A. S. Peake, "The Problem of the Old Testament", *Contemporary Review* (1907) pp. 493-509, with a reply by Orr, "The Problem of the Old Testament Restated", *ibid*, (1907), August, pp. 200-12, and a further exchange, "Dr Orr on Biblical Criticism", *Interpreter*, IV (1908) pp. 253-68, and "Professor Peake on Biblical Criticism", *ibid*, pp. 364-72.

[2]) On this compare the remarks of R. Rainy, *The Bible and Criticism*, London (1878) pp. 117-18: "Probabilities separately slight, or at least not by any means conclusive, may acquire a very high value, or may become quite conclusive, when combined. And, therefore, in any critical argument, the logic of the case is not satisfied unless the effect of the combined evidence is estimated, as well as the weight due to each separate part taken separately..." Applied to Ecclesi-astes "the separate indications of a late age in the Book of Ecclesiastes may all be separately explained away... but what [we] have to deal with is the impro-bability of a book of an early age *combining* all those separate and independent marks of a late one". (p. 118, cf. p. 167). One may wonder whether Rainy was quite loyal to his principle, when he sided against Robertson Smith. It is difficult to agree with Rainy's biographer, Carnegie Simpson, in his re-assertion after many years in a letter to J. K. Mozley, that it was Rainy's ecclesiastical statesman-ship in transferring the charge from the teaching to the man that saved the day for free enquiry in Scotland. "But for Rainy, the libel would have been carried to its judicial conclusion, and *that* would have meant not only the removal of Smith from his chair, but also a decision in principle against liberty of criticism in the Free Church. The latter—after all, the essential thing—Rainy saved" (Quoted by Mozley in *Some Tendencies in British Theology*, London (1951) p. 104). Apparently it was in order in 1882 that one man should die for the people!

[3]) J. Orr, *The Problem of the Old Testament*, Chap. X (esp. p. 335).

[4]) Peake, *op. cit*, p. 504 pointed out, however, that this had no such consequence for the Grafian reconstruction of the religion of Israel as the denial of P did.

(p. 249), but weighty theological reasons prevented the acceptance of the critic's account of its origin under Josiah, or that of P under Ezra.

It was on the theological side that Orr's work was at its strongest, as was to be expected of a dogmatic theologian, but there were not lacking those who resented the intrusion of a theologian into their field. To them the considerations adduced by Orr had no place in Old Testament science. Orr ventured the prophecy, that future generations would regard it as "one of the greatest psychological puzzles of history how such a hypothesis, loaded, with ... incredibilities, should have gained ... the ascendancy it has over so many able minds" [1]) and that

> finally the positions into which men's minds will be disposed to settle will be found nearer those advocated in... [his] pages, than... those of the advanced Wellhausen school (p. xviii).

Space precludes treatment of FINN, whose book, [2]) although one of the most comprehensive and complete, added little to the case presented by Orr, and of the many Fundamentalist works which, beginning from different presuppositions from those of the critics, could not hope to have any effect on critical opinion. It was the merit of the better Conservatives like Möller and Orr that they perceived that the case had to be argued as a matter of pure science, on the critics' own premises of an analysis of the Pentateuch into documents which they themselves did not accept.

Some others, who may be classed as Conservatives, accepted the analysis into J, E, D and P, but refused the dating and Grafian reconstruction that went with it.

> GEDEN [3]) e.g. suggested that Deuteronomy was written under David‛ and deposited in the foundation of Solomon's temple like the Book of the Dead in an Egyptian temple, until rediscovered under Josiah (pp. 330-34). JE was still earlier and must go back beyond the period of the Judges to Moses himself (p. 342). P could be any time after Deuteronomy.
>
> RULE [4]) sought an explanation of the problems raised by Graf in a thorough application of the principle of P as a priest's manual and D as a people's book. P dealt with the Levites in Jerusalem, while D devoted itself to those scattered throughout the land (Chap. 25).

---

[1]) Orr, *The Problem of the Old Testament*, p. 291.
[2]) A. H. Finn, *The Unity of the Pentateuch*, 3rd ed, London (1928).
[3]) A. S. Geden, *Outlines of Introduction to the Hebrew Bible*, Edinburgh (1909).
[4]) V. Z. Rule, *Old Testament Institutions*, London (1910).

The Levites in the temple had the tithe of P, while those "in the gates" had the third year tithe of D (Chap. 27). Moses must have been the author of the law, even if not of the Pentateuch. The literal use of the words "clean" and "unclean" must precede the figurative, and therefore the law, which knows the literal sense, must come before the prophets, who use the purely moral sense. H which combines the two uses must come between (Chap. 20).

THOMSON,[1]) like some others of the Conservative School, looked to the history of the Samaritans as supporting his position. The Samaritans would not have taken over the Pentateuch with Priestly innovations made only in the time of Ezra, nor could they have failed to have included Joshua if the critical view of a Hexateuch was true. The Pentateuch was edited under Samuel and deposited in the temple foundation to be lost until Josiah, except for traces of its history in Amos and Hosea, and of its laws in incidental references like that to firstfruits in 2 Kings 4:42. The argument from the Samaritan borrowing had already been answered by Chapman,[2]) who pointed out that as it was in the Samaritans' own interests to assert their orthodoxy, any objection on their part to the official Pentateuch was improbable.

B. JEWISH OPPOSITION

Modern Jewish Biblical science may be said to have begun with Zunz and Geiger in the first half of the nineteenth century.

ZUNZ, a student of de Wette and Wolf, regarded Leviticus "as after Ezekiel, Ezekiel as after Ezra, and the completed Pentateuch as three centuries after Josiah",[3]) and was thus a "Grafian before Graf". GEIGER argued that Leviticus was older than Deuteronomy, but allowed post-exilic additions.[4]) GRAETZ, the historian, accepted the Josianic dating for Deuteronomy, but dated the laws under Joash and Uzziah and the first four Pentateuchal books under Ahaz.[5])

---

[1]) J. E. H. Thomson, *The Samaritans*, London (1919).

[2]) A. T. Chapman, *op. cit*, pp. 277-99. The "Samaritan" argument has a history reaching back three centuries from J. I. Munro, *The Samaritan Pentateuch and Modern Criticism*, London (1911) and König on the other side in "Der samaritanische Pentateuch und die Pentateuchkritik", *JBL* XXXIV (1915) pp. 10-16, to Hengstenberg and von Bohlen (*op. cit*, I. 230), J. F. W. Jerusalem and the Deists (*op. cit*, p. 19), and van Dale and Morinus (von Bohlen, *loc. cit*). With the excavations at Shechem and the discovery of the Samaria letters in 1962 and the support they appear to give to Josephus' Alexander dating for the Samaritan temple and schism, it may now at last find a decent burial. (Cf. G. E. Wright, *Shechem*, New York (1965) pp. 178, 181; F. M. Cross, "The Discovery of the Samaria Papyri", *BA* XXVI (1963) pp. 110-21).

[3]) Cf. S. Rubaschow, "Bibel", *EncJud* Vol. IV, Berlin (1929) col. 714 and *HUCA* XXXI (1960) pp. 251-76.

[4]) M. L. Margolis, *The Hebrew Scriptures in the Making*, Philadelphia (1922) p. 50.

[5]) *Ibid*, and H. Graetz, "The Central Sanctuary of Deuteronomy", *JQR* III (1891) pp. 219-30.

Daring views like these, deviating from both conservative and critical "orthodoxy", are characteristic of Jewish scholars, if they start at all upon the path of criticism.[1])

The majority in our period did not do so, but had as their spokesmen Conservatives like LUZZATTO, who opposed de Wette from 1829, and argued for both the unity of Isaiah and the Mosaic authorship of the Pentateuch,[2]) WEISS, who in defending Mosaic authorship accepted a distinction between minor and major sanctuaries as the solution on centralization [3]) and I. M. WISE, who was prepared to concede late dates for second Isaiah and Hagiographa books, but argued for a Mosaic Pentateuch.[4])

As the Jewish presuppositions included those of the complete God-givenness of every word of the Law (see Chap. I), and the Jewish creed affirmed Mosaic authorship explicitly, [5]) a difficult situation faced scholars who wished to accept Grafian views.

One such was MONTEFIORE, who thought the essential Jewish position would be conserved if the Mosaic authorship of the Decalogue was insisted upon, [6]) and with this safeguard criticism could be both believed and taught in Judaism. [7])

The latter point became the subject of a friendly debate in the *Jewish Quarterly Review* with another friend of criticism, M. JOSEPH. Joseph had informed his congregation of the "Bible-Babel" controversy, but had found little interest, and had decided that the pulpit was not

---

[1]) Cf. Spinoza, Ibn Ezra and before them Hiwi referred to above in the first chapter.

[2]) J. Elbogen, "S.D. Luzzatto's Stellung zur Bibelkritik", *MGWJ* XLIV (1900) pp. 460-80.

[3]) S. Schechter, *Studies in Judaism*, London (1896) p. 225.

[4]) I. M. Wise, *Pronaos to Holy Writ*, Cincinnati (1891).

[5]) The eighth of Maimonides' Thirteen Articles as translated by Friedländer in *The Jewish Religion*, London (1891) was "The belief in the Divine origin of the Law: the belief that the whole Pentateuch was communicated to Moses by God, both the precepts and the historical accounts contained therein" (pp. 21, 134).

[6]) C. G. Montefiore, "Recent Criticism upon Moses and the Pentateuchal Narratives of the Decalogue", *JQR* III (1891) pp. 251-91. He felt that Friedländer's defence of total Mosaic authorship out-dated, and regretted such a stance in the only book in English on the Jewish religion by the head of the only Jewish theological college, who for twentyfive years had been responsible for training Jewish ministers ("Dr Friedländer on the Jewish Religion", *JQR* IV (1892) pp. 204-44).

[7]) Montefiore, "Some Notes on the Effect of Biblical Criticism upon the Jewish Religion", *JQR* IV (1892) pp. 293-306. He commented shrewdly that it little behoved Christians to contrast Jewish unwillingness to apply criticism to the Pentateuch with Christian readiness to do so, when Christians were equally unready when it came to *their* foundational documents, the Gospels (p. 293).

the place for critical views.[1]) Montefiore replied that although criticism
was pointless to the two groups, the liberals who did not need it and
the Conservatives who did not want it, in between there was a considerable middle group who could be helped by it.[2]) This was more true,
however, of England and America, than of Germany, where it was
still impossible to say in the Synagogue that Moses did not write the
Pentateuch.[3])

The most able of the German opponents was HOFFMANN, who
within one year of the appearance of the *Prolegomena*, and almost
before any other critique had appeared, had essayed an answer [4])
incorporating some of the traditional Jewish explanations. [5]) The

---

[1]) M. Joseph, "Biblical Criticism and the Pulpit", *JQR* XVIII (1906) pp. 291-301.
Bradley was quoted for the view that while following the truth was a duty for
oneself, suppressing it could be a duty out of consideration for others!

[2]) Montefiore, "Should Biblical criticism be spoken of in Jewish pulpits", *JQR*
XVIII (1906) pp. 302-16.

[3]) Germany's lack of interest in Biblical science is bemoaned also in "Judentum
und Bibelwissenschaft", Brüll's *Populärwissenschaftliche Monatsblätter*, Frankfurt am
Main (1907) by F. Perles, the Jewish textual critic, whose *Analekten zur Textkritik des Alten Testaments* appeared in 1895; and in "Biblical Criticism in Religious
Instruction", *JQR* XIX (1907) pp. 1-23 by F. Coblenz, who had asked "should
we Jews be inferior to men of another faith [i.e. Christians] in the knowledge
of our own peculiar treasure" (p. 13)? Unless the writer is mistaken, the only article
on criticism in the German Jewish *Monatschrift für Geschichte und Wissenschaft des
Judentums* in the thirty years before 1907 was the "safe" one on Luzzatto. In this
respect Dr Berliner's *Magazin für die Wissenschaft des Judenthums*, although opposed
to Wellhausenianism throughout its short life of twenty years (1874-1893),
served its readers better by the articles from its first issue of Hoffmann, who was
soon to be co-editor. At the same time France was carrying Halévy's powerful
anti-Wellhausen "Recherches Bibliques" in the *Revue des Etudes Juives* from
1883, and in the *Revue Semitique*, which Halévy founded, from 1893. Only in
England, with Montefiore's editorship of the *Jewish Quarterly Review* for the two
decades before 1908, was there both cognizance of, and hospitality to, criticism.
The *Jewish Encyclopedia* published about this time presents an odd appearance
with Christian scholars like Driver providing the criticism and Jews like B.
Jacob the anti-criticism in Vol. IV (1903) "Deuteronomy", and V (1903) "Exodus",
or both sides by Jews, Jacob and Hirsch "Genesis" *ibid*, and finally only the
critical view-point in "Leviticus", "Numbers", "Pentateuch". Late laws are
recognized by the article "Bible Canon" III (1902) p. 152.

[4]) D. Hoffmann, "Die neueste Hypothese über den pentateuchischen Priesterkodex", *Magazin für die Wissenschaft des Judenthums*, VI (1879) pp. 1-19, 90-114,
209-37; VII (1880) pp. 137-156, 237-254.

[5]) Cf. the interesting collection gathered from Rashi, Maimonides and others
by Manasseh ben Israel (*op. cit*) e.g. Elijah had sacrificed away from the central
sanctuary, and Joshua had perambulated Jericho on the sabbath, because
prophets could set aside law, so long as they did not induce to idolatry (Vol. I,
pp. 227-28). Josiah's law-book was new only in the sense that it alone was free
from the corruption of the divine name brought about by Manasseh (p. 297).
Chronicles says David paid six hundred shekels for Ornan's threshing floor

laws for sacrifice were given only for the central sanctuary, not for the *bamoth*. Wellhausen's deductions from sacrifices offered irregularly elsewhere, and sin offerings neglected before the Exile, missed the point that burnt offerings and only burnt offerings belonged to the central sanctuary (VI, pp. 90ff). Ezekiel, as a proved borrower, was more likely to have borrowed from P than *vice versa*. His reference to a sin of the Levites was to something very old and not just in his time (VI, pp. 209-37). Returning to the same themes in 1902-1903, [1]) Hoffmann dealt in detail with Ezekiel's use of his predecessors, including H and P (pp. 24-40), and with the inappropriateness of P in the time of Ezra-Nehemiah (pp. 63-65). Unless P preceded D we should have the unlikely spectacle of P, which centres on the temple, allowing the Passover sacrifice at home after it had been in the temple in D, and of H insisting on sacrificial slaughter after D had permitted its secularization. [2]) His work was well done and remains one of the best statements of scientific Conservatism. [3])

This can scarcely be said of the voluminous and uneven work of WIENER, which combines some of the acutest Conservative work with some of the crassest and most objectionable.

> Loewe, in editing a memorial volume of Wiener's posthumous essays,[4]) spoke of him as a firstrate historian and geographer, but it was as a lawyer that he first took the field in 1904 in his volume on *Biblical Law*.[5]) Avoiding religious questions as beyond his competence, he maintained that a knowledge of law explained many of the alleged differences between the Pentateuchal codes. His proof extended only to a few details and was of no great importance in comparison with the structure raised by Grafianism.
>
> In the years following, Wiener pressed on to other aspects of the

---

instead of Samuel's fifty, which was one twelfth, to show that although Jerusalem was in Benjamin, it was not merely the sanctuary of that one tribe, but of all twelve! (pp. 281-82).

[1]) Hoffmann, *Die wichtigsten Instanzen gegen die Graf-Wellhausensche Hypothese*, Berlin (1902-1903).

[2]) Cf. M. Waxman, *A History of Jewish Literature*, Vol. IV, New York ([2]1947) p. 645, who may also be consulted with profit on the next names.

[3]) See especially his *Das Buch Leviticus*, 2 vols. Berlin (1905-1906) and his seventeen articles in criticism of the analysis between 1914 and 1919 in the periodical *Jeschurun*, which by now seems to have replaced his *Magazin für die Wissenschaft des Judenthums*. By 1918 I. Neubauer could advise *Jeschurun's* readers that Hoffmann had made away with Wellhausen ("Wellhausen und der heutige Stand der Bibelwissenschaft", *Jeschurun* V (1918) pp. 203-33)—one of many such prophecies, with the wish apparently the father to the thought, which we shall have to record.

[4]) H. M. Wiener, *Posthumous Essays*, Oxford (1932).

[5]) Wiener, *Studies in Biblical Law*, London (1904).

subject without further hesitations about his competence. In articles
in *Bibliotheca Sacra*, which appeared later in book form he replied
in turn to the volumes of Addis,[1]) Carpenter and Harford,[2]) Wellhausen,[3]) Skinner [4]) and many others. In particular he made the field
of textual criticism his own, and confidently claimed to have overthrown Astruc's clue by his discovery of textual variants in the
Septuagint and the Samaritan.[5]) In bringing forward this argument,
as well as in his answer to historical difficulties by the theory of radical
displacement of material,[6]) he had to posit a corruption of the Massoretic Text surprising in a Jew.

Of more importance for our subject was Wiener's distinction,
taken over from van Hoonacker, between a private lay altar which
was permitted at any place, and the horned altar of the central sanctuary. [7]) This distinction was the complete answer in his opinion to
Wellhausen, who on his own admission, [8]) based his whole case on
centralization. Along with this went a distinction in the offerings
between the customary lay offerings of the pre-Mosaic times which
Moses continued and the offerings which Moses introduced—the
statutory individual offerings to be made only through the priests
at the House of God and the statutory national offerings for the whole
people. This theory fitted the facts so ingeniously that one cannot
but see it as an artificial construction made to order. [9])

Among the many other contributions made by Wiener may be noted
his essays on the Conservative and Jewish tasks in Old Testament
criticism. The first appeared in 1912.[10]) It made the pertinent point
that it was not enough to show that the critics differ on a problem,
as if the syllogism ran "A says the solution is X, B says that it is Y,
therefore there is no problem". Unless a solution Z is found, the

---

[1]) Wiener, *Notes on Hebrew Religion*, London (1907).
[2]) Wiener, *Essays in Pentateuchal Criticism*, London (1910) Chaps II-V.
[3]) Wiener, *ibid*, Chap. VI; *Pentateuchal Studies*, London (1912) Chaps XX, XXII.
[4]) Wiener, *ibid*, Chap. VIII.
[5]) Wiener, *Essays in Pentateuchal Criticism*, Chap. I.
[6]) Wiener, "Contributions to a new theory of the Composition of the Pentateuch", *Bibliotheca Sacra*, LXXV (1918) pp. 80-103, 237-66; LXXVI (1919)
pp. 193-220; LXXVII (1920) pp. 304-328, 369-402.
[7]) Wiener, *The Origin of the Pentateuch*, London (1910) Chap. III; *Essays in
Pentateuchal Criticism*, Chap. VI; "Altar", *The International Standard Bible Encyclopaedia*, Vol. I, pp. 106-110.
[8]) J. Wellhausen, Prolegomena, p. 368.
[9]) It will be interesting to see whether it survives the revision of the *ISBE*
currently being undertaken. It is dropped from the conservative case in the other
recent conservative dictionary, *The New Bible Dictionary* (IVF) (1962).
[10]) Wiener, "Some Aspects of the Conservative Task in Pentateuchal Criticism",
Pentateuchal Studies, Chap. I.

readers will decide for either X or Y. The second article, written much later,[1]) asked why there needed to be distinctively Jewish Old Testament scholarship and gave the answer that the anti-Semitism of the current German scholarship needed to be counteracted from the Jewish side. Others who interested themselves in the Jewish role in criticism were Margolis, Jastrow and Jampel. MARGOLIS, in his programmatic "The Scope and Methodology of Biblical Philology" in the first American issue of *JQR* [2],) laid down sound principles for various types of criticism, and applied them in his judicious reviews of the critical works by Driver, Chapman and others,[3]) and in his own *multum in parvo, The Hebrew Scriptures in the Making* (1922).[4]) The same is true of JASTROW's excellent "Constructive Elements in the Critical Study of the Old Testament",[5]) illustrated in this case by his works in the field of Assyriology.[6]) These two scholars represented a moderate criticism, which was repugnant to JAMPEL in his *Vorgeschichte des israelitischen Volkes*.[7]) Addressing a word to "liberal" and "conservative" Jewish Bible students in turn, he warns the first against Wellhausenian scepticism, with Graetz as his "terrible warning" [8])—when Jews are critics, they are the most extreme critics, he asserts—and the second he calls to come out of the Middle Ages, and engage in philology— Hoffmann is the "shining example"—and in archaeology, to "prove the Bible right".[9])

Jampel's claim that radical Jews would out-radical other radicals is illustrated by our next writer, BERNFELD, who moved from anti-criticism in 1899,[10]) through normal criticism with variations in 1921,[11]) to extreme criticism in his vast 2000 page Hebrew *Introduction* in 1923,

---

[1]) Wiener, "The Need of a Jewish Biblical Scholarship", *Posthumous Essays*, pp. 79-86.

[2]) *JQR* I (1910-1911) pp. 5-41. (N.S.)

[3]) *Ibid*, pp. 547-62; III (1912-1913) pp. 101-14; IV (1913-1914) pp. 249-64.

[4]) *Op. cit.*

[5]) M. Jastrow, *JBL* XXXVI (1917) pp. 1-30.

[6]) Cf. his *Hebrew and Babylonian Traditions*, New York (1914).

[7]) S. Jampel, *Die Vorgeschichte des israelitischen Volkes und seiner Religion I. Die Methoden*, Frankfurt (1913) but references are to the 1928 edition.

[8]) The Ezra correspondence, which Graetz had doubted, had now been accepted as genuine by E. Meyer.

[9]) He himself had done both the latter in his articles from 1907 on "Die bibel-wissenschaftliche Literatur der letzten Jahre", which had been the first to break the long silence and acquaint the readers of the *MGWJ* with the issues of criticism— and anti-criticism! (*MGWJ* LI (1907) pp. 659-77; LII (1908) pp. 21-36, 145-61; LIII (1909) pp. 641-56; LV (1911) pp. 641-65). The final article on "Die neuen Papyrusfunde in Elephantine", adduced the aberrations of the Elephantine community in support of the conservative defence that the non-observance of a law does not mean its non-existence, but this appeal was to prove a liability—see below.

[10]) S. Bernfeld, *Das Buch der Bücher*, Berlin (1899).

[11]) Bernfeld, *Die jüdische Literatur*, Berlin (1921). P is post-exilic and D Josianic but the divine names clue is doubted.

which allowed no part of the Pentateuch to be Mosaic or even pre-exilic, and discarded J and E.[1]) The more conventional critical view was expressed in 1925 in another Hebrew work, a history of criticism by Soloweitschik and S. Rubaschow (now President Shazar),[2]) and in the history of *Dubnow*.[3])

That it was Jampel's position rather than the critical one that was typical of Judaism in this period is clear from the increasingly conservative stance of the former liberal periodical *JQR* [4]) with its reviews of Biblical studies alternating between Hoschander and Reider. Although both scholars claimed to want a "middle way" between "nothing Mosaic" and "everything Mosaic," their position seems usually nearer the latter.

HOSCHANDER in a typical article [5]) begins with a series of *a prioris*. On the analogy of the other nations we should expect Israel to have a law code, that in her case it would be an ecclesiastical code, that as a code for priests it would differ from that for the people, that this priest's code would include instructions for a tabernacle, that the priests as the educated class would reach a higher level of spiritual thought earlier than non-priestly writers like J and E etc (p. 414). The silence of the historical books is accounted for by the dislocation created by the Disruption, Jeroboam naturally destroying copies of the Mosaic laws, and by the apostacy of Manasseh, who did the same in the South. As the Mosaic books were in the South and the rest of the Old Testament in the North, all is accounted for—[6])unless one prefers the critical disease to this radical Conservative cure!

---

[1]) Cf. Bernfeld, "Bibel", *EncJud* IV (1929) col. 495, where the late fourth century B.C. is given for the completion of the Pentateuch.

[2]) Cf. the latter's *EncJud* article on the history of Jewish criticism in *ibid*, pp. 703-17, and on these and the following scholars F. A. Levy, "Contemporary Trends in Jewish Bible Study" in H. R. Willoughby (ed.) *The Study of the Bible Today and Tomorrow*, Chicago (1947) pp. 98-115.

[3]) S. Dubnow, *Weltgeschichte des jüdischen Volkes* I. Die Orientalische Periode, Jerusalem (1925) pp. 104, 108, 119-22, 167-70 (references from 1937 edition).

[4]) This is *not* one of the changes recognized by the recent anniversary volume in its history of the review! Cf. A. A. Neuman and S. Zeitlin (ed.) *The Seventy-Fifth Anniversary Volume of the Jewish Quarterly Review*, Philadelphia (1967) p. 65 cf. p. 44. It had been transferred from England to America in 1910. *MGWJ* also, after the initial burst with Jampel's articles, apart from a few contributions from Wiener in the 1920s, again relapses into critical silence, broken only by another "demise" article on Wellhausen, a year before its own final demise in 1939.

[5]) *JQR* XVI (1925-1926) pp. 407-19.

[6]) "'Though in the Mosaic books there is scarcely anything that may be attributed to the libraries of North Israel, the literature of the latter must be regarded as a first source of information for other historical Books of the Old Testament. This is especially true of the Book of Judges, and large parts of the Books of Samuel and Kings. This fact fully answers the arguments.. that the Mosaic laws... had not yet existed in the periods of the authors of Judges, Samuel and

REIDER seems better able to appreciate critical works [1]) although not sharing their view-point. In 1936 he will contribute an article on Deuteronomy arguing against its being Josiah's law-book, or from the seventh century,[2]) but this has already taken us down beyond our 1925 date.

C. CATHOLIC OPPOSITION

The conservative nature of Catholic Biblical scholarship in this period was dictated by the attitudes of the hierarchy as expressed in various encyclicals.

In this age of *aggiornamento* it is difficult for us to realize that the century, which ended with the "modernizing" of the Second Vatican Council in 1964, had begun with Pius IX's refusal to reconcile himself to "modernity" in his *Syllabus of Errors* in 1864.[3]) Leo XIII had indeed at first encouraged the Biblical movement, but his fear of rationalistic criticism led him to draw back, so that his *Providentissimus Deus* in 1893, while calling to Bible study like that of the Apostles and Fathers, inspired confidence neither by its recommended method (tradition before internal evidence) [4]) nor its desiderated goal (to harmonize contradictions as the Fathers did).[5]) A slightly more liberal attitude to non-Catholic scholarship is indicated by his *Vigilantiae* in 1902,[6]) but the situation changes for the worse with the enthronement of Pius X in 1903. The Biblical Commission, which had been set up as a kind of a "watch-dog" by his predecessor, is now

---

Kings.. No shred of evidence for the critical theory remains [sic].. if we assume that the narratives in these Books contrary to the laws of the Pentateuch had been taken from the libraries of North Israel" (p. 416).

[1]) Cf. his reviews on the Kittel Festschrift and Gunkel's Essays *JQR* IX (1918-1919) pp. 423 ff, on the Wellhausen Festschrift XII (1921-1922) pp. 195-221, on the Kahana commentary XVII (1926-1927) p. 388, and on the Marti Festschrift XIX (1928-1929) pp. 431-37.

[2]) J. Reider, "The Origin of Deuteronomy", *JQR* XXVII (1936-1937) pp. 349-71.

[3]) Cf. A. Vidler, *The Church in an Age of Revolution*, p. 151, whose account lies in part behind what follows.

[4]) "There has arisen, to the great detriment of religion, an inept method, dignified by the name of the "higher criticism", which pretends to judge of the origin, integrity, and authority of each book from internal indications alone. It is clear, on the other hand, that in historical questions, such as the origin and the handing down of writings, the witness of history is of primary importance,... and that in this matter internal evidence is seldom of great value, except as confirmation". (*Rome and the Study of Scripture*, St Meinrad ([7]1964) p. 20).

[5]) "If then, apparent contradiction be met with, every effort should be made to remove it... the contest must not be abandoned". (*Ibid*, p. 27).

[6]) "Let them draw from this science new resources by availing themselves even of the assistance of non-Catholic scholars" (1902) *ibid*, p. 33 contrasts favourably with the 1893 warning that the latter "being without the true faith, only gnaw the bark of the sacred Scripture, and never attain its pith!" (*ibid*, p. 17).

packed with Conservatives, whose replies are uniformly in the most rigid Conservative terms,[1] until finally *Lamentabili* (1907) and *Pascendi* (1907) virtually rule out criticism altogether.[2])

On the question of the Pentateuch, the Biblical Commission in 1906 ruled for the Mosaic authorship, allowed that Moses may have used sources, but rejected a later coming together of these sources after Moses. Catholic scholarship was thus limited to the position of Astruc and could not move beyond it even to that of the early Catholics, Simon and Geddes. Grafianism was quite ruled out.

Many enlightened Catholics already on the road of criticism were embarrassed by the decision.

LOISY went the whole way and was excommunicated,[3] Lagrange was required by authority to transfer to New Testament studies,[4] and Hummelauer to other fields,[5] van Hoonacker refrained from further publication on the Pentateuch,[6] and only von Hügel, a layman, felt free to comment on the weakness of the Commission's view.[7]

---

[1]) A. Vidler, *op. cit*, p. 187.

[2]) According to Vidler the idea with which Pius X became obsessed of a "modernist plot", dictated by false philosophical presuppositions and conspiring to overthrow traditional Christianity, had little foundation in fact (pp. 179 ff). (Fuller proof is provided by Vidler in *The Modernist Movement in the Roman Church*, Cambridge (1934) pp. 1-11). A more sympathetic account is given by J. Levie who points out that the errors condemned were mainly those of Loisy, and nearly all had to do with the doctrine of Christ. (*The Bible, Word of God in Words of Men*, ET, New York (1961) pp. 70 ff, 60). The latter gives evidence of a "plot" but it was a Conservative one for the purpose of delation! (p. 73).

[3]) Loisy, who had taught Scripture at the Institut Catholique since 1884, and had welcomed Renan's Old Testament works, attacked the authenticity of the Pentateuch in his *Enseignement biblique* in 1892. (J. Levie, *op. cit*, pp. 45-46).

[4]) The full story is now available for the first time in his memoirs published in 1967 under the title *Le Père Lagrange au service de la Bible*, Souvenirs Personnels (ed.) P. Benoit, Paris (1968) (referred to hereafter as *Souvenirs*).

[5]) *Ibid*, p. 145. Lagrange, writing of Hummelauer's Deuteronomy commentary in 1901 (*ibid*, pp. 109-10) says "His ideas had completely changed since in his Genesis commentary he had distinguished an Adamic document and one from the time of Noah. Now he did not hesitate to say that the corpus of the law in Dt. 12-26 was not from Moses, but from Samuel; the Pentateuch was the work of many centuries". Hummelauer's commentaries had been *Genesis* (1894), *Exodus and Leviticus* (1897), *Numbers* (1899) and *Deuteronomy* (1901). The last-named contained a critical introduction of 159 pages.

[6]) See below.

[7]) This he did in reply to the strictures of his friend Briggs in C. A. Briggs and F. von Hügel, *The Papal Commission and the Pentateuch*, London (1906). He agreed against the Commission that the documents of the Pentateuch could not be Mosaic, when they were used for his own life, nor could they have been put together under his supervision, when they differed so much from one another (p. 42). However, Rome had what was necessary to come to see the truth of

Earlier, at a congress in Fribourg in 1897 it had been von Hügel and Lagrange, who had contributed the papers, which may be said to have precipitated the crisis in Catholic Pentateuchal scholarship. VON HÜGEL announced his conversion to source criticism as the result of six years' close study of the Pentateuch, during which he had read the books through in Hebrew, not once but in some cases several times. [1])

> Critics were not all rationalists—Simon and Astruc were not (p. 221), nor did they hopelessly disagree, (pp. 222-23).[2]) Those accepting the critical solution far outnumbered those who did not (p. 223).[3]) Pentateuchal sources are not improbable, but have their parallel in the books of Kings, Chronicles, Maccabees and Tatian (pp. 225-26).

Von Hügel also accepted the principle of a development in the laws (pp. 219-20), but it was LAGRANGE who argued this out persuasively. [4]) If such legislative evolution were not admitted Moses will have both permitted many altars and prohibited many altars. It is more reasonable to accept the critical view than to attempt to defend the Mosaic authenticity of both these laws. The words "God said to Moses" mean "in the spirit of the first legislator" and are "a justifiable fiction that harmonizes the eternal aspect of law with its changing

---

this matter as it had done in other instances. Similarly G. B. M. Coore in "The Papal Commission and the Pentateuch", *ExpT* XVIII (1906-1907) pp. 285-86, argued that while the Church could be temporarily wrong in her teaching (as with Galileo), she could not be irretrievably wrong and added: "Decisions which are scientifically, and in the abstract, erroneous, may in history be justified on pastoral grounds as necessary to protect the faith of simple souls from sudden and violent shocks", however, the educated also have a claim as children of the Church.

[1]) F. von Hügel, "The Historical Method and the Documents of the Hexateuch", *The Catholic University Bulletin* IV (1898) p. 198.

[2]) Of Astruc's 137 P (A) verses in Gn. 1-11, Kautzsch agreed with four-fifths after 140 years, and of Nöldeke's 350 P verses in 1868, nine tenths still stood thirty years later.

[3]) By 103 to 4, as the list compiled by Green contained only four professional Old Testament scholars to one hundred and three in that of Briggs.

[4]) Lagrange, who had founded the School of St Etienne in Jerusalem in 1890 and the *Revue Biblique* as its journal in 1892, had argued against Wellhausen's theory of religious evolution in an article on Hosea in *RB* in 1892 pp. 203-235 (Cf. *Souvenirs*, p. 97) but had already published articles favouring the analysis in Gn. 1-3 in 1896 and 1897, (esp. pp. 368-72) and now devoted his Fribourg lecture to a defence of this position. It appeared as "Les Sources du Pentateuque", *RB* VII, Paris (1898) pp. 10-32. In the summary given above this article is the basis, but some later expressions are included from the summaries by R. T. Murphy, *Père Lagrange and the Scriptures*, ET, Milwaukee (1946) p. 26 and E. H. Maly, "Père Lagrange and the Pentateuch", *Lagrange Lectures*, Iowa (1963) p. 78

aspect". P was from the Exile, but was no less reliable for Moses seven hundred years before than Moses was for Abraham as far before that again. D was unlikely to be from Moses, but was drawn up slightly before Josiah, [1]) but as a perfected form of the Mosaic Book was also entitled to be called Mosaic. [2]) Moses was the legislator in the sense that he laid the foundation, rather than crowned the edifice. [3])

In the wake of the Fribourg congress a spirited debate took place in a number of Catholic journals on the issues raised, [4]) but after the Commission's ruling in 1906 such articles no longer appear.[5]) Lagrange himself loyally accepted the Commission's decision and abandoned a commentary on Genesis on which he had been at work for nearly a decade. [6]) Only at the very end of his life, thirty years later, did he return to his Genesis studies, devoting to them the last article he was to publish in 1938. [7]) He gives lip-service to the Commission's ruling of documents older than Moses and used by him—a position he had rejected in 1898—but is content neither with Bea's nor Vaccari's treatment (see later). His views on the law cannot be gauged, as he deals with neither D nor P, but on Genesis he holds that Moses was responsible for both E and J. His view had always been that E rather than J was the older document. [8])

A comparison of these two articles forty years apart is a sobering commentary on the effect of the Commission's decision on the progress of Catholic scholarship. [9]) Catholic apologetic is fond of

---

[1]) "Is it likely that, once the Law was given by God on Sinai, He transformed it after only forty years, and then immobilized it for centuries?"

[2]) Lagrange's later Toulouse lecture *Historical Criticism and the Old Testament*, London (1905) p. 173.

[3]) Contra the earlier Catholic view that he had collected older laws.

[4]) See especially the article by J. Touzard, "Moïse et Josué", *Dictionnaire apologétique de la foi catholique*, Vol. III, Paris (1919) cols 732-35 for a summary.

[5]) Touzard's, which was an exception, was censured as "not safe to be taught" (A. Suelzer, *The Pentateuch*, A Study in Salvation History, New York (1964) p. 167).

[6]) It had been projected before his *Judges* but he had been advised that his recognition of sources was less likely to cause trouble if it was only in *Judges* (*Souvenirs*, p. 107). A fragment of the Genesis commentary (Gn. 1-6:4), which was already printed but did not circulate, is now a collector's item. It accepts both the Wellhausen analysis (p. 62) and dating (p. 13), but has no Introduction.

[7]) M. J. Lagrange, "L'authenticité mosaïque de la Genèse et la théorie des documents", *RB* XLVII (1938) pp. 163-83. The pen fell from his hand as he was correcting its proofs.

[8]) Cf. *RB* (1899) p. 626 but there only *some* Mosaic material is ascribed to E.

[9]) When the torso Genesis commentary is taken into account, and the revealing contemporary documents of the *Souvenirs*, it is impossible any longer to agree with R. T. Murphy in "Moses and the Pentateuch", *CBQ* XI (1949) pp. 165-78 that

attributing their church's success in Biblical studies to the restraining effect of the Commission's decision, [1]) but a less charitable view seems nearer to the facts. Only as their scholars have ignored or rationalized the decision have they made real progress. [2]) In the first year of the promulgation of the Commission's decision its effect was almost completely stultifying. [3]) Source criticism, which was permitted, did not flourish. Catholic scholarship was almost entirely in defence of the most rigid traditional view.

Aspects of Grafianism were answered by van Hoonacker and his successors Poels, Engelkemper and Landersdorfer. VAN HOONACKER dealt at length with cult centralization [4]) and the Levitical ministry. [5]) In the former of these works he advanced the novel solution soon to be taken over and elaborated by Poels, [6]) that the many sanctuaries were really the one sanctuary and that Nob and Gibeon (Gibeah = Geba) and Mizpah and Gilgal were identical with the sanctuary of the ark at Kiriath-Jearim, and that there was thus only one legitimate

---

Lagrange in 1906 had not gone beyond what the Commission allowed, and in 1938 had not changed his position.

[1]) E. J. Byrne, "Catholic Tradition and Biblical Criticism", *Mémorial Lagrange* (1940) pp. 230 ff; A. Bea, "Der heutige Stand der Pentateuchfrage", *Biblica* XVI (1935) p. 200.

[2]) For the effect of the Commission's decision the changes made between the first and second editions of W. Barry's, *Tradition of Scripture* ([1]1906 and [2]1908), as set out in parallel columns by Vidler, *The Modernist Movement*, p. 226, are illuminating. "Mosaic contributions" of 1906 becomes "Mosaic foundations" in 1908, "virtual authorship" by Moses, becomes "original authorship" by Moses, "not responsible for its historic shape" becomes "not responsible for its every line", "suppose of the 'Book of the Covenant' " becomes "far beyond the 'Book of the Covenant' ", "recensions that belong to a much later period" becomes "recensions that belong to different periods".

[3]) Lagrange obediently took up work on the Gospels with conspicuous success, but soon was in trouble with Markan priority, and on this occasion had his works named as erroneous by the S. C. Consistoriale (see *Souvenirs*, p. 203 and pp. 365-68 and F. M. Braun, *The Work of Père Lagrange*, ET, Milwaukee (1962) pp. 92-96), and had to take a break from his teaching office. In fact the *Souvenirs* throughout makes sorry reading with its spectacle of the most distinguished, but none-the-less devout, scholar of his church constantly harassed—by politicking in Rome (his constant journeys back and forth), restricted—by the take-over of his *Revue* as the Commission's organ (during his suspension the "Biblical" was removed from its title), insulted—by the permission given for the establishment of the school of a rival order along side his (this was against all church custom), and finally humiliated into submission.

[4]) A. van Hoonacker, *Le lieu du culte dans le legislation rituelle des Hebreux*, Leipzig (1894).

[5]) Hoonacker, *Le Sacerdoce Lévitique*, Louvain (1899).

[6]) H. A. Poels, *Examen critique de l'histoire de sanctuaire de l'Arche*, Louvain (1897).

sanctuary in the time of Samuel, and throughout the whole Old
Testament period (p. 66). [1])

> His other suggestion that centralization applied only to the horned
> altar, and not to the lay altars (pp. 2-32), has already been described
> in connection with Wiener, and was further elaborated by ENGEL-
> KEMPER,[2]) who sought to place the three laws of the sanctuary (Exod.
> 20; Lev. 17 and Dt. 12) at three successive stages of Israel's experience
> in the Wilderness.[3])
> LANDERSDORFER argued for the early origin of the Day of Atonement.[4])
> He found old elements in the material of the priestly vestments,
> the use of a scapegoat, and the employment of an incense censer,
> rather than the special altar. As the special altar already stood in
> Solomon's temple, the parts of P, which lack it must be older than
> the temple (pp. 43-44).
> A more general work of vast scope and detail was that of ŠANDA
> in 1924.[5]) Every aspect of Pentateuchal criticism from linguistic
> analysis to religious history was covered, but as in so many works
> of this kind the over-all picture of the wood is lost in the details of
> the trees. No one would know from the meagre thirtyfive pages
> devoted to Grafianism (pp. 281-316) towards the end of the four
> hundred and twenty page volume that this was the crux of the critical
> case. A slightly longer section on P (pp. 187-245) argues that its lack
> of order is explainable by the chronology of the Wilderness, but is
> unintelligible, like so many of its laws, on a post-exilic dating. The Book
> of the Covenant is the pre-Mosaic law of the Goshen period (p. 173).

---

[1]) Cf. E. de Knevett, "Professor Albin van Hoonacker", *ExpT* XX (1908-1909)
pp. 165-66. Lagrange, as a geographer, rejects this theory out of hand in *RB*
VI (1897) pp. 630-32.

[2]) W. Engelkemper, *Heiligtum und Opferstätten in den Gesetzen des Pentateuch*,
Paderborn (1908).

[3]) Before leaving van Hoonacker it should be noted that he too like Lagrange
had a work on Pentateuchal authorship in hand between 1896 and 1908, which
had to be set aside, but was published posthumously in 1949 twenty years after
his death (A. Suelzer, *op. cit*, p. 183). This was his *De compositione litteraria et de
origine mosaica Hexateuchi*, Brussels (1949). After his massive polemic in the volumes
above, it is surprising to find that he accepted both documents and late codification of the laws, and was content if their substance only went back to Moses,
and P was older than D. See J. Coppens, "Chronique d'Ancien Testament—
Le Problème de l'Hexateuque", *Analecta Lovaniensia Biblica et Orientalia II*,
38 pp. 3 ff, 21 and his *Le Chanoine Albin Van Hoonacker*, Paris (1935), where it is
admitted that van Hoonacker suppressed his view that Deuteronomy was post-
exilic and H was Josiah's law-book, and withdrew a commentary on Malachi
already in print. From arguing against the unity of Isaiah, he now argued for it!
Cf. Irwin's review in *JR* XVIII (1938) pp. 443-44, and in another connection
JR XIX (1939) pp. 385-86, where he remarks that the alleged Catholic freedom
was only freedom to be silent.

[4]) S. Landersdorfer, *Studien zum biblischen Versöhnungstag*, Münster (1924).

[5]) A. Šanda, *Moses und der Pentateuch*, Münster (1924).

Moses wrote Genesis, and Joshua wrote Exodus, Numbers and Deuteronomy from Mosaic data. The law was Mosaic but kept secret until Ezra-Nehemiah (pp. 107, 287-91, 395-99).

Also opposed to Grafianism was LATTEY, who in 1922 edited a small volume on *Moses and the Law* containing Catholic treatments of Pentateuchal problems [1]) Literary analysis was refuted by an article on Genesis 1-3 (pp. 10-20), centralization by an article on the ark (pp. 47-57), and Wellhausen on the priesthood by an article with this title (pp. 58-67). All the contributors are anti-Wellhausen, and this remains the verdict of most Catholic scholarship in this period. [2])

D. ARCHAEOLOGICAL OPPOSITION

The opening up of the Ancient Near East to the archaeologist in the decades succeeding Graf was to bring a flood of new light on the problems he had raised. As with other new sciences, it was some time before the bearing of archaeology was correctly estimated. [3])

The great Grafians, Wellhausen and Robertson Smith were vastly erudite on Arabian civilization,[4]) but were impatient of the claim that a layman with a spade could offer knowledge to compete with that which they had so hardly won from a study of the ancient sources in the original languages.[5]) When Conder said he would like to put

---

[1]) C. Lattey (ed.) *Moses and the Law*, London (1922).

[2]) See the articles by A. J. Maas, "Pentateuch", *Catholic Encyclopedia*, Vol. XI (1911) pp. 646-61, and E. Mangenot, "Pentateuque", *DB* Vol. V. 1. (1922) cols 50-119.

[3]) This is not always realized by the critics of Wellhausen and Robertson Smith. Writing of the latter, Pritchard says: "It must be borne in mind that in Smith's day Assyriology was not yet on a sound enough basis to afford reliable evidence of Semitic religion; the foundation stones for our knowledge of Canaanite religion had not yet been discovered; Sumerian mythology was not dreamed of in his day" (J. B. Pritchard, "W. Robertson Smith, Heretic", *Crozer Quarterly* XXIV (1947) p. 158).

[4]) Pritchard continues: "Without question pre-Islamic Arabia offered the most valuable field for study in the day in which Smith worked. So thoroughly did he deal with these sources that his labours have endured" (*ibid*). Cf. the verdict of Eissfeldt on Wellhausen above on p. 58. As early as 1756 the importance of Arabia and Egypt for Bible background had been realized by the great Michaelis, who had sent an "archaeological mission" to travel to these lands. Only one, Niebuhr, survived, but through his report on Arabia in 1774, and the inspiration he bequeathed to his more famous son, B. G. Niebuhr, he had wide influence (see J. D. Michaelis, *op. cit*, Vol. I. pp. x-xi).

[5]) It will be recalled that when Duncker essayed to rewrite his *History of Antiquity* in 1874-1877 without himself knowing Oriental languages but quoting Schrader (*Cuneiform Inscriptions and the Old Testament* (1872)) as his authority, the critic Gutschmid in his *Assyriology in Germany* (1876) attacked Schrader as

Wellhausen on a camel and show him what the East was really like,[1])
Robertson Smith retorted that it was not camping out in Palestine,
but an understanding of the sources in the original that gave access
to Semitic knowledge. He added that he did not expect this to be
appreciated by one like Conder, who was ignorant of Hebrew.[2])

This gap between the book-learned theorist, and the unlettered
man of action was to be broken down in this period. When SAYCE,
one of the brilliant philologians of his day, exchanged an Oxford
professor's chair for a *dhow* on the Nile, the new age may be said
to have begun. The world was soon to know the results in the decipher-
ment and publication of the Tel-el-Amarna tablets in 1887. The
unexpected Babylonian background revealed for the Israel of the
fifteenth century B.C. turned Old Testament research into entirely
new channels, and ensured for archaeology a fixed place in all future
discussions. Sayce himself retreated from his moderate criticism to an
increasingly conservative position, as the following writings indicate.

A major work in 1893,[3]) accepted the critical analysis into documents
but not their dating. Critical scepticism about some narratives of the
Old Testament is combatted, while on others it is accepted.[4]) The
following year found Sayce in still more conservative company

---

lacking the rigorous philological training necessary for his task. Schrader, however, by his reply, *Cuneiform Inscriptions and Historical Research*, Giessen (1878)
showed that this was not the case. (Cf. G. P. Gooch, *op. cit*, pp. 508-9, 511 and
MGWJ IX (1877) pp. 38-48).

[1]) C. R. Conder, "The Old Testament, Ancient Monuments and Modern
Critics", *Contemporary Review* LI (1887) pp. 376-93. Conder wrote: "Theories
of the scholar's chamber, which are natural to those who have never lived in the
East, often betray a modern cast of thought, which has little in common with
the facts of oriental antiquity", and claimed that the interpretation of the Song
of Songs as love-songs of rustic lovers walking in the fields like European lovers
was impossible in the East (C. R. Conder, *The Bible and the East*, London (1896)
pp. 227, 184). But one may ask if the Muslim East with its seclusion of women,
which he knew, was in fact the East of the Hebrew songs? Actually Robertson
Smith by his travels had penetrated more deeply into the heart of the East than
most Europeans, who had lived there, as his brilliant "Letters from the Hejaz"
indicate (*Lectures and Essays*, pp. 484-597).

[2]) W. Robertson Smith, "Captain Conder and Modern Critics", *Contemporary
Review* LI (1887) pp. 561-69. Conder must soon have remedied this lack, as he
appears next as a translator of the *Tell Amarna Tablets*, London (1893).

[3]) A. H. Sayce, *The 'Higher Criticism' and the Verdict of the Monuments*, 7th ed,
London (1910), first published 1893.

[4]) The publishers warned the readers against the author's view on Daniel!
He wrote: "The same monumental evidence which has vindicated the historical
accuracy of the Scriptural narrative in other places has here pronounced against
it [i.e. in the fifth chapter of Daniel]" p. 531 ([5]1895).

in the volume *Lex Mosaica*,[1]) while in 1897 he expresses scepticism as to the possibility of source analysis [2]) and in 1904 downright opposition.[3]) In 1910 he prophesied:

> in another half century Elohist and Jahwist, P and Q, Redactor etc., will have been relegated by the Old Testament scholar to that limbo of forgetfulness to which the archaeologist has already consigned them." [4])

On the question of the law, Sayce expressed himself as follows. The Levitical system had functioned in the Wilderness, but had broken down in the difficulties of the conquest. Its influence, however, is everywhere presupposed, for "only the iron fetters of a written law" and an organised cult could have held Israel together in the age of chaos in the time of the Judges.[5]) The Elephantine discoveries were held to finally disprove the post-exilic date of P, for the sacrifices of Lev. 2 (meal offering and frankincense) were in operation in Egypt at a date, which may have been as early as 655 B.C.[6]) Similarly the discovery of Hammurabi's civil code strengthened the possibility that a ritual code, which would be even closer to that of Israel might yet be discovered:

> Before long we may hope to have clear archaeological evidence that the ritual enactments of the Pentateuch, which have been assigned to different periods of history and religious development, all alike have their analogues in a ritual that was in force in Babylonia centuries before Moses was born.[7])

Sayce's inferences from archaeology were resisted by critical writers. He was a good witness but a bad logician, e.g. when he argued that because letters were written in the East, and Solomon and Hiram were in the East, therefore their letters were genuine. [8]) Accurate topography does not prove historicity, or the Book of Judith would be the most historical of all Jewish writings. [9]) Archaeology shows the possibility of a story having happened, but not that it did happen.

---

[1]) Sayce, "The Archaeological Witness to the Literary Activity of the Mosaic Age", *op. cit*, Chap. I.

[2]) Sayce, *The Early History of the Hebrews*, London (1897).

[3]) Sayce, *Monument Facts and Higher Critical Fancies*, London (1904).

[4]) Sayce, *'Higher Criticism' and the Verdict of the Monuments*, p. xv.

[5]) Sayce, *The Early History of the Hebrews*, p. 273.

[6]) Sayce, "The Jewish Garrison and Temple in Elephantine", *Expositor*, 8th series, II (1911) pp. 97-115; "The Jews and their Temple at Elephantine", *ibid*, pp. 417-34.

[7]) Sayce, *Monument Facts and Higher Critical Fancies*, p. 84.

[8]) G. B. Gray, "Prof. Sayce's Early History of the Hebrews", *Expositor*, 5th series, VII (1898) p. 342.

[9]) G. A. Smith, *The Historical Geography of the Holy Land*, 23rd ed. London (n.d.) p. 108.

It can only give direct confirmation at one or two points in Old
Testament history. In other matters its confirmation is at best in-
direct. [1]) Archaeology cannot support both of two contradictory
statements in Scripture, and this is what the critics are concerned
with. It would be of no help at all if archaeology confirmed all these
Scriptures. [2]) Elephantine in no way disturbed the critical dating of
P. At most it showed the earlier existence of some of its laws, and
this had been admitted by critics from the beginning. [3]) Hammurabi's
Code does not overthrow the Grafian dating of Israel's laws. It only
shows that a nation at a certain stage of development has a law code,
but it does not show that Israel was at such a stage of development. [4])

---

[1]) Driver, "Hebrew Archaeology", D. Hogarth (ed.) *Authority and Archaeology*,
London (1899) pp. 143-52. Driver agreed that "the consideration of the probable
age of the several institutions of P is an archaeological rather than a literary
question" (*Literature of the Old Testament* (⁹1913) p. 152), but did not feel that
archaeology had said a definite word here any more than on the historicity of
the patriarchs of which he wrote: "Formerly the world... in which the patriarchs
moved seemed to be almost empty: now we see it filled with embassies, armies,
busy cities, and long lines of traders passing to and fro between one centre of
civilization and another, but amid all that crowded life we peer in vain for any
trace of the fathers of the Hebrews; we listen in vain for any mention of their
names. This is the whole change archaeology has wrought; it has given us a
background and an atmosphere for the stories in Genesis; it is unable to recall
or certify their heroes" (quoted by G. H. Richardson, *Biblical Archaeology*, p. 53).
This is still true today after sixty more years of excavation.

[2]) A. S. Peake, "The Problem of the Old Testament", *Contemporary Review*
(1907) pp. 507-09.

[3]) C. F. Burney, "The Priestly Code and the New Aramaic Papyri from Elephantine", *Expositor*, 8th series, III (1912) pp. 97-108. The Conservative appeal
to this evidence, that important laws were not observed by Jews in close touch
with the Jerusalem temple, in support of their proposition that "non-observance
did not mean non-existence" made by Jampel (see above p. 83) was turned the
other way by A. Cowley, Sayce's collaborator in the publication, who argued
from the absence of reference to the Pentateuch that "the Pentateuch, both in
its historical and legal aspects, was unknown... [to] the populace" before
Ezra (*Aramaic Papyri of the Fifth Century B.C.*, Oxford (1923) p. xxviii). Still
more embarrassing to the Conservative case has been the conclusion of Grelot
that the Passover papyri is very close in its language to P, but not to D, and
reflects a slightly earlier date than P. (P. Grelot, "Etudes sur le "Papyrus Pascal"
d'Éléphantine", *VT* IV (1954) pp. 349-84; "Le Papyrus Pascal d'Éléphantine et
le problème du Pentateuque", *ibid*, V (1955) pp. 250-65; "La dernière étape de
la rédaction sacerdotale", *ibid*, VI (1956) pp. 174-89).

[4]) D. C. Simpson, *Pentateuchal Criticism*, Oxford (1924) p. 37, first published
1914. Cf. S. A. Cook: "The terms 'ancient' and 'primitive' are not correlative;
that which is chronologically ancient is not therefore old from the point of view
of comparative custom. Many Bedouin tribes are, sociologically, older than the
earliest historically known Israelites, and the latter, in turn, even in the sixth
century are far behind the Babylonians of the time of Hammurabi..." (S. A. Cook,
The Laws of Moses and the Code of Hammurabi, London (1903) pp. 39-40).

It will not be necessary to deal in similar detail with other archaeologists who contributed to the conservative side. HOMMEL and NAVILLE were to the fore. The first sought to oppose his knowledge of Arabia, such as the Arabian incense trade, and the Arabian names from the second millenium found in P in Numbers, to the critical theory.[1]) The second appealed to Egyptology and Assyriology in support of his theory that Moses wrote the Pentateuch on tablets in cuneiform, and that these remained in Akkadian until Ezra turned them into Aramaic, and the Rabbis in the time of Christ into Hebrew.[2]) Repetitions and transpositions are accounted for by the tablets.[3])

A cuneiform origin was also posited by KYLE,[4]) who classified the laws according to their title into judgments and statutes, and by their style into mnemonic, descriptive and hortatory. He claimed that the resulting collections exactly corresponded with JE, P and D.

Not all archaeologists supported the Conservative position. [5]) Many were eminent critics, [6]) and some, while opposing Wellhausen like the Pan-Babylonian School, outdid the radicalism of the radicals. WINCKLER [7]) and JEREMIAS [8]) were anti-Grafians and asserted an early origin for P and Israelite monotheism, but the excesses of this school

---

[1]) F. Hommel, *The Ancient Hebrew Tradition*, ET, London (1897), first published 1896.

[2]) E. Naville, *Archaeology of the Old Testament*, London (1913); *Text of the Old Testament*, London (1916); *The Law of Moses*, London (1922).

[3]) What was not accounted for, as was pointed out by W. R. W. Gardner ("Did Moses write the Pentateuch in Babylonian cuneiform?", *ExpT* XXV (1913-1914) pp. 526-27), were the references to writing that was clearly *not* cuneiform, either from the substance written on (Num. 17:2; Dt. 6:9, Dt. 27:2, 3), or from the fact that it could be wiped off (Exod. 32:32; Num. 5:23).

[4]) M. G. Kyle, "A New Solution of the Pentateuchal Problem", *JBL* XXXVI (1917) pp. 31-47; *The Problem of the Pentateuch*, Oberlin (1920); also *Moses and the Monuments*, Oberlin (1919); *The Deciding Voice of the Monuments*, Oberlin (1912).

[5]) G. E. Wright repudiates the suggestion that Palestinian archaeology was ever Fundamentalist, and points to the fact that it was mainly undertaken by the American universities, of whom this was not true. (G. E. Wright and D. Freedman (ed.) *The Biblical Archaeologist Reader* (1961) p. 16).

[6]) Or were confirmed in criticism by the discoveries e.g. Nöldeke, who was persuaded by the Elephantine discovery that the post-exilic period had not been as barren as he had imagined in 1869, and came over to the Grafians (A. S. Peake, *The Bible, Its Origin...* , p. 121), and Barton, who became convinced on the spot at Gezer and Taanach that the Levitical cities in Joshua were post-exilic, when he saw that in these supposedly Levitical cities the pillars of the Canaanite high place had never been thrown down, nor the older cult interrupted but had continued undisturbed until the Exile. (G. A. Barton, " 'Higher' Archaeology and the Verdict of Criticism", *JBL* XXXII (1913) p. 257).

[7]) H. Winckler, *Religionsgeschichtler und geschichtlicher Orient*, Leipzig (1906).

[8]) A. Jeremias, *The Old Testament in the Light of the Ancient East*, ET, 2 vols, London (²1911), first published 1904.

made their position no more acceptable to Conservatives than to their opponents. [1])

E. Critical Opposition

Other scholars besides Conservatives, were opposed to the Graf-Wellhausen reconstruction. Most tenacious of these was EERDMANS. [2]) His *Alttestamentliche Studien* on Genesis-Leviticus in the years 1908-1912 [3]) were supplemented at a much later date by studies on Numbers, [4]) Deuteronomy [5]) and the religion of Israel. [6]) In addition, a good many essays appeared in English including his treatment of the Priestly Code.

In this essay [7]) a study was undertaken of Nehemiah 8 and 10, and the differences from P outlined. Mixed marriages are condemned "as it is written" but no such law appears in P. Neither does the command against buying on the sabbath, nor the institution of the wood offering, nor the third shekel annual tax. The seventh fallow year is in H not P, the refusal of entry to Ammonite and Moabite is in D not P, while the shewbread of P does appear but not under P's name. No Old Testament text fits the law for tabernacles referred to in Nehemiah 8:15. The conclusion must therefore be drawn that Ezra's law was not P, nor the Pentateuch, nor any of the codes we have (p. 316).

On the positive side Eerdmans dates the codification of the laws to Hezekiah and thus makes them earlier than D which he leaves under

---

[1]) These were the years of the "Bibel-Babel" debate precipitated by the two lectures on this theme by FRIEDRICH DELITZSCH before the Kaiser in 1902 and 1903. Not content with deriving many Old Testament institutions from Babylon, Delitzsch went on in his second lecture to speak of the inferiority of some Old Testament attitudes e.g. to women—a foreshadowing of his *Great Delusion*, which rather gives the lie to Hoschander's explanation of his aberrations noted above (p. 38). Perhaps a nearer psychological cause is to be seen in his complaint on p. 217 of his *Babel and Bible* (ET, London 1903) that when his father, Franz Delitzsch, at the end of his life had been compelled to make concessions to Higher Criticism, he was persecuted even on his death-bed by those who had formerly been loudest in his praise.

[2]) See O. Eissfeldt, "Zwei Leidener Darstellungen der Israelitischen Religionsgeschichte", *ZDMG* LXXXV (1931) pp. 172-95.

[3]) B. D. Eerdmans, *Alttestamentliche Studien*, 4 vols, Giessen (1908-1912).

[4]) Eerdmans, "The Composition of Numbers", *Oudtestamentische Studiën* VI (1949) pp. 101-216.

[5]) Eerdmans, "Deuteronomy", *Old Testament Essays*, (1927) pp. 77-84.

[6]) Eerdmans, *The Religion of Israel*, ET, Leiden (1947), first published 1930.

[7]) Eerdmans, "Ezra and the Priestly Code", *Expositor*, 7th series, X (1910) pp. 306-26.

Josiah. [1]) His reason for this view is in part the absence of Levites in Lev. 1-8, the worshipper himself killing his own sacrifice. High priest and Day of Atonement were also not late.

Eerdmans was also distrustful of analysis based on the divine names, but it was DAHSE who made this his special field.[2]) Dahse's position, like that of Wiener was that "the Divine names are not evidence for this document or that, but are a variable element in the text", e.g. six of the seven occurrences of El Shaddai appear in the Septuagint as "my God". Other differences in the Septuagint and Samaritan threw doubt on the whole method, and suggested that a revolution of Pentateuchal criticism was at hand.[3]) Dahse's prophecy was over optimistic for in the year 1913 appeared Skinner's detailed reply *The Divine Names in Genesis*,[4]) in which he showed that the Samaritan, which was older than the Septuagint, supported the Massoretic Text in three hundred cases with only nine against, while the Septuagint itself because of the similarity of the abbreviations for *Theos* (*ths*) and *Kurios* (*ks*) was more likely to have confused the names than the Massoretic Text with Jahweh and Elohim. Dahse contributed a reply to Skinner,[5]) but was in turn answered by König,[6]) who from the beginning had been interested in linguistic considerations.[7]) He had held all along that language demanded a source hypothesis and illustrated it afresh from the failure of Dahse's attack on the integrity of the Massoretic Text. Sellin also contributed an answer in which he maintained that a more likely line for a revolution in criticism was on the question of the age of the legal material.[8])

---

[1]) Eerdmans, "Deuteronomy", *op. cit*, p. 83.

[2]) J. Dahse, "Textkritische Bedenken gegen den Ausgangspunkt der heutigen P.K." *Archiv für Religionswissenschaft*, VI (1903) pp. 305-19.

[3]) Dahse, "Näht ein Umschwung in der Pentateuchkritik?" *NKZ* XXIII (1912) pp. 748-56. Cf. also *A Fresh Investigation of Sources of Genesis*, ET, London (1914) by Dahse, and *The Name of God in the Pentateuch*, ET, London (1912) by A. Troelstra.

[4]) J. Skinner, *The Divine Names in Genesis*, London (1914), first published *Expositor*, 8th series, VI (1913).

[5]) Dahse, "A Reply to Dr Skinner", *Expositor*, 8th series, VI (1913) pp. 481-510.

[6]) E. König, *Die Moderne Pentateuchkritik und ihre neueste Bekämpfung*, Leipzig (1914). A year later he claimed that von Gall's critical edition of the Samaritan Pentateuch—the first ever—had finally disposed of the Dahse-Wiener argument by showing that the Samaritan differed rarely if at all. (E. König, "Der samaritanische Pentateuch und die Pentateuchkritik", *JBL* XXXIV (1915) pp. 10-16).

[7]) His *Habilitationsschrift* in 1879 had been on *Der Sprachbeweis in der Bibelkritik*.

[8]) E. Sellin, "Gehen wir einer Umwälzung auf dem Gebiete der Pentateuchkritik entgegen?" *NKZ* XXIV (1913) p. 146.

Sellin and König represented those critics who while accepting the Grafian dating as proved, were poles apart from Wellhausen on their estimate of the religion of Israel. [1]

As early as 1884 KÖNIG had debated the view that the beginning of Israel's religion was to be dated to the prophets.[2] In 1910 and 1921 he debated the view of its origin with Moses, and pushed it back to the patriarchal period.[3] He denied the application of evolution to the religion of Israel and asserted that some laws at least were from Moses. König thus presents, more than any other critic, the striking picture of a theological Janus, on the one hand vigorously defending critical literary views from the attacks of the Conservatives,[4] and on the other defending Conservative religious views from the attacks of the critics.[5] His maintenance of this position over nearly fifty critical years is a testimony both to the power of his mind, and to the strength and weakness of the two schools—strong in what they affirmed and weak in what they denied.

SELLIN's views were expressed particularly in his debate with Cornill on matters of Introduction in 1912. [6]

As summed up by McFadyen,[7] Cornill's part was to follow Wellhausen's datings for the documents, while Sellin took as much as he could back to Moses, and where that was impossible to the time

---

[1]) This does not mean the end of Grafianism. Peake argued against the use of "Grafianism" to describe the theory of religion held by the great Grafians and suggested it be confined to the theory that the documents were in a certain order (A. S. Peake, "Recent Developments in Old Testament Criticism", *The Servant of Yahweh*, Manchester (1931) pp. 162-63). Wellhausen also asked that it should be this view that should be associated with his name and that of Graf (*Prolegomena*, p. 366).

[2]) E. König, *Die Hauptprobleme der altisraelitischen Religionsgeschichte*, Leipzig (1884), ET, (1885).

[3]) König, "The Significance of the Patriarchs in the History of Religion", *Expositor*, 7th series, X (1910) pp. 192-207; "The Burning Problem of the Hour in Old Testament Religious History", *ibid*, 8th series, XXI (1921) pp. 81-106.

[4]) See his criticisms of Jacob, Dahse, Wiener, Yahuda etc.

[5]) See his *Introduction, O.T. Theology, History of O.T. Religion* etc. Skinner quotes König as closing an early work with the words: "I will make it impossible that irreverence towards the Holy One of Israel should come to be the order of the day in Old Testament science", and adds "He is a living refutation of the calumny that the modern criticism of the Old Testament was cradled in infidelity, and owes its hold on men's minds to a secret or open aversion to the idea of a supernatural revelation". ("The Divine Names in the Pentateuch", *ExpT* XXV (1913-1914) pp. 473-73).

[6]) C. H. Cornill, *Zur Einleitung in das Alte Testament*, Tübingen (1911); E. Sellin, *Zur Einleitung in das Alte Testament*, Leipzig (1912).

[7]) J. E. McFadyen, "Old Testament Criticism", A. S. Peake (ed.) *The People and the Book*, Oxford (1925) pp. 187-90.

of David, and where that was impossible to the time of Hezekiah. Cornill saw the religion of Israel as Wellhausen had seen it only from within, while Sellin placed it in relation to Oriental history, which had been reconstructed by archaeology since Wellhausen's time.[1]) Sellin thought the legislation of the Book of the Covenant prospective, having in view ultimate settlement in the land (pp. 11-16). Cornill argued that laws do not create conditions, but conditions laws. Both agreed with the regular datings for D and P [2]) but Sellin held the laws codified to be much older (pp. 41-46, 49-61).[3])

More radical was the view of Löhr,[4]) who argued that there was no continuous independent P source in Genesis, made in Babylon in Ezra's day. The other Pentateuchal sources were equally illusive. Ezra and his helpers had compiled the Pentateuch utilizing the ritual laws of more than one sanctuary. How Löhr understood this is indicated in a later work,[5]) which although not appearing in English until 1936, may be mentioned here. Most of the prescriptions which are to be found in Exodus, Leviticus and Numbers deal with usages in the pre-exilic temple on Zion (p. 128). Josiah's law-book was of extreme age, and was not written to reform the immediate situation—in fact there was "not the slightest connection" between the Deuteronomic provision that the local sanctuary Levites be allowed to serve at the central sanctuary, and Josiah's forcibly bringing the heathen attendants to Jerusalem and *not* allowing them to serve (pp. 110-14). The unity of the official places of worship, and the difference between sacrifice

---

[1]) Sellin's essay "Archaeology versus Wellhausenism", was included in the anti-critical volume *The Aftermath Series*, pp. 227-71 in 1924, but it limited itself to attacking Wellhausen's view of the religious evolution of Israel.

[2]) Cornill refuted the suggestion that P might have been in existence but circulating among the priests by pointing to prophets who were also priests like Jeremiah and Ezekiel, who not only showed no knowledge of it, but in the case of Ezekiel put forward a Torah of his own independent of it, which he could hardly have done had it been in existence. Where is the High Priest? Where the Day of Atonement? How were his tribal divisions to be reconciled with those of P? (C. H. Cornill, *Introduction to the Canonical Books of the Old Testament*, ET, New York (1907) pp. 108-9).

[3]) See also Sellin, *Introduction to the Old Testament*, ET, London (1923) pp. 87 ff. Cornill complained that Sellin wished to have his omelette (of critical theory) without breaking his eggs (of Conservative datings). (Quoted *ibid*, p. ix). On this the Jewish reviewer Hoschander commented "The author does not "wish" and has no cravings for the omelette, and eats it only because all the others are doing it... and he would cast away the critical premises, if he could follow his own inclinations". (*JQR* XVI (1925-1926) p. 421). The fact remains that he did not do so, and there is little evidence that he wanted to.

[4]) M. Löhr, *Der Priesterkodex in der Genesis*, Giessen (1924). It is odd to find this (critical) Saul among the (Conservative) prophets in the Du Bose volume (*op. cit*,) pp. 331-82 with his essay "The Five Books of Moses and the Question of their Origin". The editor's explanation as to what he means has little relation to what he says, and still less to his later larger clarifications.

[5]) Löhr, *A History of Religion in the Old Testament*, London (1936).

and secular killing had existed from the beginning (pp. 59, 42). However, much in the Pentateuch only dates from Ezra e.g. the extension of the old priestly purification ritual of Leviticus 16 to the whole community (pp. 60, 158).

The most significant critical opposition in this period, however, was not in the above directions, but in the attack on Deuteronomy which marked the end of the period. In accordance with the limitation imposed in the Prologue most of the work done on this book since Riehm has been left out of account, but brief reference is needed to the discussions around 1920 if the future course of criticism is to be understood. Dates both later and earlier than Josiah were suggested.

The later dating of Deuteronomy found favour with several critics in Germany and in Britain. HÖLSCHER argued, [1]) that the law of the single sanctuary was impossible in the pre-exilic period, when the community was large and scattered, and only became a possibility if dated after the Exile about 500 B.C. In England, KENNETT headed a distinguished line of Cambridge scholars favouring an exilic date for Deuteronomy. [2])

> Kennett argued [3]) that the king law of Deuteronomy, implying a time when Israel had no king and might elect one who was not an Israelite, fitted the period of political turbulence in the time of Zerubbabel and Haggai-Zechariah. Along with this went his very late dating for the whole Pentateuch.[4]) Arguing from the prophetic repudiation of sacrifice, which all strands of the Pentateuch authorize, he concluded that in the time of the great prophets no book of the Pentateuch was yet written. J was a counter blast to Josiah's Reform, E for the Aramean settlers of the seventh century, H from the Exile, D from the Return, while P as with Graf came last of all.

Other scholars among whom may be mentioned, Welch, Östreicher and Staerk favoured the earlier date for the bulk of the material. These scholars emphasised that the concern of Deuteronomy was with *"Kultusreinheit"* not *"Kultuseinheit"*.

> WELCH agreed, against Östreicher, that the present form of Deuteronomy required centralization, but regarded the solitary use

---

[1]) G. Hölscher, "Komposition und Ursprung des Deuteronomiums", *ZAW* XL (1922) pp. 161-255.

[2]) Kennett, Burkitt, Cook, Schofield.

[3]) R. H. Kennett, *The Origin of the Book of Deuteronomy*, Cambridge (1920) p. 23.

[4]) Kennett, "History of the Jewish Church from Nebuchadnezzar to Alexander", *Cambridge Biblical Essays* (1909) pp. 93-135; "Israel", *ERE* Vol. VII (1914) pp. 439-56; *Old Testament Essays*, Cambridge (1928); *The Church of Israel*, Cambridge (1933).

of the phrase "the place out of all thy tribes" in Deuteronomy (and in Kings) as a later interpolation. Everywhere else a plurality of sanctuaries was implied by the words "in any of thy tribes", and this was borne out by the laws for firstfruits in Dt. 26 which were to be brought simply to "the place", the laws for tithes, Passover, Weeks, Tabernacles, etc. and the regulations for the priesthood, the prophet and the king. He concludes that D had been a North Israelite code, while P had belonged to Jerusalem and for this reason the latter ousted the former in the return from the Exile.[1]

---

[1] A. C. Welch, *The Code of Deuteronomy*, London (1924); "When was the worship of Israel centralised at the Temple?" *ZAW* XLIII (1925) pp. 250-55; "The Problem of Deuteronomy", *JBL* XLVIII (1929) pp. 291-306.

CHAPTER EIGHT

THE POSITION IN 1925

A. The Negative Forecast

This opposition to the old positions was not without its effect. Programmatic studies calling for new approaches began to appear. Kittel [1]) and Gressmann [2]) were content to speak in general terms of the inadequacy of Grafianism, [3]) but WELCH was more specific. In 1913 he had disowned Wellhausen's conception of an evolution in Old Testament religion, [4]) although he himself still worked within the critical datings of the documents. [5]) In 1923 he felt that each of the three pillars of Graf and Wellhausen was seriously threatened. [6])

> In the first place the attack on the divine names had plausibility, in that a whole book of the Psalms had been overwritten by an Elohim redactor, and this may have happened with the Pentateuch. If Astruc's clue failed, little else that was not subjective remained for the separation of the documents (p. 349).
> The second pillar, the Josianic datings of Deuteronomy, Welch naturally regarded as disproved (p. 356). As for the third pillar, the Ezra dating of P, this was the Achilles heel of the whole theory. For one thing it rested on the authority of the Chronicler, who in all else was suspect (p. 360). For another, a continually changing Jerusalem code would not have been accepted by the Samaritans (p. 364). The exiles had more to do than to think up changes in a ritual they never practised (p. 365). These changes must be pre-exilic. Priest and prophet were not opposed as had been so long imagined

---

[1]) R. Kittel, "Die Zukunft der Alttestamentlichen Wissenschaft", *ZAW* XXXIX (1921) pp. 84-99.

[2]) H. Gressmann, "Die Aufgaben der alttestamentlichen Forschung", *ZAW* XLII (1924) pp. 1-33.

[3]) The American Conservative H. M. Du Bose, misled by statements like these and similar ones from Sellin and Löhr quoted above, felt the time opportune in 1923-1924 to publish a Conservative symposium, including contributions of the two last-named, which he hopefully called *The Aftermath Series* i.e. the "aftermath" of Wellhausen (see above under Löhr, Sellin and Kegel).

[4]) A. C. Welch, "The Present Position of Old Testament Criticism", *Expositor*, 8th series, VI (1913) pp. 518-29.

[5]) See his *Religion of Israel under the Kingdom*, Edinburgh (1912).

[6]) Welch, "On the Present Position of Old Testament Criticism", *Expositor*, 8th series, XXV (1923) pp. 344-70.

(p. 367).[1]) Codes of ritual regulations were necessary in the monarchy and must have existed at a sanctuary like Amos' Bethel.

B. THE POSITIVE FORECAST

The other survey articles which appeared at the same time as the above were less disturbed by the new trends. Peake said there had been such prophecies of the downfall of Grafianism since 1900, but nothing had been really disturbed. [2]) McFadyen felt that the opponents of orthodox Grafianism had not made out their case, but conceded that "today less than ever can the Pentateuchal problem be considered as closed". [3]) Cook was not persuaded that Kegel had made "away with Wellhausen", nor Welch with de Wette. [4])

It was HARFORD, however, who made the most elaborate answer on behalf of Wellhausen and Graf, and also the most penetrating estimate of the worth of the new arguments. This was in his articles contributed to the *Expositor* in 1925. [5])

> Taking up again the three pillars which Welch thought to be shaken, he demonstrated first that the attack on the divine names had completely failed, and that in any case other criteria for the analysis remained. Further, to dislodge D and P from the reforms of Josiah and Ezra did not overthrow Grafianism which was not built upon the date of publication of various laws, but only on the fact that the documents of the Pentateuch were in the order JEDP (p. 323). It was not fundamental that P should have been read by Ezra, but only that it should be later than D (p. 413). The Chronicler was more likely to be correct when writing of events near his own time than of those much earlier (p. 415). There was ample time between 586 and 330 B.C. for the Pentateuch to be completed before the Samaritan schism (p. 425). That modifying the ritual law was a concern during the Exile is illustrated by Ezekiel (p. 425). The existence of old laws in P had been recognized by all the critics (p. 424).

---

[1]) See also his *Prophet and Priest in Old Israel*, London (1936).
[2]) Peake, "Recent Developments in Old Testament Criticism", *The Servant of Yahweh*, Manchester (1931), first written 1924, pp. 151-93.
[3]) McFadyen, "Old Testament Criticism", *The People and the Book* (pp. 194-95).
[4]) Cook, "Some Tendencies in Old Testament Criticism", *JTS* XXVI (1925) pp. 156-73.
[5]) J. B. Harford, "Since Wellhausen", *Expositor*, 9th series, IV (1925).

SUMMARY—DIFFICULTIES OF P

Logically Harford had the better of the exchange. The prophecies of the demise of Grafianism were premature in 1925. No argument had been produced to overthrow the closely knit structure of Graf and Wellhausen, nor could such an argument be produced. The essential problem was that Grafianism had placed itself beyond the reach of all counter argument, not because its position was unassailable, but because it would admit of argument only on its own premises, and these were defined in such a way as to make counter argument impossible. [1]

Of any and every law that was proved early, criticism replied that it was only the Code, not the usage that was late, but to prove that the Code was late criticism relied on the fact that the usage was unknown earlier—an argument in a circle. Again, to base a theory on the non-occurrence of cultic references in the sources, and then to delete such cultic references when they did occur, is another circular argument. No argument is possible when all contrary evidence is already ruled out as inadmissible.

The same is the case with the argument from silence. Wellhausen claimed that it must be allowed on the ground that there could not be positive statements of non-existence. There is a difference, however, between what is known to have been in existence, and what was in existence. An Irishman charged with murder claimed to be able to produce fifty men who did not see him do it. Is one's ignorance to be made the measure of historical credibility?

Can one point to positive evidence for the existence of P in Haggai-Zechariah, in Ezra-Nehemiah or in Chronicles, when the differences in

---

[1] As an example of a neat piece of Conservative apologetic, which is convincing on Conservative presuppositions but cannot survive for a moment before critical theories of overwriting, one may take the following from W. H. Green: "As the ark of the covenant is the voucher for the unity of the sanctuary, and for the genuineness of the Mosaic legislation respecting it, so the contents of the ark form no inconsiderable bulwark for the unity of the Pentateuch. If monumental evidence is to be trusted, the Decalogue is Mosaic, and is preserved in Ex. xx in its genuine authentic form. The critics assign it to the Jehovist, [JE] and claim for it the characteristics of Jehovistic style. But it has also the peculiar phrases of Deuteronomy; and the reason annexed to the fourth commandment is based on the Elohistic [P] account of creation (Gen. i:1-ii:3). This unquestionably Mosaic document includes Elohist, Jehovist and Deuteronomist all in one". (Quoted Bissell, *op. cit*, p. 57).

the laws as revealed in these books are taken into account? [1]) Can it be concluded from the fact that Deuteronomy fits the age of Josiah that it does not also fit other ages? The fact that a key opens a door does not prove that it was the key made for the door, and not a skeleton. Can it be shown that D and no more, was the law of Josiah, and P and no more, the law of Ezra, when both may have had their influence as units of a larger whole? The greater can always include the lesser, even if the lesser cannot include the greater.

What evidence is there for the dating of J and E apart from entirely subjective considerations such as the extent to which the writer's own age has been mirrored in his description of the patriarchal?

Granting the Graf-Wellhausen presuppositions, their conclusions follow. But what recourse is open to those who do not grant these presuppositions? Is argument to be ruled out, because there are no premises, or can the dialectical deadlock be somehow by-passed so that enquiry can proceed? This was the problem in 1925, and the years following were to supply the answer.

---

[1]) The following long quotation from a work *Deuteronomy the People's Book* (1877) is cited by Boyce, *op. cit*, pp. 190-91 "If we divide the period from the days of Eli to the birth of Christ into two equal parts, we shall find that the half nearest to our own time, from 586 B.C. downwards, presents a series of quickenings and fallings away in the nation's life, exactly parallel to those which formed the outstanding features of Israel's history during the earlier half from 1170 B.C. to 586 B.C. The number of the series would seem to be almost the same in both halves. The results were clearly the same. The house of God deserted; its dues unpaid; the Levites turning to what was not their own work, or becoming lost among the other tribes; idolatry prevalent. But the law of Moses, as we now have it, was in priests' and pastors' hands through the latter half of that long period of 1170 years, although it was a dead letter until the heart of the nation was touched by a sense of duty and of danger. How then can there be a doubt in the mind of any student of history, that the quickenings and the fallings away in the earlier half, 1170 B.C. to 586 B.C. resulted from the same cause as in the more recent— regard for, and neglect of, the well-known four books"?

PART THREE

THE LAW CAME BETWEEN

THE POST-GRAFIANS (1905-1965)

CHAPTER NINE

NEW BEGINNINGS IN 1905

To take up the story of the modern period, it is necessary to go back in time to about the year 1905, when two of the movements which have become influential in recent times may be said to have taken their rise. Around this year, a century after de Wette, [1]) two of the most original critics were writing books that were to have their greatest influence only after 1925. They were Gunkel and Klostermann.

A. THE FORM-CRITICAL METHOD

The form-critical method owes its origin to GUNKEL whose great work on Genesis [2]) has been described as, "as keenly critical as Wellhausen's *Composition*". [3]) It is to form criticism more than anything else that Wellhausen's literary criticism owes its present decline, but this was no part of Gunkel's intention. Because for him Wellhausen and others had solved the literary-critical problem, [4]) Gunkel addressed himself to the pre-history of the literature. He believed a history of Hebrew literature could be written, not in the impossible old way of the personalities of the writers, but in a new way from the development of the types of literature. [5]) The general classification

---

[1]) Gasser, who published his volume (*op. cit*) in 1906 remarked that it was not only the centennial of the publication of de Wette's *Beiträge*, which first employed the historical-critical method, but also of the birth of Vatke, who applied the method most fully, and of the death of G. Bauer, who first used the term.

[2]) H. Gunkel, *Genesis übersetzt und erklärt*, 5th ed, Göttingen (1922), first published 1901.

[3]) By A. R. Gordon, "The Contribution of Germany to Old Testament Scholarship", *ExpT* XLI (1929-1930) p. 306. It is an interesting coincidence that both had a predecessor in 1753, the year from which both form criticism and source criticism may be said to take their rise. Lowth was as truly the predecessor of Gunkel, as Astruc was of Wellhausen. Others, however, prefer to think of Gunkel as "a scientific Herder", because of his attention to the aesthetic side (Cf. Suelzer, *op. cit*, p. 153). On Gunkel's debt to Herder, and for his career in general see W. Baumgartner, "Zum 100. Geburtstag von Hermann Gunkel", *VTSuppl* IX (1962) pp. 8-9 (1-18).

[4]) See *ibid*, p. 8 for Gunkel's high regard for Wellhausen—a feeling that was apparently not reciprocated.

[5]) Gunkel, "Fundamental Problems of Hebrew Literary History", *What remains of the Old Testament*, London (1928) pp. 57-68, first published *DLZ* XXVII (1906), reprinted in *Reden und Aufsätze*, Göttingen (1913) pp. 29-38.

into prose and poetry could be further subdivided into many kinds
of prose—myth, saga, folktale, romance, etc. and as great a variety
of poems—dirge, taunt, thanksgiving, etc. The basic units, in the
original oral stage, often quite small, are marked by stereotyped forms,
particularly of introduction—"ah-how", "ha-ye", "sing!" and belonged to particular functionaries in the community—the hired
female mourners, the rejoicing maidens, the priest in the sanctuary,
the elders in the gate, etc. The *Sitz im Leben* of each type is therefore
of the greatest importance. [1])

It becomes apparent that a way back beyond written sources is
opened up by this method. Gunkel began his Genesis commentary
with a long description of the forms found in Genesis (pp. vii-c). [2])
The critical dating of the documents was accepted, but this was only
the date of the collecting. The material itself was very old, as old as
1000 or 1200 B.C. Cultic needs in different sanctuaries must have
secured its preservation, if not also its origins. Aetiology was the
formative factor in the tradition.

It was somewhat remarkable that New Testament scholars were
quicker to realize the possibilities of Gunkel's form criticism than
Old Testament scholars. [3]) Even more remarkably it was Wellhausen,
now working at New Testament problems who first applied form
criticism to the Synoptic Gospels, as Bultmann has acknowledged.
Describing Wellhausen's commentaries and introductions to the Gospels which appeared between 1905 and 1911, Bultmann wrote in
summary of Wellhausen's position:

> the oldest tradition consisted almost entirely of small fragments...
> and did not present a continuous story of the deeds of Jesus or any
> complete collection of sayings. When these fragments were collected,
> they were connected so as to form a continuous narrative.... He
> showed not only that the Evangelist's narratives... were secondary,
> but also that oral tradition was already steadily producing more and
> more new sayings of Jesus.... Wellhausen brought to light the

---

[1]) See further H. Gunkel, "Die Israelitische Literatur", in P. Hinneberg (ed.)
Die Kultur der Gegenwart I, 7, Berlin (1906) pp. 51-102 and now K. Koch's excellent
Was ist Formgeschichte? Neukirchen (1964) p. 89, E.T. London, 1969.

[2]) Now translated into English as *The Legends of Genesis* with an introduction by
Professor Albright (New York (1964)).

[3]) For Gunkel's influence on New Testament scholars, especially the form critics
Bultmann, Dibelius and Schmidt in Berlin see the *Eucharistion* compiled in his
honour in 1923, where the entire second volume is by New Testament contributors.
Gunkel himself had begun his work in the New Testament field, but had concentrated on the Old Testament after 1889 (Baumgartner, *VTSuppl. op. cit*, p. 5).

principle that a literary work is a primary source only for the historical situation out of which it arose, and only secondarily for the history of the period dealt with.[1])

This method, borrowed from the Old Testament field, was not applied there by Wellhausen or others of his school for nearly a generation. Apart from Gressmann's work on Moses, [2]) it was only with the publication of Gunkel's Psalm commentary [3]) that form criticism took firm root as an Old Testament discipline. Gunkel isolated and named the various Psalm forms, and went very thoroughly into their *Sitz im Leben*. De Wette had made similar classification long before, as Kraus has pointed out [4]) and may therefore, not impossibly, be seen as the father both of Graf and the movements that were to go beyond Graf.

B. The Tradition-historical Method

To Klostermann, also, who over many years opposed Wellhausenianism, [5]) the *Sitz im Leben* of the materials was the basic question. His answer that this was to be found in the preaching of the community became the axiom of the Tradition History School. Klostermann began by maintaining that it was the mistake of all Pentateuch criticism that it accepted for the purposes of the analysis the Synagogue text—the Massoretic Text—as if it were the autograph, whereas it had been subject to modification to suit community needs until the time of Ezra (I, pp. 1-55). The sure starting point for criticism was not at the beginning with J and E, but at the end with Josiah's Reform. Deuteronomy was not the programme for the Reform but a homiletic introduction to the recovered Code (I, pp. 77-114, N.F. pp. 154-428). The rest of the Pentateuch had similarly arisen in preaching, as Exod. 24:7 and Dt. 33:9 show. *Mikra* meant "reading", not "festival". Public readings of the law, including historical matter, with regard to the origin of the ceremonies and the history of the patriarchs, were given at the festivals. In this way the

---

[1]) R. Bultmann, "The New Approach to the Synoptic Problem", *JR* VI (1926) pp. 340-44.

[2]) H. Gressmann, *Mose und seine Zeit*, Göttingen (1913).

[3]) H. Gunkel, *Die Psalmen*, Göttingen (1926).

[4]) H.-J. Kraus, *Geschichte der historisch-kritischen Erforschung*, pp. 166-67. Kraus remarks that Gunkel makes no reference to de Wette.

[5]) A. Klostermann, *Der Pentateuch*, Leipzig (1893), *Der Pentateuch*, N. F. Leipzig (1907), first published chiefly in *NKZ* between 1892 and 1907.

Mosaic ground-work of historical and legal material (J) which was regularly read before the people, received additions (E), and a large extension under Solomon (P), and its final extension under Josiah (D).[1]

The laws of the Pentateuch arose in a recital of law similar to that of the "law-speaker" in Iceland (N.F. pp. 348-428). Noth [2]) and von Rad [3]) follow him in this. Questions of date become secondary, but Klostermann sought by studies in the Jubilee, which he took as fortynine years (I, Chap. I, N.F. Chap. II), and in Pentateuchal chronology, which he thought embraced cycles of twelve times fortynine years, to show that P came from the time of Solomon. The tabernacle accounts with their distinction between *mishkan ha-eduth* and *ohel moedh* date from not long after the loss of Shiloh (N.F. pp. 41-153), and Numbers 11-36 from a time before Isaiah and Micah (I, pp. 115-52).

Needless to say this whole theory was regarded by the literary critics as quite irresponsible, and was severely criticized by Driver. [4]) Strack, however, was more sympathetic [5]) and valued Klostermann's nsights, although neither he nor any modern would follow him in he details of his construction.

---

[1]) This summary of Klostermann's views is from S. R. Driver, "Klostermann on the Pentateuch", *Expositor*, 4th series, V (1892) pp. 325-26; and F. C. Eiselen, *The Books of the Pentateuch*, New York (1916) p. 59.

[2]) M. Noth, *The History of Israel*, ET, London (1958) pp. 102-03.

[3]) G. von Rad, *Studies in Deuteronomy*, ET, London (1953) pp. 11 ff.

[4]) Driver, *loc. cit.*

[5]) H. L. Strack, "Hexateuch", *op. cit*, Vol. V (1909) pp. 264-65.

CHAPTER TEN

THE OLD METHODS CONTINUED

The most distinctive work of the past sixty years was that which took up the beginnings of Gunkel and Klostermann, but this was slow getting under way. Gunkel scarcely figures in the review discussions of 1920-1925. He was well-known for his two major commentaries but his significance as a founder of a new method of criticism with consequences for Grafianism was not yet recognized. Wright finds this to be true as late as 1938. [1]) Old Testament discussion was to continue for almost a generation on the old lines. To prevent a wrong impression being given it is necessary to postpone any description of the form-critical and tradition-historical schools until the writings of the older literary-critical school and its opponents have been traced down to the present day.

A. Critical Contributions

It is not possible for the reason given on p. 72 above, nor is it necessary, that the many contributions to orthodox Grafianism from 1925 to the present should be chronicled. It may be said without exaggeration that ninety per cent of the books on Old Testament subjects, and ninety per cent of the lectures given in Old Testament classrooms took for granted the Grafian position. In England, e.g. the joint works of Oesterley and Robinson on the *History of Israel*, *Hebrew Religion* and the *Introduction to the Old Testament* were written from this point of view, as were the chief commentary series. Space permits only the barest mention of the continuation of the work of analysis by Eissfeldt, Pfeiffer and Simpson.

In 1922 Eissfeldt isolated [2]) in the Pentateuch and Joshua a further source L (Lay Source), but as this did not affect P and was unrepresented in Leviticus, it need not be further described here. In 1930 Pfeiffer argued [3]) for an Edomite Source (S) beginning with the non-P material

---

[1]) G. E. Wright, "Recent European Study in the Pentateuch", *JBR* XVIII (1950) p. 216.

[2]) O. Eissfeldt, *Hexateuch-Synopse*, Leipzig (1922).

[3]) R. H. Pfeiffer, "A Non-Israelitic Source of the Book of Genesis", *ZAW* XLVIII (1930) pp. 66-73.

of Gn. 1-11 (p. 68). This he denied to J on the grounds that in Gn. 1-11 where fifty per cent of the material is P's, it is P that is the composer and the other material that is added, whereas in Gn. 12-50 where less than twenty per cent of the material is P's, it is P that is added to JE. This P material is unintelligible when severed from the context, and is more in the nature of marginal comments (p. 67). P as a whole was therefore an introduction and commentary to JE rather than a separate source. On P in the rest of the Pentateuch Pfeiffer in his *Introduction* [1]) follows the Graf-Wellhausen dating and general line, as does also Eissfeldt.[2]) Eissfeldt, however, goes further than Pfeiffer in his recognition of form-critical work, but in other respects these two great Introductions belong to the middle rather than the latest phase of the study.

The modern mood has not been favourable to further analysis. The division of J into J^1 and J^2 met with only moderate support,[3]) von Rad's division of P into P^A and P^B with still less,[4]) while Simpson's splinter analysis into numerous subdivisions [5]) with none at all.

Parallel with the endeavour to discover new sources was another aimed at eliminating some of those already accepted. Volz and Rudolph [6]) argued against the existence of E as a separate source. VOLZ went further and eliminated P also as a story writer. Stories like those of Gn. 22 and 23, which had been assigned to E and P belong to J. P was a legislator who supplemented the basic J document with legal material (pp. 135-42), while E if he had any existence at all was no more than an editor. RUDOLPH continued the investigation from Gn. 37 onwards and in a separate volume from Exodus to Joshua. [7]) He accepted the fact that J was the oldest and P the youngest source but like Volz found little evidence for E. [8])

WINNETT [9]) followed Volz and Rudolph in rejecting E and with it much of the analysis, but accepted a form of J, D and P. He posited an original Mosaic tradition (J—from North Israel), which was

---

[1]) Pfeiffer, *Introduction to the Old Testament*, 2nd ed, New York (1948), first published 1942.

[2]) Eissfeldt, *Einleitung in das Alte Testament*, Tübingen (^{3}1964) ET, Oxford (1965), first published 1934.

[3]) R. Smend, *Die Erzählung des Hexateuchs*, Berlin (1912).

[4]) G. von Rad, *Die Priesterschrift im Hexateuch*, Stuttgart (1934).

[5]) C. A. Simpson, *The Early Traditions of Israel*, Oxford (1948); "The Growth of the Hexateuch", *Interpreter's Bible* Vol. I (1952) pp. 185-200; "Genesis", *ibid*, pp. 439-57.

[6]) P. Volz and W. Rudolph, *Der Elohist als Erzähler: ein Irrweg der Pentateuchkritik?* Giessen (1933).

[7]) Rudolph, *Der "Elohist" von Exodus bis Josua*, Berlin (1938).

[8]) See his chart of the sources, pp. 274-81.

[9]) F. V. Winnett, *The Mosaic Tradition*, Toronto (1949).

subjected to a Judean rewriting after 722 B.C. (D—a fraudulent Judean document to push the claims of Jerusalem against the North). P was an unsuccessful compromise attempted after 586 B.C.[1])

MOWINCKEL, whose name will often recur in these chapters in connection with the many stimulating hypotheses, which have started off new lines of Old Testament study, returned again at the very close of his life to source analysis, and also concluded that E was unnecessary in large parts of the Pentateuch, where it had previously been posited [2]) —Gn. 1-11,[3]) the Jacob and Joseph stories and Exod. 1-15. Where a second source was necessary as in the Sinai and Balaam narratives, this was as likely to be oral as written, and not a continuous source like E. Of the existence of P, however, he has no doubt. A fresh investigation of key passages like the Flood narrative confirms the older analysis of J and P documents, with J the older and P retaining its Grafian position after the Exile. The framework of the Pentateuch was given, however, by J not P.

It is interesting to note here, as also with Volz, Rudolph, and Winnett how readily Pentateuchal criticism slips back into forms of the Supplementary Hypothesis, once the Wellhausenian framework is disturbed.

Despite this powerful advocacy, the elimination of E has not generally commended itself. Albright in 1963 acknowledged that the analysis, as given for example by Skinner still stood, although some of the criteria on which it was based such as the Jethro-Hobab clue might have to be called in question. [4]) L. Ruppert, a Catholic scholar, retains it in a recent study of the Joseph stories. [5])

It is true that C. H. GORDON in a popular article has announced his abandonment of the source hypothesis, and his resignation from the ranks of "the higher critics",[6]) but the spirit in which his article is written, with its aspersions on the motives of the "critics", is as little likely to commend his position, as his confused arguments are likely

---

[1]) This study had concerned itself with "the Mosaic tradition" in Exodus and Numbers, but in a much later article devoted to Genesis, Winnett has brought J down to the Exile, denied parallel strands, but allowed P in its Grafian position ("Re-examining the Foundations", *JBL* LXXXIV (1965) pp. 1-19).

[2]) S. Mowinckel, "Erwägungen zur Pentateuch Quellenfrage", *Norsk Theologisk Tidsskrift* LXV (1964) pp. 1-138.

[3]) E.g. by himself in *The Two Sources of the Pre-Deuteronomic Primeval History (JE) in Gen. 1-11*, Oslo (1937).

[4]) W. F. Albright, "Jethro, Hobab and Reuel in Early Hebrew Tradition, with some comments on the origin of 'JE'," *CBQ* XXV (1963) pp. 1-11.

[5]) L. Ruppert, *Die Josepherzählung der Genesis*, Ein Beitrag zur Theologie der Pentateuchquellen, München (1965).

[6]) C. H. Gordon, "Higher Critics and Forbidden Fruit", *Christianity Today* IV (1959-1960) pp. 131-34.

to convince his opponents. The sources J and E are unnecessary because double divine names can be paralleled elsewhere (e.g. Amon-Re (p. 132)), and doublets are a literary device (e.g. Pharaoh's and Joseph's dreams), but other sources clearly lie behind the Pentateuch, as they do behind the Gilgamesh Flood narrative (p. 133), although earlier it had been said that it was a study of the latter, which had led him to doubt the late date of P, and thus to abandon the source hypothesis (p. 131)! Another contribution of Gordon will come up in the next section.

B. CONSERVATIVE CONTRIBUTIONS

The Conservatives were not as vocal as might have been expected. There are but few works of significance to notice during the greater part of the period. Introductions to the Pentateuch by Aalders and Allis and to the whole Old Testament by Young were in the most unbending manner of the traditional position.

AALDERS [1]) like Orr was prepared to agree that the Pentateuch had been compiled from Mosaic materials at a slightly later time, that its laws had been given to Moses rather than by him (Chap. XVIII), and that the Conservative position did not necessarily coincide with traditional theories of authorship. [2]) However, when S.A. Cartledge in his *A Conservative Introduction to the Old Testament* [3]) conceded that priestly writers after the time of Moses might assign new laws, felt to be in keeping with the spirit of Moses, back to him, a Conservative reviewer asserted that this was a position "a true Conservative would reject". [4]) This is true of ALLIS, [5]) who after dealing in Part I with the Documentary Hypothesis and in Part II with the Development Hypothesis, devoted Part III of his book to the new movements, but found neither the work of Alt, Noth and von Rad on the one hand, nor that of the archaeologists Albright and Woolley on the other, acceptable.

YOUNG [6]) has one of the fullest accounts of the history of Pentateuchal criticism, on which subject he had done special work, but his rigid presuppositions prevent him from recognizing any good in the movement whatsoever. It is "the dark night of criticism" (p. 28).

---

[1]) G. Ch. Aalders, *A Short Introduction to the Pentateuch*, London (1949).
[2]) Aalders, *Recent Trends in O.T. Criticism*, London (1938).
[3]) Grand Rapids (1943), p. 70.
[4]) J. P. Free, "Archaeology and Biblical Criticism", *BibSac* CXIII (1956) p. 128.
[5]) O. T. Allis, *The Five Books of Moses*, Philadelphia ([2]1949).
[6]) E. J. Young, *An Introduction to the Old Testament*, 2nd ed, Grand Rapids (1950), first published 1949.

Wellhausen is not to be excused as "a child of his time". He should have lived under the light of eternity and accepted what God had said! [1]) An acute reviewer, noting that Young's argument seemed to be that the difficulties in criticism were greater than those in traditionalism, and that therefore it was better to abide by tradition, asked whether the Copernican theory of the universe, which also had difficulties, should likewise have been set aside for what the Bible clearly says about the firmament above and the sun's motion across it? [2])

More than a decade was to elapse before the Conservative voice made itself heard again, but what it had lacked in frequency was certainly made up in force by the attack on criticism by K. A. KITCHEN, the Egyptologist, in 1965. [3]) The critic's theories were begun by "eighteenth century dilettantes", who lacked "all knowledge of the forms and usages of Ancient Oriental literature" (p. 117); they were continued by Wellhausen, who stubbornly refused to consider comparative data even down to his sixth edition in 1905 (pp. 115, 18); [4]) and today are represented by scholars like Eissfeldt and Noth, who prefer theories to facts (pp. 59-60). [5]) Appeal is made to ancient Near Eastern literature as providing no parallel at all to the "composition-by-conflation" origin for the Old Testament posited by critical scholars, and the JEDP sequence is dismissed with a wave of the hand to Kaufmann (p. 114). [6]) As no independent proof is offered of these

---

[1]) Young, "Old Testament", Carl Henry (ed.) *Contemporary Evangelical Theology*, New York (1957) p. 19.

[2]) "Certainly the Copernican theory of our universe, or planetary system, was harder for sixteenth century minds to grasp than the Ptolemaic. And there remained some loose ends in it: Kepler had to correct Copernicus' idea of the planets' circular orbits"... (C. M. Cooper, *JQR* XLI (1950-1951) p. 114). Cooper himself had argued for an early date for Deuteronomy in the Alleman-Flack Commentary (p. 302), but had become convinced by the Lachish ostraca and a study of the Books of Kings that its style was from the sixth century (*ibid*, XLIII (1952-1953) p. 274).

[3]) In a review in *JEA* in 1961 (XLVII pp. 158-64), Kitchen had already expressed his dissatisfaction with the documentary theory but it was in his German and English editions of *Ancient Orient and Old Testament*, London (1966) that his arguments were marshalled in a systematic way.

[4]) But see above for Wellhausen's view that relevant comparisons were with Arabic culture.

[5]) "Tribal Israel as an entity in W. Palestine in 1220 B.C., pictured by the Old Testament and tacitly by the Merenptah-stela... does not suit their particular theories about Israelite origins, and they prefer these theories to the first-hand evidence of the stela" (*loc. cit*).

[6]) "Kaufmann is absolutely justified in making the supposed Priestly source earlier than both the Babylonian Exile and Deuteronomy... Hence, works that adhere to the conventional sequence and dating of J, E, D, P and exilic/post-

remarkable assertions, one can only echo Cazelle's comment "malheureusement, plus égyptologue que bibliste, n'a pas bien compris les vraies raisons qui font admettre la théorie documentaire". [1]

> When Kitchen comes to constructive argument in the central section of his book, he moves no more certainly among the Biblical difficulties than those whose views he dismisses. His discussions of the chronology of the Exodus and the patriarchs remain inconclusive, while those of the antediluvian genealogies and the Joshua conquest border on the trivial.[2] His most telling point, that theories conceived, when Israel was thought a primitive people, must look different, when her late origin in the Near Eastern cultural milieu is taken into account,[3] was in part replied to in advance by S. A. Cook above.[4] His hypothetical question based on the willingness of the critics to allow this or that detail of P to be ancient, as to what the situation will be as this is more and more the case,[5] overlooks the important distinction made by de Wette between *praxis* and written code and quoted on p. 25 above.

Kitchen desiderates a "science of comparative literature" for the Ancient Near East, and refers to W. W. Hallo's *IEJ* article "New Viewpoints on Cuneiform Literature", [6] but a perusal of the proffered "parallel" literature raises the question as to how relevant this comparative material really is. When the same periodical in earlier issues devoted a series of articles to Israelite historiography, no reason was seen to depart from E. Meyer's verdict that "no other cultural nation

---

exilic P must be considered as obsolete in their consequent presentation of... Hebrew religion and literature. This includes works that have appeared since the English version of Kaufmann's book (1960-1961) and have paid no attention to the facts marshalled by Kaufmann" (*loc. cit*).

[1] H. Cazelles, "Pentateuque", *DBSuppl* VII (1966) col. 780, first published 1963-1964. On comparative literature and Kaufmann see below.

[2] E.g. p. 69.

[3] "If the Patriarchs had lived in 7000 or 6000 B.C., and the Exodus taken place in 5000 'primitive Hebrews' would have been conceivable" but not in the second and first millenia B.C. (p. 172).

[4] See p. 94. Cf. H. J. Franken and C. A. Franken-Battershill, *A Primer of Old Testament Archaeology*, Leiden (1963) p. 149.

[5] "Suppose that every detail and aspect.. can be shown by external, objective Ancient Oriental data to be completely consistent with a general date stated or clearly implied by the biblical text—in literary structure, vocabulary and syntax, theological viewpoint and content, or social, political or legal usages, etc—and that not a scrap of residue is left over... to be labelled late. What then will become of time-honoured theory"? (pp. 26-27).

[6] *IEJ* XII (1962) pp. 13-26.

in the East created a historic literature of this kind". [1]) More recently Mowinckel too has concluded that "Israel is the only people in the whole ancient Near East, where annalistic writing developed into real historiography" and continues "neither the Babylonians nor the Assyrians took it beyond short chronicles in annalistic form; .. From Egypt we know some historical legends, but no historiography, where the historical events are seen in the larger context. Something more of a historical view is found among the Hittites, but even here in fragmentary form, as tendencies, not as realizations. The only exception is Israel". [2])

An illustration of the appeal to "comparative literature", and the limitations of such an appeal is seen in our next writer, KÜLLING, whose name has already been before us in other connections.[3]) When studies of Hittite and other ancient treaties by Mendenhall and Baltzer uncovered a basic "treaty form", which was also common to the covenant formulations of the Old Testament, Conservative interest was quickened into claiming a contemporary Mosaic origin not only for the Book of the Covenant, but also for Deuteronomy,[4]) and by Külling for P itself. After a competent survey of literature, he moves to a less convincing discussion of theories of the date of P, and comes finally to apply his "treaty form" pattern to one passage, Genesis 17. His demonstration falls far short of proof, but even had it not done so, he could scarcely draw any certain conclusions as to date, in view of the long period throughout which the treaty form was used. It is therefore an amazing *non sequitur*, when he proceeds to draw conclusions from Genesis 17 to P in Genesis, to P narrative as a whole, and so to the date of the Priestly Writing of both narrative and law.

Equally unsatisfactory as an analogy is the appeal to studies in Homer,

---

[1]) B. Maisler, "Ancient Israelite Historiography", *IEJ* II (1952) pp. 82-88, cf. U. Cassuto, "The Rise of Historiography in Israel", *Eretz Israel* I, pp. 85-88 (Heb.); E. A. Speiser, "The Biblical Idea of History in its Common Near Eastern Setting", *IEJ* VII (1957) pp. 201-16; S. N. Kramer, "Sumerian Historiography", *IEJ* III (1953) pp. 217-32. See also the chapters on Egypt, Mesopotamia and Israel in R. C. Dentan (ed.) *The Idea of History in the Ancient Near East*, New Haven (1955).

[2]) S. Mowinckel, "Israelite Historiography", *ASTI* II (1963) p. 8.

[3]) S. R. Külling, *op. cit.*

[4]) M. G. Kline, *Treaty of the Great King*, Grand Rapids (1963). But cf. now the view of Frankena that the closest parallels are not to the fourteenth century, but to the seventh, when according to the critical view Deuteronomy had its origin (R. Frankena, "The Vassal-Treaties of Esarhaddon and the dating of Deuteronomy", *OTS* XIV (1965) pp. 122-54). Frankena argues that as it was the treaty of Esarhaddon that was accepted by Manasseh, it was presumably the same treaty that was repudiated by Josiah in his Reform in 621 B.C. What more natural then that the Deuteronomists should use the same form to state the covenant with God which was to replace it?

made by YAMAUCHI, following the line laid down by C. H. Gordon in "Homer and Bible".[1]) If critics were prepared to mete out the same treatment to Astruc's analysis of Moses as they have done to Wolf's of Homer, the unity of Moses would now be recognized, as that of Homer is.[2]) As Schliemann's excavations in Troy have corroborated the historicity of Homer, so have Near Eastern excavations corroborated that of the Bible.[3]) What is not said is that Schliemann was mistaken in thinking Homer a contemporary of the Trojan War, for whereas Homer knows iron, Troy fell in the Bronze Age. In fact Homer seems to have been just about the same distance from the events, as the Jahwist posited by the critics, so that the analogy actually proves the opposite to what it is intended to prove viz. the likelihood that both the Jahwist and Homer had sources of some kind to bridge the gap.

C. JEWISH CONTRIBUTIONS

In the period following 1925 Jewish scholarship is transformed by two events—the foundation of the Hebrew University in Jerusalem in 1924, and the emergence of Yehezkel Kaufmann, "the greatest systematizer since Wellhausen", [4]) who, in Israel at least, bestrides the period like a colossus. The effect was to hold studies in Israel on the Conservative track at the very time when in Germany and America radical directions were being taken. The latter will be first surveyed.

In the last great work of German Jewry before the Nazi "scattering", the *Encyclopaedia Judaica*, (Vol. IV published in Berlin in 1929), the articles on "Bible" extending to over one hundred pages, are with one exception, in the hands of liberal scholars. [5]) In America, in the same year, E. R. TRATTNER had gone the full way with the critical hypothesis in his illuminating historical work on the unravelling of the Biblical books. [6]) The battle for criticism had been earlier won at Hebrew Union College by MORGENSTERN, who was its

---

[1]) Gordon, "Homer and Bible", *HUCA* XXVI (1955) pp. 43-108.

[2]) E .M. Yamauchi, "Do the Bible's critics Use a Double Standard"? *Christianity Today* X (1965-1966) pp. 179-82.

[3]) Yamauchi, *Composition and Corroboration in Classical and Biblical Studies*, Philadelphia (1966). This work combines the two interests of the writer, but the double themes of "composition" and "corroboration" are mingled bewilderingly, except that "composition" is always "out", and "corroboration" always "in!"

[4]) The phrase is Albright's.

[5]) Rubaschow claimed the Bible itself as the first book of Biblical criticism e.g. in Chronicles (col. 704). The discrepancies in the law of the Passover between roasting (Exod. 12: 8) and boiling (Dt. 16:7), and in the transportation of the tabernacle, whether by Levites (Num. 1:51) or by priests (2 Kings 12:11) are solved by 2 Chron. 35:13 and 23:6 by giving both!

[6]) E. R. Trattner, *Unravelling the Book of Books*, New York (1929).

president from 1922 to 1947. [1]) For Morgenstern "the oldest document of the Hexateuch" is the small Book of the Covenant in Exod. 34, but this goes back only to Asa's Reform of 899 B.C. [2]) The longer Book of the Covenant in Exod. 20-23 dates from Ahab and Jehu, about 842 B.C. [3]) H, D and P are in the customary Grafian order. P by its inclusion of a high priest dates itself from 411 B.C. when, according to his view, the high priesthood was first instituted after the Persians had organized the Jewish community into a theocracy under an anointed priest. [4])

Even more radical was the theory of AUERBACH [5]) of the working over of the Old Testament by exilic editors. D and P are both from the same time and circles, but D has not worked over the Pentateuch while P has. There were no Deuteronomic or Priestly works of history, and little secure enough to build on is to be found in the pre-exilic sources. Earlier [6]) Auerbach had sought to show from the use of the Babylonian rather than the Canaanite calendar in P, that the passages reflecting this usage, such as those dealing with the Day of Atonement, the tabernacle, the sacrificial tariff and the census must be later than 605 B.C. when, on the evidence of Jer. 36:9, the change of calendar must have taken place. Kaufmann claimed in reply [7]) that both systems were in use among the Jews from the beginning and continue to this day. D was not known to P, either in his chief idea of centralization or in any specific law. Auerbach reiterated his point in subsequent articles, and sought to establish it by a variety of proofs.[8])

---

[1]) In his *Foundations of Biblical History* in 1915, Morgenstern complained that Judaism had contributed little in Biblical scholarship and argued that a Jewish contribution was distinctive and necessary. Reform Judaism could lead the way in this, as by abrogating some laws, they had already accepted the critical principle of growth in laws (M. Lieberman, "Julian Morgenstern—Scholar, Teacher and Leader", *HUCA* XXXII (1961) pp. 3, 5. Cf. H. M. Orlinsky, "Jewish Biblical Scholarship in America", *JQR* XLV (1954-1955) pp. 374-412; XLVII (1956-1957) pp. 345-53).

[2]) J. Morgenstern, "The Oldest Document of the Hexateuch", *HUCA* IV (1927) pp. 117 ff.

[3]) Morgenstern, "The Book of the Covenant I", *HUCA* V (1928) p. 143.

[4]) Morgenstern, "A Chapter in the History of the High Priesthood", *AJSL* LV (1938) pp. 1-24, etc.

[5]) E. Auerbach, "Die grosse Überarbeitung der biblischen Bücher", *VTSuppl* I (1953) pp. 1-10.

[6]) Auerbach, "Die Babylonische Datierung im Pentateuch und das Alter des Priester-Kodex", *VT* II (1952) pp. 334-42.

[7]) J. Kaufmann, "Der Kalender und das Alter des Priesterkodex", *VT* IV (1954) pp. 307-13.

[8]) Auerbach, "Die Feste im alten Israel", *VT* VIII (1958) pp. 1-18; "Der Wechsel des Jahres-Anfangs in Juda im Lichte der neugefundenen Babylonischen Chronik", *ibid*, IX (1959) pp. 113-21; "Die Umschaltung vom judäischen auf den

A further Jewish writer, whose theory of the composition of the Pentateuch is the most complete and ambitious of all modern theories is LEWY.[1]) Disagreeing with the oft quoted dictum that the Old Testament knows no pride of authorship, he finds authors for each portion of the Pentateuch as follows—Moses (the penal, apodictic code of the Book of the Covenant), Samuel (the ethical code of the Book of the Covenant), Nathan (the humanitarian Jahwist basic document), Zadok and Abiathar (Priestly Supplements of the Jahwist), Elisha (E and the Ephraimite Deuteronomy), Jehoiada (the P narrative), a Hezekian editor (the Jerusalemite Deuteronomy), Hilkiah (the P Code), Joshua the high priest (the post-exilic P additions). This elaborate theory might be dismissed as a critical curiosity were it not for the fact that much of the new analysis has been undertaken solely to meet the difficulties encountered by the Wellhausenian view. Deuteronomy is not straightforwardly from Josiah, nor P from after the Exile. To save the Documentary Hypothesis almost as many documents as Lewy posits are necessary, but that they should so neatly fit historical characters is quite fanciful. Here again the recrudescence of the Supplementary Hypothesis should be noted together with a Grafian separation of P narrative from P law.

A final writer standing in the more liberal tradition is SANDMEL, who describes his *The Hebrew Scriptures* [2]) as "unabashedly a book of 'Higher Criticism' " (p. 19). He begins with the prophets and comes later to the Pentateuch, although warning that his order is not necessarily to be taken as chronological (pp. 21-22). Deuteronomy is exilic or after. P is late but not certainly later than D (p. 416). "The Graf-Wellhausen hypothesis remains the point of departure for scientific biblical scholarship ... not because its answers are right, but because they have reflected an awareness of the right questions".[3])

In the concession here that P is older than D we see the influence of KAUFMANN, whose views on this subject dominate all Jewish scholarship in this period. They were first stated in articles in the *Zeitschrift für die alttestamentliche Wissenschaft* in 1930 and 1933. The former of these articles [4]) was concerned to make the points that Israel had never had a hierocratic ideal, as Wellhausen had claimed and that

babylonischen Kalender", *ibid*, X (1960) pp. 69-70; "Das Zehngebot—Allgemeine Gesetzes-Form in der Bibel", *ibid*, XVI (1966) pp. 255-76.

[1]) I. Lewy, *The Growth of the Pentateuch*, New York (1955).

[2]) S. Sandmel, *The Hebrew Scriptures*, New York (1963).

[3]) This is from his article "The Haggada within Scripture", *JBL* LXXX (1961) p. 122. He would prefer a hypothesis, not of documents but of haggadic additions, but fears that its fate may be to fade into a footnote in a new Pfeiffer! (p. 106).

[4]) J. Kaufmann, "Probleme der israelitisch-jüdischen Religionsgeschichte", *ZAW* XLVIII (1930) pp. 23-43.

P predated D. Priestly rule is found neither in Ezekiel (whose head was a prince), nor in Haggai-Zechariah (where the high priest is subordinate to Zerubbabel), nor in Chronicles (whose hero was David), nor in Ezra (who was a scribe), nor in P (whose Aaron was subject to the prophetic Moses). P has no trace of D's idea of a chosen place, where tithes and firstlings must be brought and Passover eaten, but has a moving tent and a camp order for each city (pp. 32-40).

The second article [1]) offers an explanation for the indifference of the prophets to the law and stresses the priority of the latter. This is also the main point of his massive *Toledoth*, [2]) where he argues that P has too many ancient rites—the scapegoat, the red heifer and the like—to be post-exilic. P has no polemic against worship away from the central sanctuary but this was a problem in the post-exilic period (e.g. Ezra 4:2 and Elephantine (pp. 175-76)). In fact P's silence on centralization takes it back to the age before Hezekiah, when centralization first appears (pp. 175ff, 205). Summing up his arguments between pp. 175 and 205 he asserts:

> "In every detail, P betrays its antiquity. Its narrative preserves bold anthropomorphisms; its cult presupposes the existence of local altars; ... its tithes are ancient; its thousands of Levites are a reflex of a distant past" (p. 206).

On none of these points, however, are his arguments superior to Wellhausen's to the contrary. Kaufmann's rejection of a post-exilic Torah goes along with his much more fundamental attack on Wellhausen's theory of the late origin of monotheism, but the two things do not necessarily go together, and it is a defect of Kaufmann that his entire Biblical study is over-shadowed by this anti-Wellhausen polemic. [3])

---

[1]) Kaufmann, *ibid*, LI (1933) pp. 35-47.

[2]) In Hebrew, but abridged and translated into English as *The Religion of Israel*, Chicago (1960).

[3]) Cf. D. Lieber, "Yehezkel Kaufmann's Contribution to Biblical Scholarship", *Jewish Education* XXXIV (1963-1964) pp. 254-61 and "Modern Trends in Bible Study", *Conservative Judaism* XX (1965) pp. 37-46. Less discriminating were the earlier Jewish reviewers, who greeted his work as a death-blow to Wellhausen — E. Urbach "Neue Wege der Bibelwissenschaft", *MGWJ* LXXXII (1938) pp. 1-22; F. Levy in Willoughby, *op. cit.*, p. 115 who spoke of the Graf-Wellhausen hypothesis as demolished and at that by Jews; H. L. Ginsberg, "New Trends in Biblical Criticism", *Commentary* X (1950) pp. 276-78, who in the course of a valuable article on Wellhausen, Alt and Kaufmann ventured two prophecies (cf. Orr above) "The regnant hypotheses of the year 1970 [*sic*] will surely stand incomparably closer to those of Kaufmann than to those which he combats" (p. 284) and that the *Toledoth* would either be translated into English or scholars would learn "Israeli" to read it. Neither looks like being fulfilled!

Kaufmann, indeed, had accepted a good deal of Wellhausen's literary criticism e.g. the existence of the sources J, E, D and P, but no such concessions were made by many of his Jewish associates.

Standing in the Conservative tradition was HERTZ, whose discussions are to be found in additional notes added throughout his commentary on the *Pentateuch and Haftorahs*,[1]) and in an article on Deuteronomy contributed to the *Transactions of the Victoria Institute* in 1940.[2]) His concern is to answer Grafianism on sacrifice (III, pp. 42-49), the date of P (III, pp. 316-28) and centralization (V, pp. 444-55). To the arguments of his predecessors against dating P after the Exile, he adds linguistic considerations, such as the complete lack of neo-Babylonian or Persian traces. He stresses also the dissimilarity between P's exalted high priesthood and its unpopular representatives in the time of Ezra (III, pp. 318-19). He rejected the analysis entirely and in this was supported by Hebrew University professors, Segal and Cassuto.

SEGAL has devoted his retirement since 1955 [3]) to summarizing his views on "the unitary character of the Pentateuch",[4]) "El, Elohim, and Yhwh in the Bible", [5]) "the Book of Deuteronomy", [6]) and "the composition of the Pentateuch".[7]) In the last of these he speaks of the improbability of the critical view that two writers hundreds of years apart should agree to avoid the use of the name Jahweh for a specific ancient period in the interests of a theory. Law in Israel had not arisen from life, but had been an ideal given by revelation at the beginning (pp. 104-105). Deuteronomy's "one place" of worship had been generic, and did not rule out the various places of the plural altars (p. 111).[8]) Mosaic authorship of each Pentateuchal book is asserted, but with limiting exceptions that rob the assertions of much of their value.

This is even more true of CASSUTO, who is not opposed to sources in general, but only those of the Wellhausen school. As the author of the articles *Genesis, Leviticus* and *Deuteronomy* in the Hebrew Biblical encyclopaedia,[9]) and now of the stimulating commentaries *Adam to*

---

[1]) J. H. Hertz, *The Pentateuch and Haftorahs*, 5 vols, London (1930-1936).

[2]) Hertz "Deuteronomy: Antiquity and Mosaic Authorship", *Journal of Transactions of the Victoria Institute* LXXII (1940) pp. 86-103.

[3]) He died in 1968 after completing his volume *The Pentateuch: Its Composition and its Authorship*, Jerusalem (1967).

[4]) M. H. Segal, *Tarbiz* XXV-(1955) pp. 1-10.

[5]) *JQR* XLVI (1955-1956) pp. 89-115.

[6]) *JQR* XLVIII (1957-1958) pp. 315-51.

[7]) *Scripta Hierosolymitana* VIII (1961) pp. 68-114.

[8]) He claims that Dt. 12:5 etc. is using the singular for the plural like Dt. 12:18 "thy son and thy daughter" and 16:14 "the Levite and the stranger" (*JQR* XLVIII (1957-1958) p. 330), but in doing so forgets the score or so other references to centralization which Graetz found in Deuteronomy. (Cf. *JQR* III (1891) pp. 219-30).

[9]) *Encyclopedia Miqra* Vol. II (1954) pp. 318-35, 878-87, 608-19.

Noah, Noah to Abraham and *Exodus* [1] he resorts to an analysis of his own, which one would scarcely expect of the author of the *The Documentary Hypothesis* with its firm rejection of the JE analysis.[2] One wonders what advantage it is to reject paths of criticism now well worn by countless feet, to blaze new paths of one's own in source investigation, where few if any will follow, but this is what so often happens with Jewish scholars. They are not so much anti-critical, as critical in a different sense.

Modern Israeli scholars divide into three groups according to whether they follow Segal in his rejection of analysis, [3] or Cassuto in his preference for different sources, [4] or Kaufmann with his concern to date P before D. Our enquiry must limit itself to only the last of these. A convenient summary is the Kaufmann Festschrift, [5] where several articles are devoted to the history of the laws.

GREENBERG, like Kitchen, wants to see a greater use of comparative materials and takes up again the comparison of Israelite law with Hammurabi's Code. [6] Discrepancies are possible in a code published at one time, when older laws have been incorporated, but to engage in source criticism of these, as Koschaker did with Hammurabi's Code, is less helpful than to interpret the laws as they stand, as Driver and Miles did (p. 7). Apparent defects in some Israelite provisions are actually due to far-reaching principles, such as the value of human life, which are really superior. A course of development from lower to higher morality is thus ruled out. "The divergences .. appear not

---

[1] U. Cassuto, *Adam to Noah* Part I, Jerusalem (1961), *Noah to Abraham*, Jerusalem (1964), *Exodus*, Jerusalem (1967).

[2] Cassuto, *The Documentary Hypothesis*, Jerusalem (1961). A larger work on Genesis analysis had appeared in Italian much earlier.

[3] An example would be *J. M. Grintz*, who edited the Segal Festschrift (*Studies in the Bible*, Jerusalem (1964)), and has written many anti-critical articles, including most recently "Ye shall not eat *on* the blood", *Zion* XXXI (1966) pp. 1-17 (Heb and Eng). Here it is argued that Saul's words in 1 Sam. 14:23-35 had to do, not with sacrificial slaughter, but with chthonic sacrifice to goat demons, which was also the concern in Lev. 19:26 and in the scapegoat rites. He concludes that "the Priestly laws are a product of the time they reflect with such thoroughness i.e. of the period of the wanderings in the desert as the Scriptures rightly claim". Kaufmann himself "in spite of many strictures.. on the Wellhausenian view" had tended "to accept a date for the Priestly Code as a unit, that came quite near that of the School" through following Wellhausen too closely in his theory of sacrificial slaughter.

[4] E.g. Loewenstamm in his books on Exodus and Genesis (Heb).

[5] M. Haran (ed.) *Yehezkel Kaufmann Jubilee Volume*, Jerusalem (1960).

[6] M. Greenberg, "Some Postulates of Biblical Criminal Law", *ibid*, pp. 5-28.

as varying stages of progress or lag along a single line of evolution, but as reflections of differing underlying principles". [1]

SPEISER examines four long-standing cruces in the vocabulary of Leviticus, which he believes to be illuminated for the first time by Mesopotamian texts from earlier than the 15th century B.C. As the meaning had then become lost, an early origin for the chapters concerned must be posited. [2] Speiser is characteristically cautious in stating consequences, and concedes that "early" need not mean Mosaic, and that these passages are not all of P, but he is impressed by the fact that all parts of Leviticus are represented (Chaps 5, 19, 25 and 27) and thinks Kaufmann's position in general to be supported. [3]

HARAN, the editor of the Kaufmann volume, has made the most determined effort to come to terms with the cultic issues raised by Wellhausen and rebutted by Kaufmann. In his *Encyclopedia Miqra* article "Priesthood" and in many articles on the tabernacle, [4] he argued that P is different, not because it is later, but because it is a

---

[1] *Ibid*, pp. 6, 20, 22, 25. Cf. also his "A New Approach to the History of the Israelite Priesthood", *JAOS* LXX (1950) pp. 41-47 summarizing Kaufmann, whom he was later to translate, and the somewhat similar discussion of D. DAUBE in *Studies in Biblical Law*, Cambridge (1947). However in his later "Concerning Methods of Bible-Criticism", *Archiv Orientália* XVII (1949) pp. 88-99, Daube explained that he intended no disregard of the major results of Biblical criticism—JEDP and their dating—but only wanted a less mechanical application of critical methods.

[2] E. A. Speiser, "Leviticus and the Critics", *Yehezkel Kaufmann Jubilee Volume*, pp. 29-45. Cf. the similar argumentation in his Anchor Bible *Genesis*, New York (1964) e.g. pp. xxii-xxvi where JEDP are accepted but P seen as a growth of many centuries.

[3] With this essay may be compared Hurvitz' attempt to approach the date of P via the use of the synonyms for "fine linen", P using the earlier word *ses* rather than the normal late word *bus*. From this it is deduced that not only the contents of P, but also the present form of P could be early and Egyptian (A. Hurvitz, "The Usage of *šeš* and *bûs* in the Bible and its implication for the date of P", *HTR* LX (1967) pp. 117-21). But this had been discussed by the great critics as long ago as Delitzsch—cf. his introduction to Curtiss' *Levitical Priests*, Edinburgh (1877) pp. xi-xiii.

[4] M. Haran, "The Ark and the Cherubim", *IEJ* IX (1959) pp. 30-94; "The "Ohel Mo'edh' in Pentateuchal Sources", *JSS* V (1960) pp. 50-65; "The Complex of Ritual Acts performed inside the Tabernacle", *Kaufmann Volume* and *Scripta Hierosolymitana* VIII (1961) pp. 272-302; "The Uses of Incense in the ancient Israelite ritual", *VT* X (1960) pp. 113-29; "Studies in the Account of the Levitical cities II. Utopia and Historical Reality", *JBL* LXXX (1961) pp. 156-65; "Shiloh and Jerusalem. The Origin of The Priestly Tradition in the Pentateuch", *JBL* LXXXI (1962) pp. 14-24; "The Disappearance of the Ark", *IEJ* XIII (1963) pp. 46-58; "The Priestly Image of the Tabernacle", *HUCA* XXXVI (1965) pp. 191-226; "The Religion of the Patriarchs, An Attempt at a Synthesis", *ASTI* IV (1965) pp. 30-55.

work of the priests, [1]) that its locale was the Shiloh sanctuary, [2]) and its date well before the Exile, with its material much older. [3]) "I consider Ezekiel to be the borrower from H and P, since I share the conviction that both these Pentateuchal literary layers were committed to writing in the pre-Exilic period. In Ezra's time they were only edited and canonized, while Ezekiel himself is a disciple of that Priestly School in which they originated". [4])

The fact that no more can be claimed after a detailed modern investigation attests the intransigence of the cultic problem, for although the Grafian conclusions are not drawn, it is conceded that P's tabernacle was idealized, the Levitical cities were in part Utopian, the distinction between priests and Levites is late, and the divergence between many altars and the one altar of P is a fact, even if centralization was no more than a Utopian ideal. The early hope that a later article would show that Solomon's temple was later than P's tabernacle has not materialized. The data on which Graf built seem as intractable as ever. [5])

D. Catholic Contributions

This period, like its predecessor, is divided into two halves by an important Papal decision, which set the tone for Catholic scholarship, but whereas the encyclical *Pascendi* in 1907 had been a red light, *Divino Afflante Spiritu* in 1943 urged the new study of old problems, and permitted the recognition of literary forms, and thus gave a green light to the Biblical movement. [6]) The green light did indeed

---

[1]) *JBL* LXXX (1961) p. 156.

[2]) *JBL* LXXXI (1962) p. 21.

[3]) *JBL* LXXX (1961) p. 156.

[4]) *ASTI* IV (1965) p. 52. He argues that the "I am Yahweh" formula is more original in P than in Ezekiel.

[5]) A further Jewish contributor to the Kaufmann volume, M. Weinfeld, comes in for consideration more suitably later. Other important Jewish treatments are in M. Buber's *Moses*, Oxford (1946) and S. Goldman's, *The Book of Books*, 2 vols, New York (1948-1949).

[6]) From this time on a Biblical "movement" can really be spoken of. Cf. the three articles by J. M. T. Barton, "Recent Catholic Exegesis", *Mémorial Lagrange* (1940) pp. 239-44; "Roman Catholic Biblical Scholarship", *Scripture* VII (1955) pp. 50-56 and "Roman Catholic Biblical Scholarship: 1939-1960", *Theology* LXIII (1960) pp. 101-109. Writing in 1940, Barton deplored several lacks including that of a Catholic one-volume Bible commentary, but was able to report in 1955 that this need had been handsomely supplied in a volume of a million and a half words, *A Catholic Commentary on Holy Scripture*, London (1953).

change to orange with *Humani Generis* in 1950, and momentarily flickered on red with the *Monitum* of 1961, and did something of a dance at the Second Vatican Council, until it finally settled on green. [1])

A clarification as far as the Pentateuch was concerned was contained in the important letter to Cardinal Suhard in 1948, from the Secretary of the Biblical Commission, allowing a growth in the Mosaic laws even after the time of Moses. This was remarkably traced back to the 1906 concession that Moses could have used sources, and that slight post-Mosaic additions could have been made. "No one today doubts the existence of these sources or rejects a gradual increase of Mosaic laws due to the social and religious conditions of later times, a process manifest also in the historical narratives." [2]) That this was an over-optimistic estimate of the situation is apparent from the later hesitat-tions noted above, and from the continuing opposition which must first be recorded. Among scholars opposed to Grafianism may be mentioned Bea, Coppens and Steinmueller, and among those more favourable de Vaux, Cazelles, Steinmann, J. L. McKenzie and R. A. F. MacKenzie.

It will be recalled that Lagrange in his last contribution had expres-sed disagreement with BEA's estimate of the situation in critical studies. In a review article in 1935 Bea describes the ferment in Pentateuchal scholarship, and gives the impression, as Conservatives have so often done, that ferment meant confusion, and that confusion meant that Wellhausenianism was finished with. He has to admit that the Mosaic authorship of the Pentateuch has not yet been re-established, but he hopes that it will be (p. 199). [3]) Much the same may be said of the otherwise excellent review of COPPENS in 1938, [4]) which a critic rather unkindly described as "not a history of recent Old Testament criticism at all, but rather an account of what he would

---

[1]) The traffic light metaphor comes from the Catholic side, where it is used by Cardinal Alfrink in his claim that "these... stop signals [were] not intended to do more than regulate traffic in the best interests of all concerned!" (*Biblica* XLIII (1962) p. 255).

[2]) For the relevant texts see *A Catholic Commentary*, pp. 74, 74-75, 68 and the discussion by R. A. Dyson, pp. 164-76. Cf. W. M. Valk, "Moses and the Penta-teuch", *Scripture* V (1952) pp. 60-67.

[3]) A. Bea, "Der heutige Stand der Pentateuchfrage", *Biblica* XVI (1935) pp. 175-200.

[4]) J. Coppens, *The Old Testament and its Critics*, ET, Paterson (1942), first published 1938.

wish it to have been". [1]) The point at issue is whether the form-critical movement was to be seen with Coppens as a movement away from Wellhausen, or with his critic as a movement within Wellhausenianism. Coppens has subsequently revealed that his own position is substantially that of his teacher van Hoonacker. [2])

> Holding closely to the old paths still was STEINMUELLER in his three volume *A Companion to Scripture Studies* (1941-1942).[3]) Relying mainly on the arguments of Goettsberger's *Einleitung* (1928), that Josiah's lawbook was not just Deuteronomy and Ezra's not just P, he answers the various critical arguments and concludes that Moses was the author of all the Pentateuch; but had used a different style for the laws, utilized some older documents and had been subjected to a few redactional additions.[4])

The herald of the new day following 1948 is DE VAUX, who in 1953 celebrates the Astruc second centenary with an affirmation of the soundness of the analysis based on Astruc's clue. [5]) His commentary in the *Jerusalem Bible* on Genesis, and those of Cazelles on Leviticus and Deuteronomy, [6]) acknowledge the JEDP sources and their usual dating and origin. De Vaux insists, however, against Wellhausen, that Genesis relates facts not from the time written, but from the time written about and shows a real knowledge of the patriarchal period, which harmonizes well with extra-Biblical materials. [7]) In his *Ancient Israel*, [8]) he made one of the most striking positive contributions to Old Testament science in our time, but without greatly departing from the Grafian framework.

---

[1]) W. A. Irwin, Review, J. Coppens, "L'histoire critique de l'Ancien Testament" *JR* XIX (1939) p. 384.

[2]) Writing about 1952 he recorded: "The more recent study of the Pentateuch has not been favourable to the Mosaic authorship... in the strict sense, but confirms the moderate critical theses of the better Catholic exegetes in particular that of van Hoonacker. The Hebrew legislation goes back in substance to the person and work of Moses" but the codes are later. "Chronique..." (*op. cit*, p. 21).

[3]) J. E. Steinmueller, *A Companion to Scripture Studies*, Vol. I, London (1941); Vol. II (1942).

[4]) *Ibid*, Vol. II (⁸1954) pp. 59-69.

[5]) R. de Vaux, "A propos du second centenaire d'Astruc", *VTSuppl* I (1953) pp. 182-98.

[6]) De Vaux, *La Sainte Bible—La Genèse*, Paris (1951); H. Cazelles, *La Sainte Bible—Le Lévitique*, Paris (1951); *ibid*, *Le Deutéronome* (1950). Now in an English translation abridged by A. Jones, London (1966).

[7]) Cf. his "Les Patriarches hébreux et les découvertes modernes", *RB* LIII (1946) pp. 321-48; LV (1948) pp. 321-47; LVI (1949) pp. 1-36.

[8]) De Vaux, *Ancient Israel*, ET, London (1961), first published 1960.

No Catholic scholar has become more master of the whole gamut of critical studies than CAZELLES, who contributed *Deuteronomy* to the *Jerusalem Bible* in 1950. Although allowing for the existence of older laws, and at least one older codification H, being the Jerusalem law subsequent to Isaiah, Cazelles accepts the late date for Deuteronomy, and regards no part of it as the composition of Moses. The critical case has been argued out in a series of subsequent articles, [1]) which culminate in his hundred page contribution to the *Dictionnaire de la Bible* supplements in 1963 [2]) with its full answer to the objectors to Grafianism in recent years. Cazelles agrees that the Priestly Code belongs to the "second Exodus" period of the exilic Isaiah, when sabbath became the sign of the covenant, the new calendar was introduced, and a full-scale law code was necessary for the reorganized cult of the rebuilt temple. [3]) A comparison of this *Supplements* article with that of the main dictionary contributed near the end of the previous period (see above p. 91) shows the extent of the change in Catholic studies.

> Cazelles' viewpoint is also that of STEINMANN, who had written an appreciative biography of the Catholic critic, Richard Simon. Just as there is more than one style in the Pentateuch, as Spinoza discerned, so there are different law codes. "Either these laws were contemporaneous, in which case history records no other instance of such a legal tangle, or else it must be admitted that they reflect three stages in a long process of evolution".[4]) "By assigning the final version of the Priestly Code to the period immediately after the Exile,... we have simply made the divine work of revelation with its respect for times and places more intelligible..." (p. 87). It would be anachronistic today "to draw a picture of Moses' mode of worship in the desert from Leviticus... or to be surprised that Elias forgets the vetoes of Deuteronomy and the rites of Leviticus and offers a sacrifice on Mt Carmel" (p. 86). A doctrine of development from Moses, like that of Newman, is appealed to, to justify the placing of P later than D, H and Ezekiel.[5])

---

[1]) E.g. "A propos du Pentateuque", *Biblica* XXXV (1954) pp. 279-98; "La Torah ou Pentateuque", in A. Robert and A. Feuillet, *Introduction a la Bible*, I Tournai (1957) pp. 279-382; "Loi Israélite", *DBSuppl.* V Paris (1957) cols 497-530. On the Robert-Feuillet volume see W. Baumgartner, "Römisch-katholische Bibelwissenschaft im Wandel", *ThR* XXXI (1965-1966) pp. 1-14. He likens it to Robertson Smith's *Old Testament in the Jewish Church* for its disarming of suspicion of criticism (p. 1).

[2]) H. Cazelles, "Pentateuque", *DBSuppl* VII (1966) cols 687-858.

[3]) *Ibid*, cols 751, 827, 852-53.

[4]) J. Steinmann, *Biblical Criticism*, New York (1958) p. 85.

[5]) Steinmann, *Code Sacerdotal* I, Paris (1962) pp. 11-13.

Quite similar is the position of J. L. McKenzie in his magnificent, 800,000 word, one-volume, Bible dictionary,[1]) as a perusal of his articles on Moses, Law, Pentateuch, Deuteronomy, Levites and Tabernacle will reveal. The Book of the Covenant is from the Conquest rather than from the Wilderness (p. 499). Deuteronomy is a new codification of ancient Hebrew law and custom in the time of Josiah or Hezekiah (p. 197). P is from the Exile, and reflects a late interest in priestly law, which we now find attested also at Qumran (p. 657). The law was attributed back to Moses, because of his place in the covenant, but a law-giver in this sense is only known from Ezra, Nehemiah and Chronicles (pp. 589 cf. 499). The Grollenberg atlas also agrees that "the experiences of the hard years of the Exile... may have formed the psychological background to the Priestly Code",[2]) and that the present appearance of the Pentateuchal law books is an artificial one.[3])

While these are semi-popular works, there is no lack of serious work going on in Biblical criticism in Catholic circles. Nor is it only in the Dominican school of Lagrange, through his successors like de Vaux, but equally in the rival Jesuit institute, whose anti-critical orthodoxy was at the first extolled over against Lagrange's pro-criticism.[4]) The position of the Pontifical Biblical Institute's director R. A. F. MacKenzie is precisely that of the scholars just quoted [5]) and N. Lohfink's critical contributions to Deuteronomy study (during the last decade)[6],) and the Priestly Code (now beginning) are fully in the line of the Grafian tradition. The same is true of the work of L. A. Schökel.[7]) In fact the verdict of E. H. Maly that modern Roman Catholic studies "show few differences from.... non-Catholic" is abundantly borne out.[8])

---

[1]) *Op. cit.*

[2]) L. H. Grollenberg, *Atlas of the Bible*, ET, London (1956) p. 53.

[3]) "The whole legislative system of Israel seems, therefore, to have been fitted into the historical setting of the journey through the wilderness and associated with the figure of Moses... The remaining books of the Old Testament contain no further ordinances and prescriptions in the strict sense" (*ibid*, p. 52).

[4]) This is fully documented in the Lagrange *Souvenirs*, pp. 196 ff.

[5]) "In Israelite tradition, in order to express the belief that books were holy and composed under the impulse of the spirit of God, they were connected with the great names of the past... the Mosaic authorship of the Pentateuch... It is the Jewish way of expressing not the human authenticity, but the divine origin... It is hard to conceive that Moses could be in any way an *inspired* author, of say, Deuteronomy, or the Law of Holiness, if, these, as literary units, did not exist till centuries after his death". (R. A. F. MacKenzie, "Some Problems in the Field of Inspiration", *CBQ* XX (1958) pp. 4-5).

[6]) To be discussed below.

[7]) His *Understanding Biblical Research*, New York (1963) gives some interesting details of growing Catholic participation in Old Testament discussions, and notes that after all Aquinas was more critical in his Psalm studies than Luther!

[8]) E. H. Maly, "Pentateuch", *New Catholic Encyclopedia*, Vol. XI, New York (1967) p. 103.

A non-Roman reviewer therefore finds it a little devious in his Catholic counterpart that he should still want to so loudly disassociate himself from the views condemned in his predecessors. When Schökel says Catholic form criticism looks like Gunkel's, but is just the opposite, because Gunkel denied the supernatural inspiration of Scripture, yet a few pages further on can quote Gunkel's own *credo* that no irreligious historian could write effectively on Scripture, one has misgivings. [1]) When R. Brown says that Biblical criticism such as Wellhausen's was "a ... basically irreligious approach to the Bible" (p. 11) [2]) and that "no modern Catholic biblical scholar would hold the erroneous and heretical presuppositions that were the backbone of Modernism" (p. 13) and "the fact that a modern Catholic biblical scholar will occasionally accept some fact that the Modernists accepted fifty years ago proves nothing regarding his heterodoxy" (p. 12), one wonders whether Vidler is not right when he says that the modern liberal-minded Catholics have derived their view of Modernism from the distortions of *Pascendi*, rather than from the works of the Modernists themselves. [3]) The irony of the situation is reflected in a note of 1954 from officials of the Biblical Commission to the effect that in interpreting the decrees of the Commission, the date should be kept in mind. If the decree was issued during the Modernist crisis, the Commission cannot be held to maintain an attitude that is no longer justified. [4])

E. Archaeological Contributions

In the realm of archaeology new discoveries were still appealed to at the beginning of our period as substantiating the Bible records, but by the end of it, because of the ambiguous nature of the evidence, this was less often the case. Those who thought the critical case rested on the inability of Moses to write, made much of the discovery of alpha-

---

[1]) These are not allayed, when one goes on to find reiterated the charge of the rationalistic presuppositions of the older criticism, which has been shown above to be without foundation.

[2]) R. E. Brown, "Our New Approach to the Bible", *New Testament Essays*, Milwaukee (1965) p. 11.

[3]) A. Vidler, *The Church in an Age of Revolution*, p. 189. Cf. the remark quoted by Baumgartner in *ThR* XXXI (1965-1966) *op. cit*, p. 4 "Was gegenwärtig in der katholischen Kirche vor sich geht, ist im Grunde eine stillschweigende Rehabilitierung des Modernismus".

[4]) W. J. Harrington, *Record of Revelation*, Chicago (1965) p. 115.

betic inscriptions at Sinai. [1]) GARSTANG's investigations at Jericho were more grist to their mill, despite the hesitations of S.A. Cook and others, which were to be so abundantly vindicated. [2]) The Egyptian background to the Pentateuch was stressed by YAHUDA [3]) as it had been before him by Naville, Kyle. [4]) Poole [5]) and Hengstenberg, [6]) and has been since by Vergote [7]) and Kitchen, [8]) to prove that the author of the Pentateuch was familiar with Egyptian speech and customs. [9]) Much of Yahuda's material was incorporated by J. G. DUNCAN in his volume on Hebrew Origins, [10]) although the likelihood of later borrowing in the time of David and Solomon, when Israel was also in close contact with Egypt, is not overlooked. [11])

More important than any of these were the discoveries at Ras Shamra which were to illuminate the Canaanite background in a

---

[1]) E.g. H. Grimme in Germany in three titles between 1923 and 1929 beginning with *Althebräische Inschriften vom Sinai*, Hanover (1923) esp. pp. 90-96, and C. Marston in England in several works including *New Bible Evidence*, New York (1934-1935) esp. pp. 178-82. For answer see *ZDMG* LXXX (1926) pp. 24-54 by Sethe, and for a curious sidelight on how not to use archaeology, H. G. May's article on Dr Harry Rimmer in *BA* VIII (1945) "Moses and the Sinai Inscriptions". I owe these references to R. A. Bowman in the Willoughby symposium (*op. cit*, p. 12).

[2]) At the time Cook's resignation as editor of the *PEF* Quarterly was demanded by some members of the Fund, despite the fact that the original 1865 charter had stressed that its aims would be scientific rather than religious. For this, and other entertaining snippets from the "archaeology proves the Bible" debate, see J. A. Calloway, "The Emerging Role of Biblical Archaeology", *RE* LXIII (1966) pp. 200-09.

[3]) A. S. Yahuda, *The Language of the Pentateuch in its Relation to Egyptian*, ET Oxford (1933), first published 1929; also *The Accuracy of the Bible*, London (1934).

[4]) M. G. Kyle, *Moses and the Monuments* (1919).

[5]) R. S. Poole, "The Date of the Pentateuch", *Contemporary Review*, LII (1887) pp. 350-70.

[6]) E. W. Hengstenberg, *Egypt and the Books of Moses*, ET, Edinburgh (1845).

[7]) J. Vergote, *Joseph en Égypte*, Louvain (1959).

[8]) *JEA*, *op. cit*. Cf. *NBD*, pp. 656-60.

[9]) This somewhat pretentious volume received a surprisingly sympathetic reception from McFadyen (J. E. McFadyen, "The Language of the Pentateuch in its Relation to Egyptian", *ExpT* XLI (1929-1930) pp. 54-58), but was correctly estimated and answered by König (E. König, "Die sprachliche Gestalt des Pentateuches in ihrer Beziehung zur Ägyptischen Sprache", *JBL* XLVIII (1929) pp. 333-53), ever to the fore when linguistic arguments against source analysis were advanced. Neither Vergote nor Kitchen support Yahuda in many of his derivations but advance others of their own.

[10]) J. G. Duncan, *New Light on Hebrew Origins*, New York (1936). Cf. also his *The Accuracy of the Old Testament*, London (1930).

[11]) T. O. Lambdin in his important "Egyptian Loan Words in the Old Testament", *JAOS* LXXIII (1953) pp. 145-55 lists fortyfive words from all parts of the Old Testament, of which only a half are from the Pentateuch.

remarkable way, as were those at Nuzu and Mari that of the patriarchs.
Ras Shamra was important for the ritual laws of Israel, while Hurrian,
Hittite and Mesopotamian materials illustrated the civil laws. Scholars
were quick to exploit the fact that some sacrificial terms which
Wellhausen had regarded as post-exilic were found in Ras Shamra
of 1400 B.C. [1]) While recent investigators are more cautious in
drawing conclusions as to the religion of early Israel from this, [2])
it is possible that some modification of Grafianism may be necessary. [3])

That this was indeed the case was firmly asserted by W. F. ALBRIGHT
in 1938. [4]) De Wette had written in 1805 before any Ancient Near
Eastern language had been deciphered, and Wellhausen in 1878 before
any Palestinian excavation had been carried out except at Jerusalem.
The "pious fraud" postulated by the former had not been found in
the Ancient Near East, nor was Israel a "primitive people" as assumed
by the latter (p. 183). Monotheism was no later climax of a Hegelian
development process, but was early, as were individual laws, although
the dating of the codes in the order Book of the Covenant, D, Ezekiel,
P was likely to withstand the new evidence (pp. 187-88). [5]) In a less
guarded statement in 1952, Albright said that we must regard the law
as essentially Mosaic, with the Priestly Code as the ritual of the

---

[1]) J. W. Jack, *The Ras Shamra Tablets*, Edinburgh (1935) pp. 29-30; S. H. Hooke,
"The Early Background of Hebrew Religion", T. W. Manson (ed.) *A Companion
to the Bible*, Edinburgh (1947) p. 283, first published 1939; J. P. Hyatt, "The Ras
Shamra Discoveries and the Interpretation of the Old Testament", *JBR* X (1942)
p. 72.

[2]) D. M. L. Urie, "Sacrifice among the West Semites", *PEQ* LXXXI (1949)
pp. 67-82.

[3]) A full discussion will be found in the writer's *Penitence and Sacrifice in Early
Israel*, Leiden (1963) pp. 31-33, 245, 247, 248.

[4]) W. F. Albright, "Archeology Confronts Biblical Criticism", *American
Scholar* VII (1938) pp. 176-88.

[5]) In a rejoinder of the same date entitled "Higher Criticism Survives Archeology", *ibid*, pp. 409-27, W. C. Graham agreed that Wellhausen had been wrong
in assuming Israel's isolation down to the Exile, and then becoming cultic under
Babylonian influence, when Ras Shamra showed the possibility of such influence
from the beginning (p. 421), but did not agree that archaeology had either established Israel's early monotheism or overthrown Higher Criticism (pp. 420,
423). Cf. also the *JBR* articles of the same year "Biblical Criticism and Archaeology", *JBR* VI (1938) pp. 131-32, 170-71 by G. R. Berry, and "The New Trend
in Biblical Criticism", *ibid*, pp. 83-86 by T. W. Rosmarin and for factual data
in archaeology, E. H. Grant, *The Haverford Symposium on Archaeology and the Bible*,
New Haven (1938), and in criticism, O. Eissfeldt, "Die literarkritische Arbeit
am Alten Testament in den letzten 12 Jahren", *ThR* X (1938) pp. 255-91 and ET
in *Record and Revelation*, Oxford (1938) pp. 74-109.

tabernacle period, the cultic laws as older than the temple, and the civil laws than the monarchy. [1])

The question as to whether archaeology can make such affirmations has been put by NOTH [2]) to Albright as it was by others to Sayce.

Noth's own view of the kind of confirmation archaeology can give as stated in his *History of Israel* (p. 47) is perhaps too negative,[3]) but there is little justification for Albright's insinuation that the German school did not know the facts, because

> "after the middle 1930s Alt himself was cut off almost completely from direct contact with Palestine as well as from non-German research. His pupils were in much the same situation, and the attempt to replace the influx of empirical data from Palestine and the ancient Near East by systematic research along a priori lines led to increasing loss of touch with archaeological and philological fact. Today there is a very sharp cleavage between the dominant German school and the archaeological school, best represented in America and Israel". [4])

In the same vein Albright's pupil, FREEDMAN, writes in *The Bible in Modern Scholarship* [5]) "before archaeology there was no adequate alternative to the creation of hypothetical frameworks for the biblical narrative; but as the factual evidence has become available, there is less and less excuse for such exercises in ingenuity, and *in due course there will be none*".[6]) And this in a volume which many times employs two of the "hypothetical constructions" taken over from Noth and Alt—the amphictyony and "Der Gott der Väter"! And what shall we say of Albright's own theorizing about the patriarchs as donkey caravaneers, mildly rebuked, as inconsistent with the Biblical evidence, by de Vaux in the same volume,[7]) or of the "mistakes" of archaeology mentioned by Pritchard on pp. 323-24 ("Garstang's Late Bronze Walls at Jericho, Solomon's stables at Megiddo, the Jebusite

---

[1]) Albright, *The Biblical Period*, Oxford (1952) pp. 11-12. Cf. now his similar statement in connection with his forthcoming "History of the Religion of Israel" in *History, Archaeology and Christian Humanism*, New York (1964) p. 30.

[2]) E.g. M. Noth, "Der Beitrag der Archäologie zur Geschichte Israels", *VTSuppl VII Congress Volume, Oxford 1959* (1960) pp. 262-82.

[3]) Noth was perhaps reacting to an extreme work like W. Keller's *Und die Bibel hat doch recht*, Düsseldorf (1955), which in these years was having a great vogue in Germany, despite its unscientific reliance on exploded Garstang and Woolley materials. Cf. Noth, "Hat die Bibel doch recht?" *Festschrift für Günther Dehn*, Neukirchen (1957) pp. 7-22.

[4]) Albright, *History, Archaeology and Christian Humanism*, pp. 265-66.

[5]) J. P. Hyatt (ed.) *The Bible in Modern Scholarship*, Nashville (1965).

[6]) D. N. Freedman, "Archaeology and the Future of Biblical Studies", *ibid*, p. 298. Italics are ours.

[7]) *Ibid*, p. 25.

wall at Jerusalem, and the Semitic high places",) [1]) or of the Bible
records themselves which according to Pritchard (pp. 319, 317) in
the case of the three main centres connected with the conquest—
Jericho, Ai and Gibeon—have not been confirmed by excavation.[2])
It is an awareness of these facts, rather than ignorance of them,
that lies behind Noth's caution. Unlike other areas, Palestine shows
an almost complete lack of inscribed finds. Foundation stones do not
name builders, nor graves the occupants. From buildings to burying
places anonymity is the rule for all early finds.[3]) Cities fall to unnamed
conquerors, and "in no destruction of Late Bronze Age cities... which
it is chronologically plausible to ascribe to the entry of the Israelites,
is any evidence furnished as to who the enemy might have been to
whom the city in this special case fell victim." [4]) Israel's origins are
certainly to be sought in a proto-Aramaic milieu like that of Mari,[5])
but such a milieu extended from Mesopotamia to Syria-Palestine,
and over long periods, so that such research is less help in solving
the problem than the investigation of the Old Testament's own
traditions.[6])

Between the "combatants" of the American and German schools,
DE VAUX interposes himself in the Hyatt volume, as a kind of "referee"
with the statement that both have their own contribution to make
(pp. 19-20). Noth prefers to work from within, because he is at home
in the literature, but he is not against archaeology, only its abuse (p. 26).
Albright works from without, because his greatest competence is
in archaeology but, (we may add), this does not mean that he has not
made profound contributions to the history of ideas. Both the internal
and the external evidence must go hand in hand,[7]) and the claim
that "the internal evidence afforded by a document must take prece-

---

[1]) Cf. the Frankens, *op. cit*, p. 17 "The so-called 'facts' of Biblical archaeology
are often no firmer than some 'facts' of the literary interpretation of the
Bible".

[2]) Cf. Pritchard in *SEA* XXX (1965) pp. 5-20 and Freedman, *op. cit*, pp. 296-97
and the Frankens (*op. cit*, p. 80).

[3]) M. Noth, *The Old Testament World*, ET, Philadelphia (1966) pp. 142-44.
The burial customs mitigate against the preservation of names, as the grave ledges
in rock tombs were used again and again (p. 170).

[4]) *Ibid*, p. 144. In some "tells" there are almost as many destruction levels,
as there are strata, and it becomes arbitrary to seize on one that looks about the
right date!

[5]) Cf. Noth's review of Bright's *History*, *Interpretation* XV (1961) pp. 61-66.

[6]) Noth, *Die Ursprünge des alten Israels im Lichte neuer Quellen*, Köln (1961).

[7]) Cf. R. de Vaux in "Hebrew Patriarchs and History", *Theology Digest* XII
(1964) p. 228 where the coming together of the two schools is seen. "In his later
work, Martin Noth gives a more positive judgement on the historical value of
the patriarchal traditions. In the other camp, one of Albright's disciples, John
Bright, who had reproached Noth's history for its 'nihilistic' treatment of Israel's
origins himself took a more moderate position in *The History of Israel*, which he
himself wrote later".

dence over any external evidence" cannot be endorsed.[1]) De Vaux writes:

"There is no precedence between the two kinds of evidence: a correct solution must make use of both, must prove the worth of both... It is easier for the archaeologist to be objective: he is working with real material things, in real places, which have remained what they are and where they are, and he cannot alter this. A wall remains a wall, a pot remains a pot, and a coin remains a coin. If he knows his job, he can, with his coins and his pots, give a date to his walls. And he is usually more modest than his textual friend, for he is continually going to the written documents—if there are any—to guide or to test his conclusions. But the textual critic is not working on real tangible things: between him and the historical fact there are all the interpretations and possible mistakes of his author...copyists, translators... ; and on top of all this there are his own interpretations...and perhaps his mistakes. He should not...overlook, nor set aside, nor deface the walls, the pots and the coins of his brother the archaeologist".

The immense contribution that archaeology has made to Biblical studies must be freely admitted, and it is no intention of the present section to decry it, but only to establish a vantage point from which its contribution may be seen in right perspective The large areas of our ignorance, [2]) the chance element in archaeological finds, [3]) the pressure to show striking results and the danger of premature theorizings, [4]) the unlikelihood of archaeology speaking any word to the deepest level of Scripture, [5]) and the double-tongue with which it does speak when its voice is heard [6])—all warn us of the virtual impos-

---

[1]) Against G. R. Driver in *The Judaean Scrolls*. This and the following quotations are from de Vaux's review in *NTS* XIII (1966-1967) pp. 97-98.

[2]) Cf. P. W. Lapp's illuminating article, "Palestine: Known But Mostly Unknown", *BA* XXVI (1963) pp. 121-34, where it is estimated that less than two per cent of the five thousand known sites have been excavated, and more sites are being discovered each year.

[3]) No site is more than a fraction excavated, with the result that Sellin's two conclusions at Taanach in 1902 were reversed by the 1963 campaign (*ibid*, p. 130), as were Garstang's on the lack of Mycenean pottery at Hazor almost at once by Yadin.

[4]) *Ibid*, p. 132.

[5]) Cf. D. W. Thomas (ed.) *Archaeology and Old Testament Study*, Oxford (1967) p. xxviii who says that the real "truth" of the Old Testament is of a different order.. and lies in its superior religious teaching, which was of no interest to the rulers who left us inscriptions and is thus unlikely to find confirmation in archaeology.

[6]) Mesha's stone is both confirmatory of the Old Testament and in contradiction to it—it confirms Mesha's revolt, but places it before the death of Ahab, not after (*ibid*, p. xxv).

sibility of satisfactorily applying the archaeological yard-stick to our question of the history of the law.

A case in point is the excavation of the sanctuary at Arad, which is perhaps the most important for the history of the cult ever undertaken. According to excavator AHARONI (*ibid*, pp. 392-401) "the plan of the sanctuary and its contents leave no doubt that this was an Israelite sanctuary dedicated to Yahweh ... (p. 396) the first ever discovered in archaeological excavations ... (p. 395)". Its plan was precisely that of the temple, and its altar in size and materials according to the prescriptions of Exodus (pp. 395-96). But were one to hail these facts as proof of the existence of P's law, one would be immediately faced with the far more fundamental problem of what Solomon was doing, building a second temple outside the one permitted central sanctuary in Jerusalem. [1]) In fact the history of the altar as read out of the site by Aharoni is just that formulated by Wellhausen

> "it continued in existence up to the eighth or early seventh century B.C. yet its altar was ultimately neglected (in the days of Hezekiah? Cf. 2 Kings xviii. 4, 22); it was finally abandoned and deliberately destroyed... evidently after Josiah's reforms" (p. 397).

Aharoni believes that the purpose of the sanctuary had to do with the borders of the kingdom, and notes Jeroboam's Bethel and Dan at his two borders (p. 401)—cf. Dan to Beersheba. He argues that there were probably many such sanctuaries—Judean as well as Israelite— Geba, Gilgal, Ebenezer, Mizpah (Trans-Jordan), Nebo, Ataroth—the last two already attested by external evidence of Mesha's stone. [2]) If archaeology says anything, it is that centralization was not in force during the monarchy.

Reverse side of this is the failure to destroy prominent Canaanite shrines in such Levitical cities as Gezer and Taanach. [3]) Tirzah, for a time the Israelite capital, had a prominent *maṣṣebah* in the axis of the city gate, of which de Vaux writes "The *maṣṣēḇāh* was raised from one stratum to the other throughout the Israelite period, in spite of the

---

[1]) Yadin doubts the ascription to Solomon, but agrees on its being an Israelite sanctuary, so the point still remains.

[2]) Y. Aharoni, "Arad: Its Inscriptions and Temple", *BA* XXXI (1968) pp. 2-32.

[1]) Cf. p. 95 (G. Barton). Cook indeed doubted whether the standing stones at Gezer could have been rightly identified in that they survived the cleansing of Simon Maccabee, 1 Macc. 13:43-48, who did not go in for half measures (S. A. Cook, *The Religion of Ancient Palestine in the Light of Archaeology*, London (1930) p. 88).

prohibition of the Law and the condemnation of the prophets". [1] Albright, admittedly, finds what was presumably a temple in Debir destroyed, with a contemptuous disposal of cult objects as if by the Israelites,[2] and Yadin at Hazor,[3] and Wright adds Lachish.[4] Wright believes that the negative evidence in the case of Shechem—and Gezer, Taanach, Megiddo and Beth-shean—also supports the Biblical accounts, [5] and this may be granted, as far as overthrow of the cities is concerned, but it is still remarkable that so little change in cult arrangements took place when these cities were indubitably Israelite.

It is clear that no certain conclusions can be drawn from such ambiguous data, except the general one that sanctuaries are abundantly attested, and that the Conservative apologetic based on the fact that there is no archaeological evidence for any sanctuaries [6] is obviously in error. Kitchen may indeed be right in maintaining that the continuous flow of new material from archaeology may require the abandonment of long-held theories, [7] but there is no certainty thus far that it will be the critical theories that will have to be abandoned. When this Halys is crossed, the empire to be destroyed may be the traditionalist's own.

---

[1] D. W. Thomas, *op. cit*, p. 377.

[2] *Ibid*, p. 208.

[3] *Ibid*, p. 252 but elsewhere the excavators speak of this being followed by an *Israelite* cult place! (*BAR* Vol. II, p. 206).

[4] Thomas, *op. cit*, p. 362. This is confirmed as far as the destruction is concerned by excavator O. Tufnell (p. 302), but not as to its being by Israel.

[5] *Ibid*, p. 364. Cf. "Archeology and Old Testament Studies", *JBL* LXXVII (1958) p. 48. Tirzah, however, *does* show a destruction in the 13th century, (de Vaux in W. Thomas, *op. cit*, p. 375) which perhaps it should not on Wright's premises, and which can hardly be by Israel.

[6] A. Cundall, "Sanctuaries (Central and Local) in pre-exilic Israel", *Vox Evangelica* IV, London (1965) p. 18. Cf. the somewhat mystifying remark of C. R. Cross quoted in G. Cornfeld (ed.) *Adam to Daniel*, New York (1961) p. 199 "If archaeology can prove that the principle of sacrifice at a single sanctuary, outside Jerusalem, is earlier than the seventh century B.C.E., it may overthrow the critical position".

[7] As that of the Copernican cosmology did, he says (*op. cit*, p. 27).

CHAPTER ELEVEN

THE NEW METHODS APPLIED

It was not to the frontal attacks of any of the opponents mentioned in the last chapter that the eclipse of Grafianism is to be attributed, but rather to the flanking movement of the trends set in operation by Gunkel. These may be briefly classified in three groups—the Form Historical School in Germany, the Oral Tradition School in Scandinavia and what, for the want of a better name, may be called the Sanctuary Tradition representatives in England and elsewhere.

The lines between these groups are not hard and fast ones. [1]) In a sense it was the revival of cultic interest in the works of Gunkel's disciple, the Norwegian scholar MOWINCKEL, that made possible all three of the modern movements. [2]) Where Wellhausen had opposed prophet and priest, and spirit and cult, Mowinckel showed that the cult as found in such festivals as that of New Year was the spiritual centre of Israel, [3]) and that the Psalms came from the heart of the cult, where prophet and priest laboured together. [4]) The cult had a second side, hitherto unrecognized. It was concerned not only with the sacrificial—what man did, but also with the sacramental—what God had done as it was portrayed in cultic representation, and what God still did in giving the priestly oracle to the enquirer. It was in this dual recital of the acts of God in the past and in the present that scholars began to look for the origin of the narratives and the laws of the Pentateuch.

---

[1]) I. Engnell (*Gamla Testamentet*, Stockholm (1945) pp. 7-11) speaks of two modern schools—the Form-literary School and the Tradition-historical School, but the geographical division appears preferable. The German scholars of both schools are nearer to each other than they are to the Scandinavians of the latter.

[2]) Cf. D. R. Ap-Thomas, "An Appreciation of Sigmund Mowinckel's Contribution to Biblical Studies", *JBL* LXXXV (1966) pp. 315-25 and A. S. Kapelrud, "Sigmund Mowinckel and Old Testament Study", *ASTI* V (1967) pp. 4-29.

[3]) S. Mowinckel, *Psalmenstudien II. Das Thronbesteigungsfest Jahwäs*, Kristiania (1922).

[4]) Mowinckel, *Psalmenstudien III. Kultprophetie und prophetische Psalmen*, Kristiania (1923).

A. The Form Historical School

As an example of the mixture of the old method with the new the work of HEMPEL may be cited. In 1930 [1]) he recognized that Hebrew literature, apart from some old songs and poems, took its rise in priestly oracles given in the sanctuary (pp. 69-76). Codes such as the Decalogues and H could therefore be quite old, but the documents J, E, and D are to be dated to the eleventh, eighth and seventh centuries as on the older view. P, too, is exilic, but its interest in Hebron and the Aaronites suggests a conflict with Deuteronomy that is best placed soon after 586 B.C. (pp. 151-53). More recently [2]) he has suggested a date for P before 586 B.C., while friendliness to the Edomites was still possible, but from this general period, because of the language relation to Ezekiel, and perhaps after 610 B.C. when the Babylonian myths became available. The E picture of Aaron as "the great sinner" is known, to be contested, unless indeed it was P's picture of Aaron as "the called of God" which called forth E's caricature. P belongs to the anti-Jerusalemite circle of Micah and Deuteronomy and has much old material, the origin of which lies deep in the cult history.

It became obvious that much work had to be done on the units of the material and their place in the cult before over-all conclusions could be drawn, and it was to this task that a series of German scholars devoted themselves. In 1934 ALT [3]) distinguished between the two types of Hebrew laws—the "apodictic" of divine command, which he believed to be *sui generis* to Israel, and the "casuistic" or case laws, which may have had a Canaanite origin. [4]) In the same year BEGRICH [5]) isolated many examples of priestly *Heilsorakel* in Deutero-Isaiah, and

---

[1]) J. Hempel, *Die althebräische Literatur*, Potsdam (1930).

[2]) Hempel, "Priesterkodex", *Paulys Realencyclopädie*, Vol. XLIV (1954) cols 1943-1967.

[3]) A. Alt, "Die Ursprünge des Israelitischen Rechts", *Kleine Schriften I*, München (1953) pp. 278-332, first published 1934. ET now in *Essays on Old Testament History and Religion*, Oxford (1966) pp. 80-132.

[4]) The distinction between the two types of law is evident on the surface and was noted already by Gunkel in his Hinneberg article, *op. cit*, pp. 75-76: "der Dekalogue.. [hat] die Form des kategorischen Befehls 'du sollst', für den 'Mišpat' aber ist der bedingte Satz charakteristisch: 'wenn ein bestimmter Fall eintritt, so soll dies und das geschehen'". What is more questionable is the suggested ethnic backgrounds cf. I. Rapaport, "The Origins of Hebrew Law", *PEQ* LXXIII (1941) pp. 158-67 and E. Gerstenberger, *Wesen und Herkunft des "Apodiktischen Rechts"*, Neukirchen (1965).

) J. Begrich, "Das priesterliche Heilsorakel", *ZAW* LII (1934) pp. 81-92.

showed how phrase for phrase they corresponded as answers to petitions offered by sufferers in the Psalms. He carried his discussion of priestly oracles further in 1936, [1]) by showing that the *Torah* was a priestly verdict of "clean" or "unclean" in relation to eligibility for cultic participation. From this beginning VON RAD went on in 1950 [2]) and 1951 [3]) to argue for an Old Testament conception of imputed righteousness spoken in the priestly verdict "he is righteous" or conversely "he is guilty".

Two pupils of von Rad, Rendtorff and Koch, have extended the investigation further into the laws. RENDTORFF [4]) investigated chiefly the sacrificial *Torah* (Lev. 1-7) and concluded that its stylizing manner could be understood only on the theory of its recitation in the temple. KOCH [5]) gave attention to the tabernacle chapters and other parts of the *Priesterschrift* and the code of Ezekiel, and found similar evidences of stylizing suggesting the presence of much old cultic material in P. These two investigators have departed from the older method of studying the post-history of P (P's supplements) and have taken up what promises to be the more fruitful question of its pre-history.

A third form-critical investigation, this time of the Holiness Code, by REVENTLOW is less friendly to source criticism, and claims that neither Koch nor Rendtorff has gone far enough in freeing himself from it. [6]) He makes a thoroughgoing application of Klostermann's principle that the law was not a literary composition, but the deposit of preaching, and seeks to show that H as a whole, not just in some details; in its end-form, not just in its materials; was a worship document from the cultic life of Israel (p. 165). As this worship came to an end in 586 B.C., a pre-exilic date is necessary; this date could be before 725 B.C., if Begrich is right about the date of the calendar change (p. 166); but for the core even a Mosaic date may not be old

---

[1]) Begrich, "Die priesterliche Tora", *Werden und Wesen des Alten Testaments*, Berlin (1936) pp. 63-88.

[2]) G. von Rad, " 'Gerechtigkeit' und 'Leben' in der Kultsprache der Psalmen", *Gesammelte Studien zum Alten Testament*, München (1958) pp. 225-47, first published 1950. ET, *The Problem of the Hexateuch and other Essays*, Edinburgh (1966) pp. 243-66.

[3]) Von Rad, "Die Anrechnung des Glaubens zur Gerechtigkeit", *ibid*, pp. 130-35, first published 1951. ET, *op. cit*, pp. 125-30.

[4]) R. Rendtorff, *Die Gesetze in der Priesterschrift*, Göttingen (1954).

[5]) K. Koch, *Die Priesterschrift von Exodus 25 bis Leviticus 16*, Göttingen (1959); also "Die Eigenart der priesterschriftlichen Sinaigesetzgebung", *ZThK* LV (1958) pp. 36-51.

[6]) H. G. Reventlow, *Das Heiligkeitsgesetz formgeschichtlich untersucht*, Neukirchen (1961) p. 166.

enough (p. 165). The ruling idea that the law is exilic, or just before, and the youngest part of the Old Testament, is challenged by his investigations. The Pentateuch was a cultic text of many generations, not the product of a writing table. [1])

Parallel to this work on the laws, has been the very significant work on the narratives of the Pentateuch undertaken by von Rad and Noth. After the earlier work of a literary analysis of P [2]) and a study of the theology of Deuteronomy which left out of account analysis altogether, [3]) VON RAD came in 1938 to his form-historical study of the oldest *credos* in the Pentateuch. [4]) These he found in Dt. 26:5-9, Dt. 6:20-24 and Josh. 24:2-13. The rhythm and alliteration in these passages showed them to be older than their context, as old perhaps as the period of the Judges. Three great themes are reflected here— Israel's Aramean origin, her deliverance from Egypt and her taking of the Promised Land. The events of Sinai are missing from this original outline, as also from similar summaries in the Psalms. [5]) Von Rad credited the Jahwist with having added to the material which he received the Sinai, patriarchal and primeval traditions. With these additions he constructed a narrative in the framework of the *credo*. This Jahwistic work is the basis of the Pentateuch. It was supplemented by E and P, but, as these writers added nothing essentially new, the determination of their contribution is a literary-critical problem, while that of J the form-historical one. [6])

---

[1]) His arguments on H have been found wanting by the most recent Leviticus commentator K. Elliger, *Leviticus, HZAT*, Tübingen (1966) pp. 14-15, and fellow form critic N. Lohfink, who wants to posit this kind of origin for Deuteronomy, rather than H, and asks "Müsste man da nicht klären, wieso das gleiche Fest zwei trotz ihrer Verwandschaft auch wieder so grundverschiedene Grössen wie D und H nebeneinander ertragen konnte?" (N. Lohfink, "Die Bundesurkunde des Königs Josias (Eine Frage an die Deuteronomiumsforschung)", *Bibl* XLIV (1963) p. 487).

[2]) See above p. 114.

[3]) G. von Rad, *Das Gottesvolk im Deuteronomium*, Stuttgart (1929).

[4]) Von Rad, *Das Formgeschichtliche Problem des Hexateuchs*, München (1938). ET, *The Problem of the Hexateuch and other Essays*, pp. 1-78.

[5]) For Weiser's answer that the Sinai events were in the tradition although unmentioned because they did not rate as "saving acts", see his *The Old Testament: Its Formation and Development*, ET, New York (1961) pp. 83-90, and W. Beyerlin, *Die Kulttraditionen Israels in der Verkündigung des Propheten Micha*, Göttingen (1959) and *Herkunft und Geschichte der ältesten Sinaitraditionen*, Tübingen (1961), ET, Oxford (1965).

[6]) A more fundamental criticism of von Rad's presentation is that which questions the antiquity or separate existence of the *credos* on the grounds that they are typically Deuteronomic in style and standpoint, are not "creeds" and are

Von Rad's view of Deuteronomy is essentially that of Klostermann, that it is not a law code but a preaching about the law, material for a public proclamation of the law in a cultic festival. [1]) Its combined military and priestly provenance suggests a North Israelite origin among the country Levites, [2]) and this makes it quite impossible, as Welch had perceived, that centralization was its original motive (pp. 67-68). [3]) For one thing the command in Dt. 27 to set up an altar on Mt Ebal *sperrt sich* against such a theory (p. 68). The theory of the prophetic origin of the book was not worth serious consideration (p. 69). Its connection to Josiah's Reform was doubtful, although in its present form the book is a revival for a later time. [4]) On H and P von Rad is less definite. H also is a paranetic work, which P is not, but P nevertheless reflects the theology of centuries of priesthood of the *kabod* and "tent" type at Jerusalem or Hebron (pp. 41-43). Its present form is also late.

NOTH worked along the same lines as von Rad, but thought that the three original themes of the outline inherited by the Jahwist should be extended to five. [5]) The themes of Sinai and the Wilderness are in both J and E, and seeing neither document builds on the other, must go back to a common *Grundlage* (G), which from its "all Israel" motif may be dated soon after the *Landnahme*. Where von Rad had seen the Hexateuch as one work, with the *Landnahme* fulfilled in Joshua, Noth found no traces of P in Joshua or Deuteronomy apart from the displaced final chapters. [6]) P had edited a Tetrateuch, and

---

not set in the context of any festival, (Cf. T. C. Vriezen, *The Religion of Ancient Israel*, ET, London (1967) pp. 126-27; G. Fohrer, *Introduction*..., p. 118; R. E. Clements, *God's Chosen People*, London (1968) pp. 55 ff).

[1]) Von Rad, *Studies in Deuteronomy*, ET, London (1953) p. 15, first published 1948.

[2]) Unlike H and P, the whole book is military, and is redolent of the North, where the fight against Canaan was most intense. That the Levites preached is clear from Neh. 8:1 ff, and that this preaching included the speeches before battle from Dt. 20:1 ff. (Von Rad, *Deuteronomy*, *ATD*, ET, London (1966) pp. 24-25).

[3]) Only six "blocks" require centralization (*ATD*, p. 16).

[4]) This is made more explicit in the *ATD* commentary. The book comes from the century before 621 B.C., not earlier (p. 26). It is not from the old amphictyony, when the "call-up" was in use, nor from the early monarchy when it was replaced by the mercenary army, but from the revived popular "call-up" reinstituted by Josiah, after the Assyrian invasions had removed the mercenaries (p. 25). Mosaic origin is unlikely because of "the burden of the immense traditions which speak to us out of very verse" (p. 20).

[5]) M. Noth, *Überlieferungsgeschichte des Pentateuch*, Stuttgart (1948).

[6]) See von Rad's review "Hexateuch oder Pentateuch", *Verkündigung und Forschung* (1947-1948) pp. 52-55. Von Rad's point is that the *Landnahme* motif

D a work of history running from Deuteronomy to the end of Kings. [1]) Noth accepted the Grafian dating of P, but like so many others doubted if it was Ezra's lawbook. What this was remains a mystery. It could not be P which was a narrative work in which the legal sections are only secondary. [2]) Nor could it be the Pentateuch, which would not have been compiled in Babylon. Probably some legal portions, now imbedded in the Pentateuch, best fulfil the requirements. [3])

ELLIGER's view of P was similar. [4]) It was narrative, not law, and did not appear in Joshua. The laws were inserted in various blocks by later disciples. In this there is a return to something like Graf's first position, except that the P narrative is now post-exilic, while the blocks of law are of varying ages and not all late. It is an open question where these laws originated, and how old they are. The patient investigation of this problem which has been begun by Rendtorff and Koch is altogether necessary. With it must come a re-examination of the dating of the P narrative which, when divorced from the laws is not the easiest matter, if the history of criticism is any guide. The last word on this side of the problem has certainly not yet been said.

---

is a "bow of promise" from Gn. 12 to Joshua, one end of which would be left up in the air if Joshua is severed from the Pentateuch.

[1]) Noth, *Überlieferungsgeschichtliche Studien* I, Halle (1943). While the supposition of a D-work finds support in the Deuteronomic nature of Joshua, Judges and Kings, and perhaps in the double introduction to Deuteronomy, it has against it the non-Deuteronomic books of Samuel. Against a P Tetrateuch stands the reappearance of the Pentateuchal sources at the end of Deuteronomy, and of Pentateuchal themes (the inheritance of the nine and half tribes, the figure of Joshua, the bones of Joseph) in Joshua. (Cf. the Introductions of Eissfeldt, who prefers an Octateuch, pp. 241-48 and Fohrer, who wants a Hexateuch, pp. 192-95, and for the connection of Deuteronomy to Joshua A. C. Tunyogi, "The Book of the Conquest", *JBL* LXXXIV (1965) pp. 374-80)).

[2]) Noth, "Die Gesetze im Pentateuch", *Gesammelte Studien*, München (1957) p. 110, first published 1940. ET, *The Laws in the Pentateuch*, Edinburgh (1966) p. 83.

[3]) Noth, *History of Israel*, ET, London (1958) pp. 334-35, first published 1950. Cf. *Laws*, pp. 3 and 8 where passages like Exod. 12; Lev. 16 and Num. 28-29 are thought to be post-exilic, the codes D and H from the end of the monarchy, the sections of Lev. 1-7 and 11-15 earlier in the monarchy, when the two classes were only priests and laymen not priests and Levites, and The Book of the Covenant from the pre-monarchic period. But see also *Leviticus*, *ATD*, ET, London (1965) for individual variations.

[4]) K. Elliger, "Sinn und Ursprung der priesterlichen Geschichtserzählung", *ZThK* XLIX (1952) pp. 121-43.

B. The Oral Tradition School

Kraus has said that von Rad moved the form-historical question from the aesthetical-archaic sphere of Gunkel to that of Old Testament creed and tradition history. [1] The movement in this direction continued also in Scandinavia where questions of the literature were closely bound up with those of cult and ritual patternism in the Ancient Near East as a whole. [2] Not only Mowinckel but PEDERSEN also, from a different point of view, looked to an old Israelite festival as the centre of the year's religious round. This he found in the Passover. [3] Exod. 1-15, the old cult legend enshrining the ancient usage, was a unity as were many other passages normally divided by analysis. [4] Wellhausenianism was to be rejected *in toto* [5] although J, E, D and P sources might be allowed to stand. Deuteronomy, however, did not belong to Josiah's Reformation. Its attitude to the gods of other nations and its law for a king who would be an obedient pupil of the priests placed it after the Exile (pp. 176-81). [6] P is also from this time, but is evidence for pre-exilic temple *praxis*, and may like a modern Bedouin sheik, preserve laws a thousand years old (p. 176). All the sources of the Pentateuch are both pre-exilic and post-exilic. Their material is parallel, rather than successive (pp. 178-79).

It was a short step from this position to the further one that the Pentateuchal material had existed only in oral form before the Exile. This step was taken by ENGNELL in his *Gamla Testamentet* [7] in 1945.

---

[1] H.-J. Kraus, *op. cit*, p. 403. Cf. Kraus, *Worship in Israel*, ET, Oxford (1966) pp. 234-35, where he deplores the tendency to "consider the 'sources' of the Pentateuch from the stand-point of modern literary criticism and to overlook the requirements of the cult, which rests on the basis of historical and legal documents . . . Is it not a fact that the great 'source documents' of the Pentateuch had a basic connection with this founding of the cult in the Temple sanctuary?" (The Elohist with a sanctuary of the pre-monarchic period, the Jahwist with Solomon's temple, Deuteronomy with the restored 'amphictyonic cult' in the time of Josiah, and P or P including JE with Ezra's post-exilic cult).

[2] For this section see further G. W. Anderson, "Some Aspects of the Uppsala School of Old Testament Study", *HTR* XLIII (1950) pp. 239-56.

[3] J. Pedersen, "Passahfest und Passahlegende", *ZAW* LII (1934) pp. 161-75; also *Israel III-IV*, London (1940) pp. 725-50, first published 1934.

[4] His arguments have not convinced Martin Noth in *Exodus*, *ATD*, ET, London (1962), or G. Fohrer, *Überlieferung und Geschichte des Exodus: Eine Analyse von Ex. 1-15*, Berlin (1964), who reasserts the case for JEDP plus an additional source N in this passage.

[5] Pedersen, "Die Auffassung vom Alten Testament", *ZAW* XLIX (1931) pp. 161-81.

[6] Pedersen, *Israel III-IV*, pp. 585-87, 750-52.

[7] I. Engnell, *Gamla Testamentet I*, Stockholm (1945).

Already in 1938 Nyberg in a study of the text of Hosea [1]) had come to the conclusion that the written Old Testament was post-exilic, and the prophets had done little, if any, writing at all. Writing existed before the Exile, but it was doubtful if it was used for purely literary purposes (p. 8). Birkeland and later Mowinckel [2]) carried the discussion into the prophetic books. It was Engnell, however, who drew the conclusions for the Pentateuch, and elaborated his own theory along the lines of Pedersen and Noth. [3]) There were in the Pentateuch two main collections of material—a P work of the priestly type (but not P) which centred in Exod. 1-15, and a D work, of which Deuteronomy was the beginning, extending into the history. Both were compiled in the time of Ezra-Nehemiah and then united. The date of Deuteronomy and its demands for centralization has no bearing on the date of P, but is simply an evidence of different interests and viewpoints, which can quite well lie alongside one another in time. J and E were a fiction and all attempts at analysis astray. In the strongest possible way Engnell affirmed that Wellhausen and literary criticism had been outdated by the recognition of the place of oral tradition. [4])

This attitude to Wellhausenianism has become so prevalent in Scandinavia, that in some cases scholarly work by-passes problems of source analysis and redaction, and accepts the Old Testament as it stands. [5]) More logical would be an attitude of complete scepticism concerning Israelite literature, but such a conclusion would, of course, be the end of all discussion and has not in fact been drawn. A number of scholars recoiling from this conclusion have asked whether written tradition could not have existed side by side with oral. Mowinckel, [6])

[1]) H. S. Nyberg, *Studien zum Hoseabuche*, Uppsala (1935).

[2]) S. Mowinckel, *Prophecy and Tradition*, Oslo (1946).

[3]) Engnell, "Moseböckerna", *Svenskt Bibliskt Uppslagsverk* Vol II (1952) pp. 324-42.

[4]) Engnell offers a clarification of the "tradition-historical method" in "Methodological Aspects of Old Testament Study", *VTSuppl* VII (1960) pp. 13-30, and in the course of it claims that it is a misunderstanding of his position to set oral tradition over against writing as if they were mutually exclusive alternatives to be played off against one another (p. 23). On the method as a whole see now R. A. Carlson, *David the Chosen King*, Uppsala (1964) pp. 1-19 (on oral tradition) and 20-37 (on the D work), and on oral tradition in comparative religion J. Vansina, *Oral Tradition*, London (1965).

[5]) E.g. G. A. Danell, *Studies in the Name Israel in the Old Testament*, Uppsala (1946).

[6]) S. Mowinckel, *Prophecy and Tradition*, pp. 1-36. Outside Scandinavia an important critique was offered by J. van der Ploeg, "Le rôle de la tradition orale dans la transmission du texte de l'ancien testament", *RB* LIV (1947) pp. 5-41. He concluded that although oral tradition had had a place in Israel especially

Widengren, Ringgren and Laessøe in particular have followed out this line.

WIDENGREN [1]) beginning from Arabic materials showed that even in pre-Islamic Arabia writings had existed, although transmission was mainly oral. Mohammad's method was to recite to his followers, so that they learned the revelation by heart. At the same time, however, he had it recorded by a scribe (p. 47). We may suppose some such method to have been employed by the Old Testament prophets in view of the references to writing in the books of Isaiah, Jeremiah and Ezekiel (p. 77). Probably a variety of methods were employed, but writing was always one of them.

RINGGREN's discussion [2]) consisted of a study of the passages in the Old Testament which occur in the same form in different contexts. He asked whether the slight variations of text that are discoverable can best be explained by oral or written transmission. Writing was found to be less often the probable cause, but it was difficult to say whether auditory errors may not have originated in the memories of scribes rather than in oral transmission. There had always existed an oral tradition alongside the written (p. 59).

MURTONEN [3]) working on a different line came to opposite conclusions. Beginning from the Uppsala position he began investigating the use of the *matres lectionis* and on the assumption that the use increases with the latest documents, found himself forced back into literary criticism. It was impossible that the Pentateuch was not fixed in writing until the Exile.

LAESSØE added a study of Mesopotamian practice to those already undertaken on Arabia, and showed that here also written traditions existed alongside oral. Literature and the full achievement of the art of writing had risen together. Preference for written sources in later Greece is expressed by Diodorus Siculus.[4])

---

in the Wilderness and nomad period, this was less the case later, and rather improbable for sacred texts, which even outside Israel were written, where possible, to prevent corruption e.g. Enûma Elish and the Koran.

[1]) G. Widengren, *Literary and Psychological Aspects of the Hebrew Prophets*, Uppsala (1948). Widengren adduces additional Arabic evidence and other materials from Ugarit and Mesopotamia, including those cited by some of the scholars below, in his article "Oral Tradition and Written Literature among the Hebrews in the Light of Arabic Evidence, with Special Regard to Prose Narratives", *Acta Orientalia* XXIII (1959) pp. 201-262. Cf. Engnell's remarks on this in *VTSuppl* VII (1960) pp. 24-27.

[2]) H. Ringgren, "Oral and Written Transmission in the O.T.", *Studia Theologica* III (1949) pp. 35-59.

[3]) A. Murtonen, "The Fixation in Writing of Various Parts of the Pentateuch", *VT* III (1953) pp. 46-53.

[4]) J. Laessøe, "Literacy and Oral Tradition in Ancient Mesopotamia", *Studia Orientalia Ioanni Pedersen*, Hauniae (1953) pp. 205-18.

With the absence of a reliable control in this type of discussion it becomes a matter of balancing probabilities from ancient history. Nielsen takes a negative view of the place of writing in ancient Palestine and believes that it was confined to experts. [1]) North in reviewing this book asks whether the Bible writers were not in fact such experts. [2]) D. J. Wiseman argued from the scribal schools of Mesopotamia in the third millennium B.C. that literary tradition was more important than oral, but Ellison replied that unless he could demonstrate that the period from Exodus to Solomon was comparable to Mesopotamia a thousand years earlier this did not help much. [3]) Engnell refuses parallels drawn from profane sources as not applicable to the cult literature of the Old Testament at all. Bevan in a much earlier, classic discussion had pointed out that the question of literacy had no bearing on the date of a nation's historical literature. Both Greeks and Arabs had a literature for centuries before they produced any historical writing, and the same is likely to have been true in Israel. [4]) While this is of course true, the probable origins of Israel lie so far back that this development could conceivably have taken place before David, or even before Moses for that matter. The balance of probabilities must be said to be against such a development being late in Israel. [5])

C. The Sanctuary Tradition Representatives

The question of oral and written tradition had been taken up as early as 1943 by the British scholar, ROBERTSON, in connection with his comprehensive reinvestigation of the whole Pentateuchal problem. [6]) Beginning from the methods of the Mishna, in which both

[1]) E. Nielsen, *Oral Tradition*, London (1954).

[2]) C. R. North, "Oral Tradition and Written Documents", *ExpT* LXVI (1954-1955) p. 39 reviewing Nielsen; also "The Place of Oral Tradition in the Growth of the Old Testament", *ibid*, LXI (1949-1950) pp. 292-96.

[3]) H. L. Ellison, "Some Major Modern Trends in Old Testament Study", *Journal of Transactions of the Victoria Institute* LXXXVIII (1956) p. 160, cf. pp. 32-46. A similar argument to Wiseman's was advanced by E. C. Richardson, "Oral Traditions, Libraries and the Hexateuch", *Presbyterian Review* III (1905) pp. 191-215; also *ibid*, X (1912) pp. 581-605.

[4]) A. A. Bevan, "Historical Methods in the Old Testament", *Cambridge Biblical Essays*, London (1909) p. 6.

[5]) For a full discussion see K. Koch, *Was ist Formgeschichte?* Neukirchen (1964) pp. 84-100. ET, *The Growth of the Biblical Tradition*, London, 1969.

[6]) E. Robertson, *The Old Testament Problem*, Manchester (1950), first published in the *Bulletin of the John Rylands Library* between 1936 and 1950.

oral and written tradition were used, he showed that this had always been the case in Israel, as the *halakhic* and *haggadic* additions in the second form of the Decalogue testify. The Book of the Covenant was a Midrash to the Decalogue, and most of the other laws arose in the same manner as homilies on the written law. The differences in the laws were to be accounted for by the origin of these traditions in different sanctuaries (pp. 100-101). Similarities are due to the similar problems handled (p. 138).

> On Robertson's view Israel passed from centralization to a localization of her cult in the exigencies of the entry into the land.
>
> Shechem retained the Aaronite priesthood, and some functions of the central sanctuary of the Wilderness period (pp. 163-82), but administration and justice, worship and offerings were also of necessity carried on at such places as Shiloh, Gibeon, Mizpah, Nob, Bethel, Ophrah and Beersheba. The unification of the kingdom under Saul enabled Samuel to bring forward a programme for a unified cult, which is to be found in the book of Deuteronomy—a book which suits the time of Samuel much better than that of Josiah (pp. 44-45). The united kingdom, however, was short-lived, and Deuteronomy naturally fell into disuse during the entire period of the divided kingdom. The older *praxis* of the local cult was reverted to in this period, and only the cessation of the Northern kingdom in 721 B.C. opened the way to the recovery of Deuteronomy (pp. 48-49).
>
> The time of Samuel also saw the bringing together of the other strata of the Pentateuch—J and E from the narrative material collected in the sanctuaries, and P from the laws. That there were such documents in the Pentateuch no one who has studied the evidence will venture to deny (pp. 34-35), but the clue to the divine names must not be pushed too far (pp. 153 ff), nor the process of editing and re-editing favoured by the critics, which would have been impossible in authoritative and sacrosanct liturgical documents (pp. 35-36).

The work of Robertson was continued by BRINKER, [1]) with somewhat more attention to the religious history and the issues raised by Graf and Wellhausen. In the course of a very full history of the major Israelite sanctuaries he offered alternative explanations of the problems of centralization, sacrifice and priests and Levites.

> He agreed with Robertson that the conditions of the conquest sufficiently explained the growth of the sanctuaries,[2]) particularly if Burney's theory of stages of conquest be accepted (pp. 20-22). The specifically

---

[1]) R. Brinker, *The Influence of Sanctuaries in Early Israel*, Manchester (1946).

[2]) A similar explanation is offered by Cundall, *op. cit*, pp. 15, 17, 18 and Uffenheimer "On the question of centralisation of worship in ancient Israel", *Tarbiz* XXVIII (1958) pp. 138-53 (Heb and Eng). *Uffenheimer* distinguishes three periods

P emphasis on expiatory sacrifice is explained if we accept the view that P was the code of the Gibeon sanctuary before the monarchy (p. 95). When Zadok the priest of Gibeon brought P to Jerusalem, it was an alien law that could not be enforced. *Asham, Chattath* and Day of Atonement were known, but were in abeyance until after the Exile (pp. 126-36). Ezekiel's programme for the reduced status of the Levites and their substitution for Canaanite temple servants is also explained if we recall that it was at Gibeon that Canaanites had been given the rank of servants of the sanctuary. As the original occupiers of the shrine, the Gibeonites were to receive their tithe before the priests, a procedure incredible on the usual view of P (pp. 101-110). A similar explanation of some of these difficulties was offered by WELCH,[1] whose earlier work was reviewed on pages 100 ff above. P was the usage of the priests in Jerusalem, and parallel to the Northern Deuteronomy rather than its successor. It was Jerusalem that maintained the expiatory tradition. Its beginning may be traced to the origin of the cult there in the propitiatory sacrifice on the floor of Araunah. Its continuation may be seen in the sense of sin in Solomon's prayer, and in the Southern prophets Isaiah and Micah, whose sixth chapters show an interest in sacrifice and propitiation unrepresented in the North (pp. 291-306).

Another scholar who regards D, H, and P as parallel rather than successive is WRIGHT, who in his Deuteronomy commentary [2] explains the difference between the codes in this way (p. 325). Jerusalem held to the Aaronite descent of the priesthood and subordinated others. D in the North was not so different, as he also distinguished two orders of Levites—"the priests the Levites" who were altar clergy; and teacher Levites, whose functions were as described by

---

in the history of centralization. From the entry down to the fall of Shiloh (Joshua to 1 Sam. 8) only one sanctuary had been permitted but its location had rotated. Other altars were not permanent sanctuaries. From the fall of Shiloh to the building of the temple a multiplicity of sanctuaries had of necessity been allowed, but from the beginning of the temple to its destruction only one. Deuteronomy belonged to the first period. *Cundall* argues that the disorder due to the Philistine invasion and the disruption of the kingdom, accounts for the plurality of sanctuaries, but believes that some were legitimate e.g. Gibeon, where according to Josh. 9:24 the Gibeonites were to serve "in the place where the Lord chooses", those authorized in other parts of Deuteronomy (the Dt. 12 verses are taken to mean "in each place" following Brinker) (p. 10), and Beersheba and Hebron (p. 20). Deuteronomy is held to be Mosaic (its disorder is daunting to unitary authorship, but Israel was large and Moses kept preaching! pp. 7-8), but all the Pentateuch need not be, nor all its laws. Why not some from Aaron, Miriam, Joshua and Phinehas? (p. 26). A similar conservative viewpoint is found in M. H. Woudstra, *The Ark of the Covenant from Conquest to Kingship*, Philadelphia (1965).

[1] A. C. Welch, *Post-Exilic Judaism*, Edinburgh (1935).
[2] G. E. Wright, "Deuteronomy", *Interpreter's Bible* Vol. II (1953).

von Rad (pp. 444-46). [1]) Wright thus seeks to refute the critical view that Deuteronomy knows no difference between priests and Levites. [2])

Similarly MENDENHALL argued from the nature of ancient law that Israel may have had simultaneous law codes. [3]) Ancient law was not a code for a judge or for a court of law, but was a private or royal formulation. Amendments rather than existing usage were codified. He thought that Deuteronomy was "the continuity of the legal practice in some community which had escaped the changes in law which came in with the monarchy" (p. 21).

This attempt to explain the differences of the laws by contemporary rather than successive usage was of course not new. It will be remembered that de Wette had suggested this way through the difficulties in 1837:

> die örtliche Praxis bildete sich zum Theile verschieden aus, war auch wohl unter verschiedenen Priestern etwas verschieden, und daraus sind gewisse Verschiedenheiten in den vorhandenen Gesetzen zu erklären. So könnte an dem einen heiligen Orte der Gebrauch der Sündopfer, an dem anderen der der Schuldopfer entstanden, und beide dann in eine Gesetzgebung zusammengezogen werd seyn.[4])

---

[1]) Wright, "The Levites in Deuteronomy", *VT* IV (1954) pp. 325-30.

[2]) But see J. A. Emerton, "Priests and Levites in Deuteronomy", *VT* XII (1962) pp. 129-38 for a refutation and re-establishment of the critical view. "Wright has produced no convincing evidence that there was [in Dt] a sharp distinction in principle between altar-priests and client-Levites, and that the latter were not qualified to exercise priestly functions" [as was the case in P] (p. 138).

[3]) G. E. Mendenhall, *Law and Covenant in Israel and the Ancient Near East*, Pittsburgh (1955).

[4]) W. M. L. de Wette, Rec. "Vatke, George, von Bohlen...", *ThStKr* X (1837) p. 974, see above p. 25.

CHAPTER TWELVE

THE NEW METHODS APPRAISED

With the history of the development of criticism as related in Part I in mind one cannot but see a curious resemblance between the theories of this century and those of the last, even as to the order of their appearance. Gunkel wrote exactly one hundred years after Vater, and there were not lacking those who saw in his work on the units of the tradition a revival of the *Fragment Hypothesis*. If these units had stereotyped forms, what happens to the whole method of identifying documents by stylistic criteria? Surely questions of authorship become irrelevant, and one must think rather of a community product. Can a form-critical approach rightly continue to use a framework of documents established by methods it denies? [1])

Noth and von Rad, however, talk about authorship and regard the Jahwist, Elohist and Deuteronomist as individual authors rather than schools. In such a construction we have passed beyond the Fragment Hypothesis to the second stage. Here too, as before, it may best be described as a *Supplementary Hypothesis*. One basic document, in this case the Jahwist, has been supplemented by the other sources. This is more true of von Rad than Noth, who in his theory of a JE *Grundlage* specifically rejected Volz's reduction of E to a mere supplementation. Von Rad, also, does not speak of E as a supplementer, but his view that he is "bound by tradition", and less likely to originate than J, comes close to it. [2])

---

[1]) This is even more true of the later developments which are better called "formula criticism" than form criticism. Commenting on the fact that Gunkel did not use the term "Form" but "Gattung", Noth writes "This difference in terminology is not altogether a matter of no consequence. For Gunkel, concern was by no means merely with 'forms', but with kinds of discourse, each of which belonged to a specific life situation (*Sitz im Leben*), which in turn had its own historical presuppositions. But now the danger exists [in the writings of Reventlow and Baltzer] that interest will be directed no longer at the 'forms' but at the 'formulae', with the result that 'form history' will be turned into 'formula history' " —and this in turn into "formula non-history". Such form criticism is inferior to literary criticism. (M. Noth, *Developing Lines of Theological Thought in Germany*, Virginia (1963) p. 8). Cf. now K. Koch, *Was ist Formgeschichte?*

[2]) G. von Rad, *The Problem of the Hexateuch*, p. 75; *Genesis (ATD)* p. 25. For the opposite view that E is *not* always more fragmentary than J, see G. Fohrer, *Introduction*, p. 155.

It has been debated whether supplementation or *agglomeration* best describes the joining together of ancient sources. Bevan had argued that the Arabic parallels show the constant use of the method of putting of sources side by side—agglomeration. [1]) Olmstead, on the other hand, insisted that all ancient historiography was by supplementation of one major source:

> each book or section of a book was based upon one source, generally unacknowledged, which was filled out here and there by additional bits of information derived from other sources regularly cited by exact title.[2])

Olmstead claimed that the Graf-Wellhausen Hypothesis was therefore an unwarrantable intrusion in the sound method of historic development of the last century (p. 11). [3])

The same impatience with the stage of *literary dissection* is apparent in the work of Engnell, but on other grounds. For him the work of Hupfeld, and the precise source analysis of Wellhausen was a vast mistake. It was a modern "bookish" approach which was quite anachronistic. A literary composition like Tatian's was inconceivable in the ancient Orient. [4])

An objection made to pre-Grafian criticism was that it obscured *the pattern of development* in the Old Testament by giving a flat surface without depth, and the same charge can also be laid at the door of Engnell and his school. [5]) Some ideas must be early and some late,

---

[1]) A. A. Bevan, *op. cit*, pp. 12-17.

[2]) A. T. Olmstead, "History, the Ancient World and the Bible", *JNES* II (1943) pp. 1-34. Cf. also W. C. Graham, *op. cit*, p. 411, who also prefers a theory of accretion by supplementation to the "scissors and paste" of an RJE.

[3]) Commenting in 1953 on Hupfeld's discovery of a century before, Rylaarsdam also expressed misgivings that a whole century had had to elapse—from 1753 to 1853—before a second Elohist was discovered. Why too had P so often been thought to precede D and even E, and why did sources so often tend to break up into the fragment hypothesis? (J. Rylaarsdam, "The Present Status of Pentateuchal Criticism", *JBR* XXII (1954) p. 242).

[4]) I. Engnell, *Gamla Testamentet I* p. 208. Rylaarsdam in comment on the Scandinavian school continues: "Skinner's famous reply to Dahse a generation ago confirmed the documentary theory; a similar reply to Mowinckel [*sic* ? Engnell] today would do no such thing. The attempt has not been made" (*op. cit*, p. 247).

[5]) C. R. North, "Pentateuchal Criticism", H. H. Rowley (ed.) *The Old Testament and Modern Study*, Oxford (1951) p. 77. Cf. O. Eissfeldt, *Introduction* p. 143 "That instead of chronological sequence... we should think of a co-existence of the strands... that the third [?P] was roughly contemporary with the second [?D], but in another locality and in another stratum of society... [is] possible, but not, very probable".

but we cannot tell which. The whole position becomes one of uncertainty. Graf thought that he had a fixed point for tracing development in the Josianic date of Deuteronomy and the relative dating of
the other laws, but almost every representative of the modern school
has tilted a lance at the former—Bentzen, [1]) Pedersen, von Rad,
Engnell, Robertson, Brinker and Wright. Admittedly most still pay
lip service to de Wette's discovery as applicable to the present form
of Deuteronomy, but it is quite improbable that the meagre support
they now allow for centralization would ever have established the
Josianic dating a century ago.

The explanation of *parallel laws* in D and P is certainly a possible
alternative to that offered by Graf, but one should recognize just what
it means to accept it. Graf offered an explanation which, granted his
premises, was capable of logical demonstration, as Wellhausen so
brilliantly showed. The modern school can only offer in return
assumptions built upon assumptions. It is assumed that the cult and
sanctuaries occupied a certain place in the life of the people, and on
this the further assumption, that the laws and legends occupied a
certain place in the cultic celebrations, is built. Here is something
that can be neither proved nor disproved. One may prefer an agnosti-
cism that is content never to really know, to the omniscience of
Wellhausen, but must recognize with it that this is a "walking by
faith" where the Grafians claimed to be able to "walk by sight".

It is not surprising therefore that the very end of our period has
seen something like a *return to the older Grafian questions*. Although
some older scholars like Mowinckel have been also represented (see
above p. 115), it has been mainly on the part of the younger scholars,
who are no longer content to by-pass source questions as their fathers
did in the intermediate generation but want to return to where their
grandfathers left off. [2]) Typical are the writings of the 1960's on the
origin of Deuteronomy. A remarkable consensus on the Josianic
dating is evident in a whole series of younger scholars.

LOHFINK takes issue with von Rad, and puts forward the formidable
alternatives—either Northern preaching or Jerusalem covenant

---

[1]) A. Bentzen, *Die Josianische Reform*, Copenhagen (1926).
[2]) Literally true in at least one case. R. Smend, grandson of the critic of that
name, has written on de Wette, and re-published Wellhausen's most typical
writings, with a laudatory preface in 1965 (R. Smend (ed.) *Julius Wellhausen,
Grundrisse zum Alten Testament*, München (1965)).

source,[1]) and feels that the evidence is stronger for the latter.[2]) His view of a covenant source can also find a place for its use in preaching, in a way that a mere preaching source theory cannot accomodate the Josianic covenant (p. 496). Hezekiah's reform added centralization to the old Deuteronomic core, but the bringing of the country priests to Jerusalem was only later (p. 473). The date is fixed by the obvious connections to the Esarhaddon treaty form (p. 482).[3])

CLEMENTS also agrees that theories of a Northern origin have been carried too far. Northern materials may be contained in it, but the book was put together in Jerusalem and with Jerusalem in mind.[4]) Its theology of election, of the land as gift and of the ark as container points to Jerusalem.[5]) NICHOLSON is no less convinced of the connection to Josiah's Reform, and its theme of centralization—*ein Gott, ein Volk, ein Kult*—the one people should worship the one God in the one sanctuary.[6])

Even more emphatic is the support of de Wette by the Jewish scholar WEINFELD:

> "Since De Wette,...to the criterion of centralization of cult, which was used as the first key for understanding the book, two other criteria were added: the stylistic criterion and the ideological one. Both of these criteria give additional support to De Wette's hypothesis but with one important reservation: one can no longer speak of a new book written in the time of Josiah, but about compiling old traditions and reworking them in the spirit of a new historical and social reality".[7])

---

[1]) N. Lohfink, "Die Bundesurkunde des Königs Josias (Eine Frage an die Deuteronomiumforschung")", *Bibl* XLIV (1963) pp. 261-88, 461-98. Cf. also his *Das Hauptgebot: Eine Untersuchung literarischer Einleitungsfragen zu Dtn 5-11*, Rome (1963) on Dt. 5-11, and numerous articles.

[2]) His view is "that there was kept in Jerusalem, for a considerable period prior to Josiah's reign, a covenant document which was revised from time to time", and that "Deuteronomy was the form which this had attained by Josiah's time". "Deuteronomy was therefore of Jerusalem origin, contrary to the widely held scholarly opinion that its real background lay in the Northern Kingdom". Clements, who is quoted here, adds that the thesis fails to carry conviction because of lack of evidence for the existence of such a document prior to Josiah's time. (*God's Chosen People*, pp. 100 ff).

[3]) See above p. 119.

[4]) R. E. Clements, "Deuteronomy and the Jerusalem Cult Tradition", *VT* XV (1965) pp. 300-12; *God's Chosen People*, London (1968) pp. 20 ff. He recognizes, however, that the authors were northerners, who had migrated to Jerusalem.

[5]) Clements is sceptical about an earlier centralization in the amphictyony in view of the changing location of the shrine (*God's Chosen People*, p. 76) and points out that what Deuteronomy requires is not a central sanctuary but a *sole* sanctuary.

[6]) E. W. Nicholson, "The Centralisation of the Cult in Deuteronomy", *VT* XIII (1963) pp. 380-89, and *Deuteronomy and Tradition*, Oxford (1967) esp. p. 55.

[7]) M. Weinfeld, "Deuteronomy—the Present State of Inquiry", *JBL* LXXXVI (1967) p. 262.

Elaborating his reference to style, Weinfeld writes: "It remains a fact that the style peculiar to Deuteronomy is nowhere to be found in Biblical literature prior to the seventh century".[1] The ideology he finds to be that of the Wisdom school,[2] and the date again that of Josiah's revolt from Assyria, following the repudiation of a treaty like Esarhaddon's.[3]

The plan of this Part in speaking of a "continuation of the old methods" as well as "applying of new methods" has thus been vindicated by this illustration that the old methods have not ceased. In fact at every point of climax in our description of the various groups in the modern scene, even in those formerly most conservative, we have found fingers pointing in this direction, as reference back to Mowinckel, Haran, Lohfink, Aharoni, Elliger, Noth and FOHRER will show. The lastnamed may perhaps be allowed to speak for all when he expresses dissatisfaction with form critical procedures in the prophetic books, and something like a nostalgia for Wellhausen. [4] Against von Rad's order "law-prophets" he remarks:

> "At the time of the pre-exilic prophets the historical traditions were to be found only in fragmentary form.... The most recent—the Deuteronomic theology and the Priestly Code—...were not able to exert a strong influence on the prophets but were rather themselves influenced by prophetic theology..." [5]

While preferring to speak of "strata" rather than "documents", the dates given in his *Introduction* are still close to Graf and Wellhausen. He thinks the various theories of the origin of the Pentateuch are not

---

[1] Weinfeld, "The Period of the Conquest and of the Judges as seen by the earlier and the later sources". *VT* XVII (1967) p. 97.

[2] Cf. his articles on the dependence of Deuteronomy on the Wisdom literature, *Kaufmann Jubilee Volume* (Heb.), reward in Deuteronomy, *Tarbiz* XXX (1960) pp. 8-15, religion in Deuteronomy, *ibid*, XXXI (1961) pp. 1-17, humanism in Deuteronomy, *JBL* LXXX (1961) pp. 241-47, and the scribes and Deuteronomy, *ibid*, LXXXVI (1967) pp. 249-62.

[3] "The fact, however, that both the subject matter and the sequence of maledictions in this section of Dt Ch. 28 is identical with the parallel series of curses in the Vassal Treaties of Esarhaddon attests that there was a direct Deuteronomic borrowing from the Assyrian treaty documents". (There is no parallel elsewhere and the Mesopotamian setting is more original—p. 423). (M. Weinfeld, "Traces of Assyrian Treaty Formulae in Deuteronomy", *Bibl* XLVI (1965) pp. 417-27).

[4] G. Fohrer, "Remarks on Modern Interpretation of the Prophets", *JBL* LXXX (1961) p. 318. For the limitations of Pentateuchal form criticism see his *Introduction*, pp. 27 ff.

[5] *JBL*, p. 314.

so much "hypotheses", excluding one another, as methods used conjointly in one place or another. Agglomeration—or the putting of sources side by side—played the principal role; supplementation accounts for the data of the law codes; and composition for the mosaic-like joining of individual parts to form a greater whole.[1])

[1]) *Introduction*, pp. 113-16. Similarly Eissfeldt, *Introduction*, pp. 177-82.

CHAPTER THIRTEEN

THE POSITION IN 1965

This may be variously estimated. In a letter to the writer in 1960, H. H. Rowley summed up the situation as follows. Modifications have been made in some details of the Grafian hypothesis.

> "*Archaeology* has shown that the pentateuchal narratives of J and E reflect the customs of the age with which they deal, and while it has not proved the accuracy of the history, it has disproved the dictum of Wellhausen that they give us little knowledge of the age about which they write but much of the age in which they were written. This is reinforced by the arguments of the *oral tradition* school, which are relevant for the period between the events and their deposit in literature, but insufficient to establish that writing did not take place until the post-exilic age. The sharp line between *the priests and the prophets* is disputed by many scholars today, but this does not mean the collapse of literary criticism. The recognition that much of *the ritual of P* was ancient has always been made by the literary critics and the evidence in support of this is stronger today than it ever was".

On essentials, however, Rowley thinks that the Grafian hypothesis still stands.

> "What none of the critics has shown is that there was any *centralization* of the cultus before Hezekiah (who appeals to no law book) and Josiah (who does). This is not an argument from silence, since there is ample evidence of a multiplicity of shrines throughout the period from the settlement to Hezekiah, and again between Hezekiah and Josiah. Again what none of the critics has shown is that there was an exclusively *Aaronite priesthood* before the exile, whereas it can be shown that there was not. It seems inescapable that on the priesthood the sequence JED Ezekiel P is established. Again no critic has seriously overthrown the view that D shows knowledge of JE both in its law and in its history, but not of P".

Rowley's conclusion is that "none of the rival views can accommodate so many of the facts, or can escape far more difficulties". [1]

For the period since 1960 a wealth of material has become available through a series of major publications. The early 1960s have seen a spate of publishing not unlike that of the decade around 1900. Some

---

[1] H. H. Rowley, *The Growth of the Old Testament*, London (1950) p. 46.

of the great reference works produced near the latter date [1]) have been rewritten, and they, together with new dictionaries, provide ample materials for a statement of the present position. The works to be referred to are the new editions of the *Hastings One Volume Dictionary* [2]) and *Peake's Commentary* [3]) and the *New Bible Dictionary* [4]) and the *Interpreter's Dictionary of the Bible*. [5])

A. VIEWS OF THE RELIGIOUS DEVELOPMENT

The three areas of sacrifice, sanctuary and priesthood canvassed by Wellhausen and his predecessors are the subject of articles, which are in the main confirmatory rather than critical, although in each case at least one dissentient opinion is found.

On *sacrifice*, T. H. Gaster in the *IDB* takes no particular issue with Grafian views, except in his rejection of Robertson Smith's commensal theory. [6]) N. Porteous in the *New Peake* thinks that the prophets presuppose amphictyonic law [7]) and that substitution, although not present in the legislation, must have been in the mind of the worshipper. [8]) J. Barr in the *New Hastings* thinks the post-exilic origin of sin offering and guilt offering unlikely. [9]) While the element of expiation was increased by the Exile, it was not new then. [10]) P is, however, post-exilic, but the difference before and after the Exile was not expiation, but centralization. [11])

---

[1]) See above p. 70.

[2]) J. Hastings (ed.) *Dictionary of the Bible* (One Volume), Edinburgh Rev. ed. (1963). First published 1909.

[3]) M. Black and H. H. Rowley (ed.) *Peake's Commentary on the Bible*, London rewritten 1962. First published 1919.

[4]) J. D. Douglas (ed.) *The New Bible Dictionary*, London (1962).

[5]) G. A. Buttrick (ed.) *The Interpreter's Dictionary of the Bible*, 4 vols, New York (1962).

[6]) T. H. Gaster, "Sacrifices and Offerings", *IDB* Vol. IV, p. 151.

[7]) N. Porteous, "The Theology of the Old Testament", *Peake's Commentary* (1962) pp. 154, 155.

[8]) *Ibid*, p. 158.

[9]) J. Barr, "Sacrifice and Offering", *NHDB* (One Volume) (1963) pp. 873-74.

[10]) *Ibid*, p. 870. Also pp. 77, 79. A similar conclusion is reached by the present writer in his work *Penitence and Sacrifice in Early Israel*, and in the article "Sacrifice and Offering", *NBD* (1962) pp. 1113-22. See also H. Ringgren, *Sacrifice in the Bible*, London (1962) pp. 35 ff and *Israelite Religion*, Philadelphia (1966) p. 174; R. de Vaux, *Studies in Old Testament Sacrifice*, Cardiff (1964) pp. 103-06 and *Ancient Israel*, pp. 425 ff; H- J. Kraus, *Worship in Israel*, (1966) pp. 118, 119, 122; E. E. Evans-Pritchard, *Theories of Primitive Religion*, Oxford (1965) p. 52.

[11]) J. Barr, *op. cit*, p. 870.

On *centralization*, a variety of opinion is expressed. G. Henton Davies in the *New Peake Commentary* on Deuteronomy thinks that the differences between Deuteronomy and the other codes are due to "geographical apartness" rather than to "chronological development", [1]) and in the *IDB* article on "Tabernacle" argues that P's tabernacle is Davidic rather than exilic. [2]) Von Rad in the *IDB* article "Deuteronomy" allows that there had been a kind of centralization in the amphictyony at Shiloh in the times of the Judges, but finds a more extreme type in the present form of Deuteronomy dating from Josiah. [3]) C. A. Simpson in the *New Hastings* article "Deuteronomy" also allows that an earlier demand for centralization associated with Shechem lies behind Deuteronomy, but dates this only to the period following the fall of Samaria in 721 B.C. [4]) S. H. Hooke in the *New Peake* doubts if the amphictyony ever had a single centre for all twelve tribes before the monarchy, [5]) and H. H. Rowley is not convinced there ever was an amphictyony. [6])

---

[1]) "Deuteronomy is a stream rather than a gusher". *Peake's Commentary* (1962) pp. 269-270. A footnote by editor, H. H. Rowley, directs the reader to the more orthodox Grafian view-point in $ 69c.

[2]) G. H. Davies, "Tabernacle", *IDB* Vol. IV (1962) pp. 498-506. Attention is drawn to the excellent article of Frank Cross, *Biblical Archaeologist Reader*, p. 221 where a similar dating is suggested in the course of a comprehensive critique of the Graf dating of P. (F. M. Cross, "The Tabernacle", first published *BA* X (1947) pp. 45-66). Cross' conclusion, however, is noteworthy: "The broad outlines of the Documentary Hypothesis (JE, D, and P) remain intact, and in fact have been strongly supported by the implications of Biblical archaeology" (p. 48). P dates only from the Exile but did not exist as an independent code so much as a commentary and systematic expansion of the JE tradition in the Tetrateuch (pp. 57-58). The search for an earlier "nuclear" P should at all events proceed (p. 59).

[3]) G. von Rad, "Deuteronomy", *IBD* Vol. I, pp. 834 ff. In *Deuteronomy*, *ATD*, pp. 16-17 he is more explicit. "The lawgiver is aware of the fact that he is demanding something quite new in his own time. Nevertheless we must ask whether the centralization of the cult was really something so completely new in the history of Israel. During the period of the judges, when Israel was a sacral, tribal union, there was, after all, the ark (finally at Shiloh) as the cultic centre to which the tribes made their way at the great pilgrimage festivals. Centralization was, of course, unknown at that early period in the extreme form demanded by Deuteronomy". If A. H. J. Gunneweg is right in speaking of a de-centralization with the Jahwizing of Canaanite sanctuaries, (*Leviten und Priester*, Göttingen (1965) p. 76) the term for what happens in the seventh century would be "re-centralization".

[4]) C. A. Simpson, "Deuteronomy", *NHDB* (One Volume) p. 215.

[5]) He thinks each tribe had its own ark (S. H. Hooke, "The Religious Institutions of Israel", *Peake's Commentary* (1962) p. 145).

[6]) "It is doubtful if we should speak of a central sanctuary, indicated by the

On *priesthood*, there are new articles in the *New Hastings* by D. R. Jones, and in the *IDB* by R. Abba. The former accepts the Grafian development of priests and Levites, [1]) but the latter joins issue with it. Abba claims that Deuteronomy does distinguish priests and Levites, [2]) and that Ezekiel, who has the Levites as sacrificants, as in Chronicles, is later than P, where the offerer still sacrifices his own victim. P is earlier than both D and Ezekiel. [3]) A full-scale reply to Wellhausen is attempted by Hubbard in the *NBD*. [4])

B. Views of the Literary Development

The Grafian view of the literary development continues to be represented in the articles on Pentateuch, Genesis, Exodus, Leviticus, Numbers. The *IDB* article by Freedman wants a *Grundlage* source behind JE, but does not otherwise disturb the order JEDP. [5]) The *New Peake* represents the Grafian viewpoint, except in the treatment by Henton Davies of Deuteronomy. [6]) The *New Hastings* similarly is Grafian, although the existence of a greater number of scholarly Conservatives than ever before is recognized. [7]) Some of the latter are represented in the *New Bible Dictionary*, where the articles on Exodus, and Deuteronomy still argue for Mosaic authorship. However, the writers on Leviticus and Numbers think this claim less necessary, [8]) while those on Genesis and Pentateuch leave the question open.

---

presence of the Ark, in the period of the Judges". H. H. Rowley, *ExpT* LXIX (1957-1958) p. 49. Cf. *Worship in Ancient Israel*, London (1967) pp. 58-59.

[1]) D. R. Jones, "Priests and Levites", *NHDB* (One Volume) pp. 793-97.

[2]) R. Abba, "Priests and Levites", *IDB* Vol. III, pp. 887-88. Further, on this problem see the writer's *Penitence and Sacrifice*, p. 210.

[3]) *Ibid*, p. 888. The normal critical order is restated by N. H. Snaith in his commentary, *Leviticus and Numbers*, London (1967). He thinks the Zadokite priesthood of the monarchy and Ezekiel was deported in the Exile and the Aaronites, who had formerly functioned at Bethel, moved into Jerusalem, and thus into P (p. 14). The connection of Aaronites and Bethel, which has some support in the Golden Calf link, is favoured also by Jones in *NHDB* (One Volume) p. 795 and by many other recent discussions. See Gunneweg, *op. cit*, p. 90.

[4]) D. A. Hubbard, "Priests and Levites", *NBD* (1962) pp. 1028-34. Hubbard concludes that "it is... tenuous to hold that because laws were not enforced they did not exist" (p. 1034).

[5]) D. N. Freedman, "Pentateuch", *IDB* Vol. III, pp. 711-27.

[6]) See above, p. 161, fn. 1.

[7]) C. R. North, "Pentateuch", *NHDB* (One Volume), p. 744.

[8]) *NBD*, p. 731 (W. H. Gispen); p. 899 (N. H. Ridderbos).

In 1965 then, a century after its publication, the Grafian hypothesis is still favoured by the majority of scholars. Prophecies of its demise by Orr in 1905, Sayce in 1910, Neubauer in 1918, Du Bose in 1923, Urbach and Coppens in 1938, Levy in 1947 and Ginsberg in 1950 have not been fulfilled. Instead it has turned the tables on its critics and eroded the Conservative bastions in Jerusalem and Rome and made inroads into evangelical Protestantism. Whether this is a matter for regret or satisfaction is the question to which we will turn in the Epilogue.

SUMMARY—THE DATE OF P

On the date of P a wide variety of arguments have been appealed to in our period in support of a post-exilic dating. [1]) The *linguistic* argument has not been advanced, except in the unsatisfactory instance of Hurvitz. Grelot, has however, appealed to terminology in his comparison of P laws with those in use at Elephantine. Auerbach has argued from a literary form—that of the ten-point enumeration of law—as well as from the use of the Babylonian calendar, but it is Kapelrud who has made the most use of the argument from terminology in an article not thus far surveyed. [2]) Kapelrud believes he can pinpoint the date of P or at least some parts of it to between Ezekiel and Deutero-Isaiah. The latter's use of such P terms as *bara, tohu, reshith,* "spring forth," "firmament" (in verbal form) as well as his allusions to P narrative—the drowning of the Egyptians, the covenant at the Flood, and at creation, the sabbath as sign—support a date for P of about 550 B.C.

While this might enable a dating of particular portions, more general considerations would be necessary to fix a date for the code as a whole, and these are found in the *milieu* argument advanced by Cazelles. The return from Babylon in the second Exodus, the need of a new Sinai, with instructions for a renewed cult, a new sanctuary, a new priesthood and a new offering tariff would provide a *Sitz im Leben* (witness the alternative formulation already attempted in Ezekiel 40-48). An extension of this argument would take into account the concern of the Persian emperors with the establishment of law, as noted by Mendenhall (see above p. 41) and Noth. [3]) The latter sees in Ezra a Persian appointed "secretary" entrusted with this mission, and remarks the Persian loanword now used for "law" *dat*. [4]) *Dat*, however, has a fixity and a binding character ("the laws of the Medes and Persians that change not") unknown to *torah* in the old Israelite sense, which was rather "guide-lines", precedents, case-

---

[1]) For the following cf. but with caution Külling *op. cit*, pp. 166-227.

[2]) A. S. Kapelrud, "The Date of the Priestly Code (P)", *ASTI* III (1964) pp. 58-64.

[3]) M. Noth, *The Laws in the Pentateuch*, p. 75.

[4]) Cf. especially Ezra 7:26 where the "law of thy God" is now equated with the law (*dat*) of the king.

law. As *dat* comes to take over from *torah*, Judaism, "the religion of the law" is born. [1] It is an attractive hypothesis that part of the process of turning *torah* into *dat* is the writing of the P code.

What then was the origin of the law? Two names and two only stand in the Biblical tradition as lawgivers—the names of Moses and Ezra. Is it too much to say that Moses gave the *torah* and Ezra the *dat*? Investigations like those of von Rad, [2] Horst and others have shown how often the layers in a book like Deuteronomy can be removed, so that in section after section a nucleus remains, with one, two or three expansions. Many of these nuclei could indeed be Mosaic, the interpretative materials come from the following centuries, and the final form only at the late date. [3] This is not just a case of all the schools winning and thus all getting prizes, but rather seems to arise from the facts of the case. Something is needed to justify the ascription to Moses, but much must equally be later than Moses. The determining of the relationship between these two foci is an absorbing task for the criticism of tomorrow

In a parallel discipline it has been said that there is "a quest to be resumed"—the quest of the historical Jesus, which had been prematurely abandoned a generation ago. "The quest of the historical Jesus" was a translator's inspired rendering of Schweitzer's more prosaic title "From Reimarus to Wrede". The name of Reimarus is also one of the first names in this work, and at time of writing it is the two hundredth anniversary of his death. Is there not also a quest to be resumed in *Old* Testament studies—the quest of the historical Moses? [4]

---

[1] Modern Hebrew uses *dat* for "religion".

[2] Von Rad, *Studies in Deuteronomy*, pp. 15 ff.

[3] The name suggested by Eissfeldt for a hypothesis like this is "crystallisation hypothesis" (*Introduction*, p. 167).

[4] What the writer has in mind is illustrated by Vriezen, *The Religion of Ancient Israel*, pp. 135 ff, where it is recognized that the relevant data include not only the tomb tradition, favoured by Noth, but also that of the Egyptian name and the Kenite connection; and Henton Davies, *Exodus* (Torch Commentary), London (1967) pp. 11, 31, 65, where against Noth's "nihilism", it is asserted that his choice of the tomb tradition, rather than that of the Egyptian name, is "the great divide in this scholar's work", that mitigates against his entire reconstruction of the early history of Israel. To the data mentioned by these scholars should now be added Moses' connection to the law. Cf. R. Smend, *Das Mosebild von Heinrich Ewald bis Martin Noth*, Tübingen (1959).

CHAPTER FOURTEEN

EPILOGUE

If we are to resume "the quest for the historical Moses" as suggested in the last chapter, has the long journey which criticism has undertaken, been really necessary? Could we all along have done without Graf, Wellhausen and the rest? Not a few authors, wearied with present uncertainties, seem to imply this by their works, if not by their words. [1]) For example, the sumptuous Israeli publication *Adam to Daniel*, [2]) explains its method to the reader thus:

> Generally we do not resort to the "documentary" hypothesis of much modern commentary. This is not to be taken as a refutation of this discipline. Instead, we believe that the most fruitful road to an understanding of Biblical traditions is to place them firmly in their setting and interpret the narrative as an integral part of the whole Biblical concept. This cannot be done by literary criticism alone... We do not consider that this discipline is essential to understanding the original text for the purpose of our exposition.[3])

The findings of the present work do not bear this out, and must therefore be briefly restated, before some applications are made from these for the task ahead in Pentateuchal criticism.

A LOOK BACK

i. *Source criticism is here to stay*

Alan Richardson is surely right, when he says that the patristic or pre-critical view of the Bible is no more an option open for us today than Ptolemaic cosmology has been since Copernicus. [4]) Repetitions in the Pentateuch are more simply explained by a hypothesis of

---

[1]) By the latter also occasionally. Cf. the popular book title *Let's Return to the Mosaic Authorship of the Pentateuch* (By E. Z. Browne, New York (1962)).

[2]) G. Cornfeld (ed.) *Adam to Daniel*, New York (1961).

[3]) *Ibid*, Foreword. Similarly the Old Testament commentaries of the Tyndale series, unlike their New Testament counterparts on the Gospels, have thus far proceeded without the help of the critical analysis e.g. D. Kidner, *Genesis* (Tyndale Commentary) London (1967).

[4]) A. Richardson, "The Rise of Modern Biblical Scholarship", S. L. Greenslade (ed.), *The Cambridge History of the Bible*, Cambridge (1963) p. 310.

sources than by such implausible harmonizations as two wives for Adam, and a rock that moved! [1])

When it is asked why Samuel hesitated to anoint a king, when he had Dt. 17 in his hand; or why Elijah built an altar away from the legitimate central sanctuary; or why Hezekiah quoted no law-book for his reform, whereas Josiah did; or why Deuteronomy permits Levites to come to the altar, where Leviticus does not; for answer to these questions, resort must be made to the critical hypothesis. [2])

The fear frequently expressed that once analysis was permitted, the personalities of the Biblical authors would be lost, and in their stead would be an army of sources, strands and redactors, exhausting the alphabet for their enumeration, has proved groundless. On the modern view five figures only are required to account for the historical books—the Jahwist and Elohist, whose works run in parallel through Genesis, Exodus and Numbers; the Deuteronomist, whose work continues from Deuteronomy to the end of Kings; the Priestist, whose work frames the JE Pentateuch; and the Chronicler, who is responsible for Chronicles, Ezra, and Nehemiah.

The alleged advantage of being able to attach the books to well-known characters like Moses, Joshua, Samuel, Jeremiah and Ezra, was in fact illusory, because the life of Jeremiah does not illuminate the very different Books of Kings and Lamentations, nor Samuel's the narratives later than his death, nor Moses' the laws belonging to life in Canaan. Instead of these tenuous connections, the books now stand as the deposit of the greatest movements of Israelite history. The coming in of Judah to form a united kingdom under David is the background for the merging of traditions by the Jahwist; the fall of the Northern Kingdom in 721 B.C., for the merging of the Northern and Southern traditions in the document JE; the fall of the Southern Kingdom in 586 B.C., for the Deuteronomic Work of History, which runs down to 550 B.C.; and the re-institution after the Exile, for the priestly and temple reform of the Priestly Code and the later Chronicler.

---

[1]) Cf. B. W. Bacon, *Genesis of Genesis*, Hartford (1892) p. 23 and F. Baumgärtel, *Ist die Kritik am Alten Testament berechtigt?* Schönberg (1927), where a score of such difficulties on unitary theories are alleviated by criticism. Baumgärtel argues that the Christian is therefore not only justified in using literary criticism, but has a solemn duty to do so, if the Bible is to stand. It is not just impiety or caprice that actuates the critics, but Christian responsibility (p. 22).

[2]) Cf. J. Steinmann, quoted above on p. 130.

When critics are challenged to prove their methods by exercising their skills on contemporary works, what is forgotten is that the documents posited for the Old Testament are not contemporary, but may be anything from five hundred to a thousand years apart, and reflect real historical differences. [1]) It is an advantage and altogether necessary that these works be closely related to the history. This has been the solid gain of the method begun by de Wette and Graf.

ii. *The aim of source criticism is theological insight*

This point is well put by James Barr, when he writes:

> "Even if it were true [as people say] that you can't preach J, E, D and P (though I am by no means sure it is true)...it would not be decisive. The fact of working on a level where it is known that J, E, D and P are realities, where therefore the reasoning that leads to their identification is valid reasoning or probably so, means a whole different basis for contact with the text. It means a level which...can say something to theology which it would not otherwise know,... Where this sort of link is absent, the use of scripture... can easily degenerate into no more than elaboration, illustration and presentation of knowledge that the Church already has". [2])

This was the situation before the rise of criticism, [3]) and is still largely the case where it is outlawed. [4])

In contrast, interpretation has been rejuvenated by criticism, as the writings of Westermann and Zimmerli, and the sermons of Thielicke, Luthi, Wolff and Kraus testify.[5]) A pair of quite minor illustrations must suffice. It has been pointed out by Vermes that the estimate of Balaam in the Rabbinic tradition varies between that of "Balaam the tragic hero", and "Balaam the villain", and that these go back to the different pictures given by JE and P in Numbers. [6]) Is it possible correctly to

---

[1]) This point, made by Graf in his opening pages, was conceded also by Delitzsch, who argued that if sources were needed for the Gospels, how much more necessary were they for the Pentateuch, where the period covered was ten centuries not one. (*ZKWL* I (1880) p. 620).

[2]) J. Barr, *Old and New in Interpretation*, London (1966) p. 198.

[3]) Cf. the "constancy" of interpretation in, for example, the parables from Augustine to Archbishop Trench.

[4]) Barr continues: "There is no more severe self-indictment of fundamentalism than that it has produced no really interesting discussion of biblical interpretation. In this regard historical criticism, even of the most 'destructive' kind, has been a thousand times more fruitful..." (pp. 203-04).

[5]) Cf. the excellent *Alttestamentliche Predigten* series arising out of the severe critical disciplines of the preparation of the volumes of the *Biblische Kommentar*.

[6]) G. Vermes, *Scripture and Tradition in Judaism*, Leiden (1961) pp. 175-77.

estimate the Balaam references, even in the New Testament. without this knowledge? Is it not also important, when dealing with the teaching of Genesis on original sin, to know that the pessimistic J view may be directed to the over-confidence of David's Golden Age, and the optimistic P view, to the period of depression following the Fall of Jerusalem in 586 B.C.? [1])

The kind of "theology of the Old Testament", which traces "the theology of the oldest traditions", as von Rad's has done, is altogether necessary. Even theology, however, is not the end of our interest.

iii. *Theological insight is in order to the advancement of religion*

"The theological interpretation of the Bible, which is often called for ... is not sufficient", writes H. H. Rowley, "For the Bible is more than a theological book. It is a religious book; and religion is more than theology. Its study should do more than develop right views about God, man and duty; it should nurture right relations to God". [2]) Quite similar are the words of Ebeling: "that whereof the Bible witnesses and which is its object is not theology but something that happens to man between God and the world". [3]) Our study of the human words of Scripture, is only so that the divine word may break through and speak to our condition.

When Manson speaks of "the failure of liberalism to interpret the Bible as the Word of God", [4]) and Packer says that while criticism may have thrown light on the human side of the Bible, it has done nothing at all to enhance man's acceptance of it as the Word of God, [5]) these scholars do no more than highlight a difficulty expressed by Westphal at the beginning of the critical movement. He spoke of the tension between science and faith as the modern Martha and Mary. Following Westphal, Wedgwood wrote:

> But it will generally be found that the power of analysing a complete whole into the work of various writers tends to quench the vision

---

[1]) Cf. M-L. Henry, *Jahwist und Priesterschrift*: *Zwei Glaubenszeugnisse des Alten Testaments*, Stuttgart (1960).

[2]) H. H. Rowley, "The Relevance of Biblical Interpretation", *Interpretation* I (1947) p. 16.

[3]) G. Ebeling, "The Meaning of 'Biblical Theology' " in L. Hodgson and others, *On the Authority of the Bible*, London (1960) p. 63.

[4]) T. W. Manson in C. W. Dugmore (ed.) *The Interpretation of the Bible*, London (1944) pp. 92-107.

[5]) J. I. Packer, *'Fundamentalism' and the Word of God*, Grand Rapids (1958) pp. 112-13.

of their common revelation... It is impossible for Martha to sit at
the feet of the Teacher while she is occupied with the work of providing
for outward needs.[1]

In the light of our study, we should want to emend "impossible"
to "difficult". Difficult as it is to combine criticism with reverence
for revelation, it is by no means impossible, as the examples of many
quoted in these pages reveal. [2] Our task is incomplete, until the word
of revelation is heard. Kidner speaks to critics, as well as to Conservatives, when citing Peter's preoccupation with Moses and Elijah
on the Mount, he says:

> "whether we are tempted, in our pentateuchal studies, to erect many
> tabernacles or few, for Moses or a multitude, the answer of heaven is,
> 'This is my beloved Son: hear him!' " [3]

A Look Forward

Corresponding to the above propositions, are three specific questions for future Pentateuch studies. [4]

i. *What is the meaning of the unity of the Pentateuch?*

Scholars as different as Ewald and Ranke, A. H. Finn and M. H.
Segal have asked this question, and sometimes have come to their
answer too quickly, by failing to give sufficient weight to the diversity.
The unity of Biblical Theology's *Heilsgeschichte* may be too simple, [5]
but if the Oral Tradition and History of Tradition Schools are right,
the constant repetition and restatement of the tradition in worship
and life must have proceeded from some principle. If the unifying
vision was not simply that of the saving acts of God in history, [6]
was it that of the covenant, or the covenant people, the covenant
land or the covenant God? What were the words or ideas accompany-
ing or even preceding the acts?

---

[1] J. Wedgwood, *op. cit*, pp. 27-29 in comment on Westphal, *Les Sources du
Pentateuque*, pp. iv ff.
[2] Cf above on pp. 45, 67, 98.
[3] D. Kidner, *op. cit*, pp. 25-26.
[4] For help with the following suggestions, my thanks are due to an Auckland
colleague J. J. Lewis. James Barr's *Old and New in Interpretation* has also provided
stimulation. Cf. also now N. E. Wagner, "Pentateuchal Criticism: No Clear
Future", *Canadian Journal of Theology* XIII (1967) pp. 225-32.
[5] J. Barr, *Old and New in Interpretation*.
[6] *Loc. cit.*

In asking for further study of the Pentateuchal documents in terms of "the history of ideas", one realizes that the term "ideas" is inadequate to describe the rich texture of faith and life that needs to be uncovered. The carrier of the traditions was the worshipping community, and we need to penetrate beyond purely literary questions to the life of that community. The traditions must have gathered around particular shrines, just as the Gospel traditions seem to have gathered around certain centres in the Roman Empire, but for the Pentateuch thus far there is little agreement as to the role played by Bethel, Gilgal, Shechem, Shiloh and Gibeon. History of tradition studies must continue.

Beyond the study of these disparate traditions, lies the question of the centripetal force which gathered them together, first by identifying the El deities of the sanctuaries with the Fathers'-God and Jahweh, and then by superimposing the Zionist ideology of the election of Jerusalem on the earlier election ideologies. In calling for a recognition of the place of worship in the growth of the Pentateuch, Kraus asked if each of the source documents of the Pentateuch may not have had a connection with the founding of the cult in the temple sanctuary (see footnote on p. 146 above). This seems easier to demonstrate for Deuteronomy and the Priestly Code than for the Jahwist and Elohist, but an investigation of the latter from this point of view might be fruitful. If the Exodus and Sinai election themes had thus early been merged with those of Jerusalem and "the sure mercies of David", could not the focus of the Pentateuch's unity lie here?

ii. *What is the contribution of the Pentateuch to theological understanding?*

The unity of the Pentateuch is not just a matter of an aggregation of its parts, as revealed by analysis, but of their integration by the Biblical redactors, and for the study of this, redaction criticism must be employed. Helen Gardner in a well-known passage stated the dissatisfaction with source criticism in general literature as a "dissatisfaction with a criticism which seemed to be always discussing something other than the work: its sources, or the author's life, or social and political history as reflected in it ..." These keys certainly open a door; but only into another room, which is not the heart of the work, and which in turn is locked with a lock that the keys do not fit. [1] "Trends in literary scholarship thus gives support to critics who

---

[1] H. Gardner, *The Business of Criticism*, Oxford (1959) p. 132.

regard it as their duty to see works as integrated wholes". [1]) The rule is "make sense of what you have." [2])

While this cannot be applied directly to the Old Testament, because of the vast tracts of time involved as indicated above, it is salutary to recall with Snaith that there was "a method in the madness which so thoroughly dovetailed together" the sources which "we have been so very energetic in isolating from each other". [3]) Important as the bricks are, which have been revealed to us by source and form criticism even more important is the mortar that joins them. What was the vision of the priestly compilers? What was the significance e.g. of taking the covenant back to the Flood or earlier, and of adding Gen.1 ? Why did they speak to their age in this way?

Good work has been done by von Rad and others on the theology of the Jahwist, the theology of the Elohist and the theology of the Priestist, but this is a continuing task, as advances are made in our knowledge of the history of the traditions. Further study is required of the historical and social reasons that led to the various collations and restatements.

iii. *How does revelation advance religion in the Pentateuch?*

It is becoming clear that the retreat of "religion of Israel" studies before "Old Testament theology" has been too precipitate, [4]) and the balance needs to be redressed. What can be done by using the insights of the one to illumine the other, is illustrated by Vriezen's outstanding recent contribution. [5]) The extent to which Israel is both like and unlike her neighbours emerges only in such comparative study. To study the history is not enough, for, as has been well said, of no nation does the history provide so little explanation of her uniqueness as of Israel. Reviewing Driver's *Genesis*, S. A. Cook wrote:

> "Israel's history appears comparatively trifling compared with that of these old-world monarchies, [of the Ancient Near East], but...

---

[1]) *Ibid*, p. 99.

[2]) *Ibid*, p. 97. Helen Gardner continues: "There has been a strong reaction against the study of even extant and known sources, much more against the discussion of hypothetical ones. Why should we trouble ourselves with sources on which a poet worked, it is asked: what matters is what he made of his material, not where he quarried his stone, or what was the shape of the unsightly lumps before his chisel transformed them into a significant masterpiece" (p. 98).

[3]) N. H. Snaith, *Distinctive Ideas of the Old Testament*, London (1944) p. 13.

[4]) Cf. J. Barr, *Old and New in Interpretation*, p. 97. Cf. p. 29.

[5]) T. C. Vriezen, *The Religion of Ancient Israel*, ET (1967). Cf. his *Outline of Old Testament Theology*, ET (1958).

its teaching... has played a grander part... than all the heritage of Egypt and Mesopotamia..." "In proportion as the Promised Land shrinks in size when we view it by the side of the mighty empires of Babylonia, Assyria, and Egypt, it gains in dignity of thought and grandeur of religion".[1])

To spell out these differences is a task for scholars of tomorrow. While Kaufmann may have gone too far with his theory of a "meta-divine", accepted by Israel's neighbours, but rejected by Israel, [2]) and van Leeuwen similarly with his "ontocratic" and "theocratic" patterns, [3]) they point to important distinctions that need further study. In a world in which nationhood, lawgiving, priesthood and kingship were traced back to time's beginning and beyond, and thus given near-divine status, what does it mean that Israel knew that none of these institutions were primeval, but all had their beginning in the remembered history—in the call of Abraham, the covenant at Sinai, the sin of the Golden Calf, and the pressure of the Philistines? The very "mistakes of Moses"—the anachronisms in the Pentateuch, which cast doubt on his authorship—"the Canaanite was then in the land", "before there reigned any king over Israel", "light before the sun" [4])—were all along bearing silent testimony to the uniqueness of Israel's religion, and to the revelation of God recorded in the Pentateuch.

---

[1]) S. A. Cook, "S. R. Driver's *Genesis*", *JQR* XVII (1905) p. 185.
[2]) J. Kaufmann, *The Religion of Israel*.
[3]) A. T. van Leeuwen, *Christianity in World History*, Edinburgh (1964).
[4]) In Egypt and Babylon the sun was primeval and divine.

BIBLIOGRAPHY

Aalders, G. C., *Recent Trends in Old Testament Criticism*, London, 1938.

——, *A Short Introduction to the Pentateuch*, London, 1949.

Abba, R., "Priests and Levites", G. A. Buttrick (ed.) *Interpreter's Dictionary of the Bible*, Vol. 3, New York (1962) pp. 876-89.

Addis, W. E., *The Documents of the Hexateuch*, 2 vols, London, 1892-1898.

Aharoni, Y., "The Negeb", in D. W. Thomas (ed.) *Archaeology and Old Testament Study*, Oxford (1967) pp. 385-403.

Albright, W. F., "Archeology Confronts Biblical Criticism", *American Scholar* VII (1938) pp. 176-88.

——, "The Ancient Near East and the Religion of Israel", *JBL* LIX (1940) pp. 85-112.

——, *From the Stone Age to Christianity*, Baltimore, 1940.

——, *Archaeology and the Religion of Israel*, Baltimore (³1953), first published 1941.

——, "The War and Biblical Studies", in H. R. Willoughby (ed.) *The Study of the Bible Today and Tomorrow*, Chicago (1947) pp. 162-74.

——, *The Archaeology of Palestine*, Harmondsworth (³1956), first published 1949.

——, "The Bible After Twenty Years of Archeology (1932-1952)", *Religion in Life* XXI (1951-1952) pp. 537-50.

——, *The Biblical Period*, Oxford (1952), first published 1949.

——, "Jethro, Hobab and Reuel in Early Hebrew Tradition (With Some Comments on the Origin of 'JE')", *CBQ* XXV (1963) pp. 1-11.

——, *History, Archaeology and Christian Humanism*, New York, 1964.

Alfrink, B., "Dedication" (to A. Bea and A. Vaccari) *Biblica* XLIII (1962) pp. 255-63.

Allis, O. T., *The Five Books of Moses*, Philadelphia, (²1949), first published 1942.

Alt, A., „Die Ursprünge des Israelitischen Rechts", *Kleine Schriften zur Geschichte des Volkes Israels I*, München, 1953, first published 1934. ET now in *Essays on Old Testament History and Religion*, Oxford (1966) pp. 80-132.

Anastasius the Sinaite. „Viae Dux", Chap. XXII, J. P. Migne (ed.) *Patrologia Series Graeca* LXXXIX (1865) p. 286.

Anderson, G. W., "Some Aspects of the Uppsala School of Old Testament Study", *HTR* XLIII (1950) pp. 239-56.

Anderson, R., *The Bible and Modern Criticism*, London, ²1903.

Andrews, E. B., "On the New Pentateuch-Criticism", *The Hebrew Student* II (1882) pp. 97-104.

Ap-Thomas, D. R. "Pentateuchal Criticism: Some Recent Trends", *ExpT* LXII (1950-1951) pp. 67-71.

——, "An Appreciation of Sigmund Mowinckel's Contribution to Biblical Studies", *JBL* LXXXV (1966) pp. 315-25.

Astruc, J., *Conjectures sur les Memoires Originaux dont il paroit que Moyse s'est fervi pour composer le Livre de la Genèse*, Bruxelles, 1753.

Auerbach, E., „Die Babylonische Datierung im Pentateuch und das Alter des Priesterkodex," *VT* II (1952) pp. 334-42.

——, „Die grosse Überarbeitung der biblischen Bücher", *VTSuppl I*: *Congress Volume Copenhagen 1953*, Leiden, (1953) pp. 1-10.

——, „Die Feste im alten Israel", *VT* VIII (1958) pp. 1-18.

——, „Der Wechsel des Jahres Anfangs in Juda im Lichte der neugefundenen Babylonischen Chronik", *VT* IX (1959) pp. 113-21.

Auerbach, E., „Die Umschaltung vom judäischen auf den babylonischen Kalender", *VT* X (1960) pp. 69-70.
——, „Das Zehngebot — Allgemeine Gesetzes-Form in der Bibel", *VT* XVI (1966) pp. 255-76.
Bacon, B. W., *The Genesis of Genesis*, Hartford, 1892.
Barr, J., "Sacrifice and Offering", J. Hastings (ed.) *Dictionary of the Bible* (One Volume) Rev. ed, Edinburgh (1963) pp. 868-76.
——, *Old and New in Interpretation*, London, 1966.
Barton, G. A., " 'Higher' Archaeology and the Verdict of Criticism", *JBL* XXXII (1913) pp. 244-60.
Barton, J. M. T., "Recent Catholic Exegesis", *Mémorial Lagrange*, Paris (1940) pp. 239-44.
——, "Roman Catholic Biblical Scholarship", *Scripture* VII (1955) pp. 50-56.
——, "Roman Catholic Biblical Scholarship: 1939-1960", *Theology* LXIII 1960) pp. 101-09.
Baudissin, W.W. Graf, „Höhendienst", J.J. Herzog, and G. L. Plitt (ed.) *Realencyclopädie für protestantische Theologie und Kirche*, Vol. VI, Leipzig (²1880) pp. 181-93.
——, „Reuss 'Die Geschichte der heiligen Schriften des Alten Testaments' ", *ThStKr* LVI (1883) pp. 818-45.
——, *Die Geschichte des Alttestamentlichen Priesterthums*, Leipzig, 1889.
——, "Priests and Levites", *HDB* Vol. IV, Edinburgh, 1902.
Baumgärtel, F., *Ist die Kritik am Alten Testament berechtigt?* Schönberg, 1927.
Baumgartner, W., „Wellhausen und der heutige Stand der alttestamentlichen Wissenschaft", *ThR* N.F. II (1930) pp. 287-307.
——, „Alttestamentliche Einleitung und Literaturgeschichte", *ThR* N.F. VIII (1936) pp. 179-222.
——, „Zum 100. Geburtstag von Hermann Gunkel", *VTSuppl* IX (1962) pp. 1-18.
——, „Römisch-katholische Bibelwissenschaft im Wandel", *ThR* XXXI (1965-1966) pp. 1-14.
Baxter, W. L., *Sanctuary and Sacrifice*, London, 1895.
——, "Professor Peake on the Reply to Wellhausen", *ExpT* VII (1895-1896) pp. 505-12.
Bea, A., „Der heutige Stand der Pentateuchfrage", *Biblica* XVI (1935) pp. 175-200.
Beer, G., „Graf, Karl Heinrich", *Realencyclopaedie für protestantische Theologie und Kirche*, Vol. XXIII (1913) pp. 588-92.
Begrich, J., „Das priesterliche Heilsorakel", *ZAW* LII (1934) pp. 81-92.
——, „Die priesterliche Tora", P. Volz, F. Stummer and J. Hempel (ed.) *Werden und Wesen des Alten Testaments*, Berlin (1936) pp. 63-68.
Bennett, W. H. and others. *Faith and Criticism*, London, 1893.
Benoit,P.(ed.). *Le Père Lagrange au service de la Bible*,Souvenirs Personnels, Paris, 1968.
Bentzen, A., *Die Josianische Reform und ihre Voraussetzungen*, Copenhagen, 1926.
——, *Introduction to the Old Testament*, ET, Copenhagen, 1948.
——, „Skandinavische Literatur zum Alten Testament, 1939-1948", *ThR* N.F. XVII (1948-1949) pp. 273-328.
Bernfeld, S., *Das Buch der Bücher*, Berlin, 1899.
——, *Die jüdische Literatur I*, Berlin, 1921.
——, „Bücher der Bibel", *Encyclopaedia Judaica* IV (1929) cols 485-511.
Berry, G. R., "Biblical Criticism and Archaeology", *JBR* VI (1938) pp. 131-132, 170-71.
Bevan A. A., "Historical Methods in the Old Testament", H. B. Swete (ed.) *Cambridge Biblical Essays*, London (1909) pp. 1-19.
Beyerlin, W., *Die Kulttraditionen Israels in der Verkündigung des Propheten Micha*, Göttingen, 1959.

Beyerlin, W., *Herkunft und Geschichte der ältesten Sinaitraditionen*, Tübingen, 1961. ET now in *Origins and History of the Oldest Sinaitic Traditions*, Oxford, 1965.
Bissell, E. C., *The Pentateuch. Its Origin and Structure*, New York, 1885.
Black, M. and Rowley, H. H. (ed.) *Peake's Commentary on the Bible*, rewritten London (1962), first published 1919.
Black, J. S. and Chrystal, G., *The Life of William Robertson Smith*, London, 1912.
Bleek, F., *Einleitung in das Alte Testament*, Berlin, 1860. ET, 1869, from 2nd ed. 1865. 4th ed. by Wellhausen, 1878.
Böhl, E., *Zum Gesetz und zum Zeugniss*, Wien, 1883.
Böhmer, E., *Das Erste Buch der Thora*, Halle, 1862.
Bohlen, P. von. *Die Genesis historisch-kritisch erläutert*, Königsberg, 1835. ET now in *Introduction to the Book of Genesis*, 2 vols, London, 1855.
Boschwitz, F., *Julius Wellhausen, Motive und Massstäbe seiner Geschichtsschreibung*, Marburg, 1938.
Bose, H. M. du, *The Aftermath Series*, Parts 1-12, Nashville, 1923-1924.
Bowman, R. A., "Old Testament Research Between the Great Wars", H. R. Willoughby (ed.) *The Study of the Bible Today and Tomorrow*, Chicago (1947) pp. 3-31.
Boyce, W. B., *The Higher Criticism and the Bible*, London, 1881.
Branscomb, B. H., *Jesus and the Law of Moses*, New York, 1930.
Braun, F. M., *The Work of Père Lagrange*, ET, Milwaukee, 1962, first published 1943.
Bredenkamp, C. J., *Gesetz und Propheten*, Erlangen, 1881.
Briggs, C. A., Review of Dillmann's *Numeri, Deuteronomium und Josua*, *Presbyterian Review* VIII (1887) pp. 339-42.
——, *General Introduction to the Study of Holy Scripture*, Edinburgh, 1899.
——, and Hügel, F. von, *The Papal Commission and the Pentateuch*, London, 1906.
Bright, J., "Modern Study of Old Testament Literature", in G. E. Wright (ed.) *The Bible and the Ancient Near East*, New York (1961) pp. 13-31.
Brinker, R., *The Influence of Sanctuaries in Early Israel*, Manchester, 1946.
Brooke, S. A., *Life and Letters of Frederick W. Robertson*, 2 vols, London, ²1880.
Broomall, W., *Biblical Criticism*, Grand Rapids, 1957.
Brown, R. E., *New Testament Essays*, Milwaukee, 1965.
Browne, E. Z., *Let's Return to the Mosaic Authorship of the Pentateuch*, New York, 1962.
Brownlee, W. H., *The Meaning of the Qumrân Scrolls for the Bible*, New York, 1964.
Buber, M, *Moses*, Oxford, 1946.
Bultmann, R., "The New Approach to the Synoptic Problem", *JR* VI (1926) pp. 337-62.
Burney, C. F., "The Priestly Code and the New Aramaic Papyri from Elephantine", *Expositor* 8th series III (1912) pp. 97-108.
Buttmann, P., *Mythologus oder gesammelte Abhandlungen über die Sagen des Alterthums*, Vol. I, Berlin, 1828.
Buttrick, G. A., (ed.) *The Interpreter's Dictionary of the Bible*, 4 vols, New York, 1962.
Byrne, E. J., "Catholic Tradition and Biblical Criticism", *Mémorial Lagrange*, Paris (1940) pp. 230-37.
Calloway, J. A., "The Emerging Role of Biblical Archaeology", *RE* LXIII (1966) pp. 200-09.
Calvin, J., *Commentaries on the Four Last Books of Moses arranged in the Form of a Harmony*, ET, Vol. I, Edinburgh, 1852.
Carlson, R. A., *David, The Chosen King*, Uppsala, 1964.
Carpenter, J. E. and Harford, G. B., *The Composition of the Hexateuch*, London, 1902.
Carpenter, J. E., *The Bible in the Nineteenth Century*, London, 1903.

Cartledge, S., *A Conservative Introduction to the Old Testament*, Grand Rapids, 1943.
Cassuto, U., "Genesis", *Encyclopedia Miqra*, Vol. II (1954) pp. 318-35.
——, "Leviticus", *Encyclopedia Miqra*, Vol. II (1954) pp. 878-87.
——, "Deuteronomy", *Encyclopedia Miqra*, Vol. II (1954) pp. 608-19.
——, *The Documentary Hypothesis*, Jerusalem, 1961.
——, *Adam to Noah*, Jerusalem, 1961.
——, *Noah to Abraham*, Jerusalem, 1964.
——, *Exodus*, Jerusalem, 1967.
Cazelles, H., *Le Deutéronome-La Sainte Bible*, Paris, 1950.
——, *Le Lévitique-La Sainte Bible*, Paris, 1951.
——, „A propos du Pentateuque", *Biblica* XXXV (1954) pp. 279-98.
——, „La Torah au Pentateuque", in A. Robert and A. Feuillet (ed.) *Introduction a la Bible*, Tournai, 1957, pp. 279-382.
——, „Loi Israélite", *DBSuppl* V, Paris (1957) cols 497-530.
——, „Pentateuque", *DBSuppl* VII, Paris (1966) cols 687-858.
Chadwick, H., „Der Einfluss der deutschen protestantischen Theologie auf die englische Kirche im 19. Jahrhundert", *EvTh* XVI (1956) pp. 556-71.
——, (ed.) *Lessing's Theological Writings*, London, 1956.
Chadwick, O., *The Victorian Church*, Part I, London, 1966.
Chambers, T. W., (ed.) *Moses and His Recent Critics*, New York, 1889.
Chapman, A. T., *Introduction to the Pentateuch*, Cambridge, 1911.
Charlier, C., *The Christian Approach to the Bible*, ET, Westminster, 1959.
Cheyne, T. K., *Founders of Old Testament Criticism*, London, 1893.
——, and Black, J. S., (ed.) *Encyclopaedia Biblica* 4 vols, London, 1899-1903.
Clements, R. E., "Deuteronomy and the Jerusalem Cult Tradition", *VT* XV (1965) pp. 300-12.
——, *God's Chosen People*, London, 1968.
Coblenz, F., "Biblical Criticism in Religious Instruction", *JQR* XIX (1907) pp. 1-23.
Cockshut, A. O. J., *Anglican Attitudes. A Study of Victorian Religious Controversies*, London, 1959.
Cohon, S. S., "Zunz and Reform Judaism", *HUCA* XXXI (1960) pp. 251-76.
Colenso, J. W., *The Pentateuch and the Book of Joshua Critically Examined*, 7 vols, London, 1862-1879.
Coleridge, S. T., *Confessions of an Inquiring Spirit*, London (1956), first published 1840.
Conder, C. R., "The Old Testament: Ancient Monuments and Modern Critics", *Contemporary Review* LI (1887) pp. 376-93.
——, *The Bible and the East*, London, 1896.
Cook, S. A., *The Laws of Moses and the Code of Hammurabi*, London, 1903.
——, "S. R. Driver's *Genesis*", *JQR* XVII (1905) pp. 184-87.
——, "The Criticism of the Old Testament", *Expositor* 7th series I (1906) pp. 524-43.
——, "Literary and Historical Criticism", *JQR* XIX (1907) pp. 342-62.
——, "The Present Stage of Old Testament Research", H. B. Swete (ed.) *Cambridge Biblical Essays*, (1909) pp. 53-90.
——, Review of Naville, E. "Higher Criticism in Relation to Pentateuch", *JTS* XXV (1924) pp. 432-39.
——, "Some Tendencies in Old Testament Criticism", *JTS* XXVI (1925) pp. 156-73.
——, *The Religion of Ancient Palestine in the Light of Archaeology*, London, 1930.
——, *The Old Testament a Reinterpretation*, Cambridge, 1936.

Cooper, C. M., Review of Young, E. J. "Introduction to the Old Testament", *JQR* XLI (1950-1951) pp. 111-15.

Coore, G. B. M., "The Papal Commission and the Pentateuch", *ExpT* XVIII (1906-1907) pp. 285-86.

Coppens, J., *Le Chanoine Albine van Hoonacker*, Paris, 1935.

——, *The Old Testament and the Critics*, ET, New Jersey (1942), first published 1938.

——, „Chronique d'Ancien Testament — Le Problème de l'Hexateuque", *Analecta Lovaniensia Biblica et Orientalia*, II 38, pp. 3-21.

Cornfeld, G. (ed.) *Adam to Daniel*, New York, 1961.

Cornill, C. H., *Introduction to the Canonical Books of the Old Testament*, ET, New York (1907) 5th ed, first published 1891.

——, *Zur Einleitung in das Alte Testament*, Tübingen, 1911.

Cowley, A., *Aramaic Papyri of the Fifth Century B.C.*, Oxford, 1923.

Cox, G. W., *The Life of John William Colenso*, 2 vols, London, 1888.

Crehan, F. J., "The Bible in the Roman Catholic Church from Trent to the Present Day", S. L. Greenslade, (ed.) *The Cambridge History of the Bible*, Cambridge (1963) pp. 199-237.

Cross, F. M., "The Tabernacle", *BA* X (1947) pp. 45-66, now in G. E. Wright and D. N. Freedman, *The Biblical Archaeologist Reader*, New York (1961) pp. 201-28.

——, "The Discovery of the Samaria Papyri", *BA* XXVI (1963) pp. 110-21.

Cundall, A. E., "Sanctuaries (Central and Local) in Pre-exilic Israel, with particular reference to the Book of Deuteronomy", *Vox Evangelica* IV, London (1965) pp. 4-27.

Curtis, E. L. and Madsen, A. A., *A Critical and Exegetical Commentary on the Books of Chronicles (ICC)* Edinburgh, 1910.

Curtiss, S. I., *The Levitical Priests*, Edinburgh, 1877.

——, "Delitzsch on the Origin and Composition of the Pentateuch", *Presbyterian Review* III (1882) pp. 553-88.

——, "Sketches in Pentateuchal Criticism", *BibSac* XLI (1884) pp. 1-23 (Jan.), 660-97 (Oct.), XLII (1885) pp. 291-326.

——, "Professor Julius Wellhausen and his theory of the Pentateuch", *Expositor* 3rd series III (1886) pp. 81-98.

——, "History of Israel from the Standpoint of Modern Criticism", *Expositor* 3rd series VI (1887) pp. 321-39.

Dahler, J. G., *De Librorum Paralipomenōn Auctoritate atque Fide Historica*, Lipsiae, 1819.

Dahse, J., „Textkritische Bedenken gegen den Ausgangspunkt der heutigen Pentateuchkritik", *Archiv für Religionswissenschaft* VI (1903) pp. 305-19.

——, „Näht ein Umschwung in der Pentateuchkritik?", *NKZ* XXIII (1912) pp. 748-56.

——, "A Reply to Dr Skinner", *Expositor* 8th series VI (1913) pp. 481-510.

——, *A Fresh Investigation of Sources of Genesis*, ET, London, 1914.

Dale, A. van, *Dissertationes de Origine ac Progressu Idolatriae et Superstitionum*, Amstelodami, 1696.

Danell, G. A., *Studies in the Name Israel in the Old Testament*, Uppsala, 1946.

Daube, D., *Studies in Biblical Law*, Cambridge, 1947.

——, "Concerning Methods of Bible-Criticism", *Archiv Orientálni* XVII (1949) pp. 88-99.

Davidson, I., *Saadia's Polemic Against Hiwi Al-Balkai*, New York, 1915.

Davidson, S., *Introduction to the Old Testament*, 3 vols, London, 1862-1863.

Davies, G. Henton, "Deuteronomy", M. Black and H. H. Rowley (ed.) *Peake's Commentary on the Bible*, London (1962) pp. 269-84.

Davies, G. Henton, "Tabernacle", G. A. Buttrick (ed.) *The Interpreter's Dictionary of the Bible*, Vol. 4, New York (1962) pp. 498-506.

——, *Exodus* (Torch Commentary) London, 1967.

Delitzsch, F., "Pentateuchkritische Studien I-XII", *ZKWL* I (1880) pp. 3-10, 57-66, 113-21, 173-83, 223-34, 279-89, 337-47, 393-99, 445-49, 503-09, 559-89, 617-26.

——, „Urmosaisches im Pentateuch", *ZKWL* III (1882) pp. 113-36, 225-35, 281-99, 337-47, 449-57, 561-73.

——, *Neuer Commentar über die Genesis*, Leipzig, 1887.

——, „Die nordamerikanischen pentateuchkritischen Essays", *ZKWL* IX (1888) pp. 222-31.

Delitzsch, Friedrich, *Babel and Bible*, ET, London, 1903.

Dentan, R. C., (ed.) *The Idea of History in the Ancient Near East*, New Haven, 1955.

Dillmann, A., *Die Bücher Numeri, Deuteronomium und Josua*, KEH, Leipzig, ²1886.

Dodd, C. H., *Romans*, Moffatt NT Commentary, 1932.

Douglas, J. D., (ed.) *The New Bible Dictionary*, London, 1962.

Driver, S. R., Review of J. Wellhausen, "Israel", Encyclopaedia Britannica, in *The Academy* XXI (1882) pp. 131-32.

——, "On Some Alleged Linguistic Affinities of the Elohist", *Journal of Philology* XI (1882) pp. 201-36.

——, *An Introduction to the Literature of the Old Testament*, 7th ed, Edinburgh (1898), first published 1891.

——, "Klostermann on the Pentateuch", *Expositor* 4th series V (1892) pp. 320-42.

——, "Hebrew Archaeology", D. G. Hogarth (ed.) *Authority and Archaeology*, London (1899) pp. 143-52.

——, "Deuteronomy", *Jewish Encyclopedia*, Vol. IV, London (1903) pp. 539-43.

——, "Exodus", *ibid*, Vol. V, London (1903) pp. 301-03.

Dubnow, S., *Weltgeschichte des jüdischen Volkes I*, Die Orientalische Periode, Jerusalem (1937), first published 1935.

Duff, A., *History of Old Testament Criticism*, New York, 1910.

Dugmore, C. W., (ed.) *The Interpretation of the Bible*, London, 1944.

Duhm, B., *Die Theologie der Propheten*, Bonn, 1875.

Duncan, J. G., *The Accuracy of the Old Testament*, London, 1930.

——, *New Light on Hebrew Origins*, New York, 1936.

Dyson, R. A. and Sutcliffe, E. F., "Introduction to the Pentateuch", *A Catholic Commentary on Holy Scripture* (1953) pp. 164-76.

Ebeling, G., "The Meaning of Biblical Theology", in L. Hodgson and others *On the Authority of the Bible*, London (1960) pp. 49-67.

Eerdmans, B. D., *Alttestamentliche Studien*, I-IV, Giessen, 1908-1912.

——, "The Book of the Covenant and the Decalogue", *Expositor* 7th series VIII (1909) pp. 21-33, 158-67, 223-30.

——, "A New Development in O.T. Criticism", *Hibbert Journal* VII (1909) pp. 812-16.

——, "Ezra and the Priestly Code", *Expositor* 7th series X (1910) pp. 306-26.

——, "Deuteronomy", *Old Testament Essays*, London, (1927) pp. 77-84.

——, *The Religion of Israel*, ET, Leiden, 1947, first published 1930.

——, "The Composition of Numbers", *OTS* VI (1949) pp. 101-216.

Eichhorn, J. G., *Einleitung ins Alte Testament*, 3 vols, Leipzig, 1781-1783.

Eichrodt, W., *Die Quellen der Genesis von Neuem Untersucht*, Giessen, 1916.

Eiselen, F. C., *The Books of the Pentateuch*, New York, 1916.

Eissfeldt, O., *Hexateuch Synopse*, Leipzig, 1922.

——, *Einleitung in das Alte Testament*, Tübingen, (³1964), first published 1934. ET now in *Old Testament Introduction*, New York, 1965.

Eissfeldt, O., „Die literarkritische Arbeit am Alten Testament in den letzten 12 Jahren", *ThR* X (1938) pp. 255-91 = "Modern Criticism" in *Record and Revelation*, Oxford, 1938, pp. 74-109.

——, „Julius Wellhausen", *KS* I, Tübingen (1962) pp. 56-71, first published 1920.

——, „Vom Lebenswerk eines Religionshistorikers — (Wolf Wilhelm Graf Baudissin)", *KS* I, Tübingen (1962) pp. 115-42, first published 1926.

——, „Hegel-Kritik und Pentateuch-Kritik", *KS* II, Tübingen (1963) pp. 112-22, first published 1938.

——, „Das Gesetz ist zwischeneingekommen: Ein Beitrag zur Analyse der Sinai-Erzählung Ex 19-34", *ThLZ* XCI (1966) cols 1-6.

Elbogen, J., „S.D. Luzzatto's Stellung zur Bibelkritik", *MGWJ* XLIV (1900) pp. 460-80.

Elliger, K., „Sinn und Ursprung der priesterlichen Geschichtserzählung", *ZThK* XLIX (1952) pp. 121-43.

——, *Leviticus, HZAT*, Tübingen, 1966.

Elliott-Binns, L. E., *English Thought 1860-1900*, London, 1956.

Ellis, P. F., *The Men and the Message of the Old Testament*, Minnesota, 1962.

Ellison, H. L., "Some major modern trends in Old Testament study", *Journal of Transactions of the Victoria Institute* LXXXVIII (1956) pp. 32-46 and 153-60.

Emerton, J. A., "Priests and Levites in Deuteronomy", *VT* XII (1962) pp. 129-38.

Engelkemper, W., *Heiligtum und Opferstätten in den Gesetzen des Pentateuch*, Paderborn, 1908.

Engnell, I., *Gamla Testamentet I*, Stockholm, 1945.

——, „Profetia och Tradition", *Svensk Exegetisk Årsbok* XII (1948) pp. 94-123.

——, „Moseböckerna", I. Engnell and A. Fridrichsen (ed.) *Svenskt Bibliskt Uppslagsverk* Vol. II, Stockholm (1952) pp. 324-42.

——, "Methodological Aspects of Old Testament Study", *VTSuppl* VII, Leiden (1960) pp. 13-30.

Epstein, I. (ed.), *The Babylonian Talmud* Bab. Bathra I, London, 1935.

——, *Essays and Reviews*, F. Temple and others, London, [8]1861.

Ewald, H. A., *Die Komposition der Genesis*, Braunschweig, 1823.

——, *The History of Israel*, ET, Vol. I, London, (1869) from the 2nd ed, first published 1843.

Ewing, W., "The Samaritan Pentateuch and the Higher Criticism", *Expositor* 8th series XVIII (1919) pp. 451-69.

Fairbairn, A. M., *The Place of Christ in Modern Theology*, London, [6]1894.

Farrar, F. W., *History of Interpretation*, London, 1886.

——, "Higher Criticism", Ch I. I Kings, *Expositor's Bible* Vol. II, Grand Rapids (1947) pp. 217-19, first published 1893.

——, "Professor Sayce and the Higher Criticism", *Expositor* 5th series III (1896) pp. 30-48.

Finn, A. H., "The Tabernacle Chapters", *JTS* XVI (1915) pp. 449-82.

——, *The Unity of the Pentateuch*, 3rd ed. London (1928), first published 1917.

——, "The Mosaic Origin of the Pentateuch", *Journal of the Transactions of the Victoria Institute* L (1918) pp. 32-50.

——, *The Author of the Pentateuch*, London, n.d.

Finsler, R., *Darstellung und Kritik der Ansicht Wellhausen's von Geschichte und Religion des Alten Testaments*, Zürich, 1887.

Fohrer, G., "Remarks on Modern Interpretation of the Prophets", *JBL* LXXX (1961) pp. 309-19.

——, *Überlieferung und Geschichte des Exodus: Eine Analyse von Ex 1-15*, Berlin, 1964.

Fohrer, G., Sellin-Fohrer, *Introduction to the Old Testament*, ET New York (1968).
Franken, H. J. and Franken-Battershill, C. A., *A Primer of Old Testament Archaeology*, Leiden, 1963.
Frankena, R., "The Vassal-Treaties of Esarhaddon and the dating of Deuteronomy", *OTS* XIV (1965) pp. 122-54.
Free, J. P., "Archeology and Biblical Criticism", *BibSac* CXIII (1956) pp. 123-39, 214-26, 322-38.
——, "Archeology and Biblical Criticism" contd. *BibSac* CXIV (1957) pp. 23-39, 123-32, 213-24.
Freedman, D. N., "Pentateuch", G. A. Buttrick (ed.) *The Interpreter's Dictionary of the Bible*, Vol. 3, New York (1962) pp. 711-27.
——, "Archaeology and the Future of Biblical Studies 1. The Biblical languages", in J. P. Hyatt (ed.) *The Bible in Modern Scholarship*, Nashville (1965) pp. 294-312.
Freedman, H. and Simon, M. (ed.) *Midrash Rabba, Deuteronomy*, London, 1939.
French, R. V. (ed.) *Lex Mosaica*, London, 1894.
Friedländer, M., *The Jewish Religion*, London, 1891.
Gardner, H., *The Business of Criticism*, Oxford, 1959.
Gardner, W. R. W., "Did Moses write the Pentateuch in Babylonian Cuneiform?", *ExpT* XXV (1913-1914) pp. 526-27.
Gasser, C., *Das Alte Testament und die Kritik*, Stuttgart, 1906.
Gaster, T. H., "Sacrifices and Offerings", G. A. Buttrick (ed.) *The Interpreter's Dictionary of the Bible*, Vol. 4, New York (1962) pp. 147-59.
Geddes, A., *The Holy Bible or the Books accounted sacred by Christians and Jews . . . faithfully translated with various readings, Explanatory Notes and Critical Remarks*, Vol. I, London, 1792.
Geden, A. S., *Outlines of Introduction to the Hebrew Bible*, Edinburgh, 1909.
George, J. F. L., *Die älteren jüdischen Feste mit einer Kritik der Gesetzgebung des Pentateuchs*, Berlin, 1835.
Gerstenberger, E., *Wesen und Herkunft des „Apodiktischen Rechts"*, Neukirchen, 1965.
Giesebrecht, F., „Zur Hexateuchkritik", *ZAW* I (1881) pp. 177-276.
Ginsberg, H. L., "New Trends in Biblical Criticism", *Commentary* X (1950) pp. 276-84.
Gispen, W. W., "Leviticus", J. D. Douglas (ed.) *The New Bible Dictionary*, London (1962) pp.731-32.
Gladstone, W. E., *The Impregnable Rock of Holy Scripture*, Rev. London, 1890.
Glover, W. B., *Evangelical Nonconformists and Higher Criticism in the Nineteenth Century*, London, 1954.
Goldman, S., *The Book of Books—an Introduction*, 2 vols, New York, 1948-1949.
Gooch, G. P., *History and Historians in the Nineteenth Century*, London, ²1952.
Gooding, D. W., *The Account of the Tabernacle*, Cambridge, 1959.
Gordon, A. R., „Wellhausen", *Expositor* 6th series XI (1905) pp. 177-94.
——, "Ewald", *ExpT* XXV (1913-1914) pp. 511-16.
——, "The Contribution of Germany to Old Testament Scholarship", *ExpT* XLI (1929-1930) pp. 303-06.
Gordon, C. H., "Homer and the Bible", *HUCA* XXVI (1955) pp. 43-108.
——, "Higher Critics and Forbidden Fruit", *Christianity Today* IV (1959-1960) pp. 131-34.
Gore, C., (ed.) *Lux Mundi*, London, ¹⁰1890.
Graetz, H., "The Central Sanctuary of Deuteronomy", *JQR* III (1891) pp. 219-30.
——, *History of the Jews*, ET, Vol. I, London, 1901.
Graf, K. H., *Der Prophet Jeremia*, Leipzig, 1862.
——, *Die geschichtlichen Bücher des Alten Testaments*, Leipzig, (1866), actually published 1865.

Graf, K. H., „Zur Geschichte des Stammes Levi", A. Merx (ed.) *Archiv für wissenschaftliche Erforschung des Alten Testaments*, Halle (1867) I, pp. 68-106, 208-36.

——, "Die sogenannte Grundschrift des Pentateuchs", A. Merx (ed.) *Archiv für wissenschaftliche Erforschung des Alten Testaments*, Halle (1869) I, pp. 466-77.

——, K. Budde and H. J. Holtzmann (ed.) *Eduard Reuss' Briefwechsel mit seinem Schüler und Freunde Karl Heinrich Graf*, Giessen, 1904.

Graham, W. C., "Higher Criticism Survives Archeology", *American Scholar* VII (1938) pp. 409-27.

Gramberg, C. P. W., *Die Chronik nach ihrem geschichtlichen Charakter und ihrer Glaubwürdigkeit neu geprüft*, Halle, 1823.

——, *Kritische Geschichte der Religionsideen des Alten Testaments*, 2 vols, Berlin, 1829-1830.

Grant, E. H. (ed.), *The Haverford Symposium on Archaeology and the Bible*, New Haven, 1938.

Grant, R. M., "Historical Criticism in the Ancient Church", *JR* XXV (1945) pp. 183-96.

——, *A Short History of the Interpretation of the Bible*, Rev. ed, London (1965), first published 1948=*The Bible in the Church*.

Gray, E. M., *Old Testament Criticism: Its Rise and Progress from the Second Century to the End of the Eighteenth*, New York, 1923.

Gray, G. B., "Prof. Sayce's 'Early History of the Hebrews' ", *Expositor* 5th series VII (1898) pp. 337-55.

Green, W. H., *Moses and the Prophets*, New York, 1882.

——, "Professor Robertson Smith on the Pentateuch", *Presbyterian Review* III (1882) pp. 108-56.

——, *The Hebrew Feasts*, New York, 1886.

——, "The Pentateuchal Question", *Hebraica* V (1888-1889) pp. 137-89, VI (1889-1890) pp. 109-38, 161-211, VII (1890-1891) pp. 1-38, 81-103, VIII (1891-1892) pp. 15-64, 174-243.

——, *The Higher Criticism of the Pentateuch*, New York, 1895.

Greenberg, M., "A New Approach to the History of the Israelite Priesthood", *JAOS* LXX (1950) pp. 41-47.

——, "Some Postulates of Biblical Criminal Law", in M. Haran (ed.) *Yehezkel Kaufmann Jubilee Volume*, Jerusalem, 1960.

Greenslade, S. L. (ed.), *The Cambridge History of the Bible* (The West from the Reformation to the present day), Cambridge, 1963.

Grelot, P., "Etudes sur le 'Papyrus Pascal' d'Éléphantine", *VT* IV (1954) pp. 349-84.

——, „Le Papyrus Pascal d'Éléphantine et le problème du Pentateuque", *VT* V (1955) pp. 250-65.

——, „La dernière étape de la rédaction sacerdotale", *VT* VI (1956) pp. 174-89.

Gressmann, H., *Mose und seine Zeit*, Göttingen, 1913.

——, „Die Aufgaben der alttestamentlichen Forschung", *ZAW* XLII (1924) pp. 1-33.

Grimme, H., *Althebräische Inschriften vom Sinai*, Hanover, 1923.

Grintz, J. M. and Liver, J. (ed.), *Studies in the Bible*, (Segal Festschrift) Jerusalem, 1964.

Grintz, J. M., "Ye shall not eat *on* the blood", *Zion* XXXI (1966) pp. 1-17, Heb and Eng summary.

Grollenberg, L. H., *Atlas of the Bible*, ET, London, 1956.

Gunkel, H., *Genesis übersetzt und erklärt*, 5th ed, Göttingen (1922), first published 1901. ET of Introduction, *The Legends of Genesis*, New York, 1964.

Gunkel, H., „Die Israelitische Literatur", in P. Hinneberg (ed.) *Die Kultur der Gegenwart I* (VII) Berlin, 1906.

——, *Reden und Aufsätze*, Göttingen, 1913.

——, *Die Psalmen*, Göttingen, 1926.

——, *What Remains of the Old Testament*, ET, London, 1928.

Gunneweg, A. H. J., *Leviten und Priester*, Göttingen, 1965.

Hävernick, H. A. C., *A Historico-Critical Introduction to the Pentateuch*, ET, Edinburgh, 1840, first published 1837.

Hahn, H. F., *The Old Testament in Modern Research*, Philadelphia, 1954.

——, "Wellhausen's Interpretation of Israel's Religious History", J. L. Blau (ed.) *Essays on Jewish Life and Thought* (for S. W. Baron), New York (1959), pp. 299-308.

Halévy, J., „Esdras et le Code Sacerdotal", *Revue de l'Histoire des Religions* IV (1881) pp. 22-45.

——, „Esdras a-t-il promulqué une Loi Nouvelle?" *Revue de l'Histoire des Religions* XII (1885) pp. 26-38.

——, „Le Code Sacerdotal pendant l'Exil", *Revue de l'Histoire des Religions* XIV (1886) pp. 189-202.

——, *Recherches Bibliques*, 2 vols, Paris, 1895 and 1901.

Hallo, W. W., "New Viewpoints on Cuneiform Literature", *IEJ* XII (1962) pp. 13-26.

Haran, M., "The Ark and the Cherubim: Their Symbolic Significance in Biblical Ritual", *IEJ* IX (1959) pp. 30-94.

——, "The Nature of the " 'Ohel Mo'edh" in Pentateuchal Sources", *JSS* V (1960) pp. 50-65.

——, "The Complex of Ritual Acts performed inside the Tabernacle", *Scripta Hierosolymitana* VIII (1961) pp. 272-302.

——, "The Uses of Incense in the ancient Israelite Ritual", *VT* X (1960) pp. 113-29.

——, "Studies in the Account of the Levitical cities, I. Preliminary Considerations", *JBL* LXXX (1961) pp. 45-54, II. "Utopia and Reality", pp. 156-65.

——, "Shiloh and Jerusalem. The Origin of the Priestly Tradition in the Pentateuch", *JBL* LXXXI (1962) pp. 14-24.

——, "The Disappearance of the Ark", *IEJ* XIII (1963) pp. 46-58.

——, "The Priestly Image of the Tabernacle", *HUCA* XXXVI (1965) pp. 191-226.

——, "The Religion of the Patriarchs; An Attempt at a Synthesis", *ASTI* IV (1965) pp. 30-55.

——, (ed.) *Yehezkel Kaufmann Jubilee Volume*, Jerusalem, 1960.

Harford, J. B., "Since Wellhausen," *Expositor* 9th series IV (1925) pp. 4 ff, 83 ff, 164 ff, 244 ff, 323 ff, 403 ff.

Harper, W. R., "The Pentateuchal Question", *Hebraica* V (1888-1889) pp. 18-73, 243-91, VI (1889-1890) pp. 1-48, 241-95.

——, *The Priestly Element in the Old Testament*, Chicago, Rev. ed, 1902.

Harrington, W. J., *Record of Revelation*, Chicago, 1965.

Hastings, J. (ed.), *A Dictionary of the Bible*, 5 vols, Edinburgh, 1898-1904.

——, (ed.) *Dictionary of the Bible* (One Volume) Rev. ed, by F. C. Grant and H. H. Rowley, Edinburgh, (1963), first published 1909.

Hempel, J., *Die althebräische Literatur*, Potsdam, 1930.

——, „Chronik", *ZAW* LI (1933) pp. 284-301.

——, „Priesterkodex", *Paulys Realencyclopädie der Classischen Altertumswissenschaft* Vol. XLIV, Stuttgart (1954) cols 1943-1967.

Hengstenberg, E. W., *Egypt and the Books of Moses*, ET, Edinburgh (1845), first published Berlin, 1841.

Hengstenberg, E. W., *Dissertations on the Genuineness of the Pentateuch*, ET, 2 vols, Edinburgh (1847), first published 1836-1839.

Henry, M-L., *Jahwist und Priesterschrift*: Zwei Glaubenszeugnisse des Alten Testaments, Stuttgart, 1960.

Herder, J. G., *Aelteste Urkunde des Menschengeschlechts*, 3 vols (Müller ed.) Stuttgart, 1827-1828, first published 1774-1776.

——, *Salomons Lieder der Liebe*, die ältesten und schönsten aus Morgenlande. Nebst vierundvierzig alten Minneliedern und einem Anhang über die ebräische Elegie, 2 vols (Müller ed.) Stuttgart (1827), first published 1778.

——, *Briefe, das Studium der Theologie betreffend*, 3 vols (Müller ed.) Stuttgart (1829), first published 1780.

——, *Vom Geist der ebräischen Poesie*, 3 vols, Leipzig, 1782-1783. ET, *The Spirit of Hebrew Poetry*, 2 vols, Burlington, 1833.

Hertz, J. H. (ed.), *The Pentateuch and Haftorahs*, 5 vols, London, 1929-1935.

——, "Deuteronomy: Antiquity and Mosaic Authorship", *Journal of Transactions of the Victoria Institute* LXXII (1940) pp. 86-103.

Hicks, F. N., *The Fullness of Sacrifice*, London, ³1953.

Hill, S. S., "The Southern Baptists: Need for Reformulation, Redirection", *The Christian Century* LXXX (1963) pp. 39-42.

Hinchliff, P. B., *John William Colenso*, London, 1964.

Hirsch, E. G. H., "Genesis", *Jewish Encyclopedia* Vol. V, London (1903) pp. 610-11.

Hölscher, G., „Komposition und Ursprung des Deuteronomiums", *ZAW* XL (1922) pp. 161-255.

Hoffmann, D., „Die neueste Hypothese über den pentateuchischen Priesterkodex", *Magazin für die Wissenschaft des Judenthums* VI (1879) pp. 1-19, 90-114, 209-37, VII (1880) pp. 137-56, 237-54.

——, *Die wichtigsten Instanzen gegen die Graf-Wellhausensche Hypothese*, Berlin, 1902-1903.

——, *Das Buch Leviticus*, 2 vols, Berlin, 1905-1906.

——, „Probleme der Pentateuchexegese", *Jeschurun* I-VI (1914-1919).

Holzinger, H., *Einleitung in den Hexateuch*, Freiburg, 1893.

Hommel, F., *The Ancient Hebrew Tradition as illustrated by the Monuments*, ET, London (1897), first published 1896.

Hooke, S. H., "The Early Background of Hebrew Religion", T. W. Manson (ed.) *A Companion to the Bible*, Edinburgh (1947) pp. 271-86, first published 1939.

——, "The Religious Institutions of Israel", M. Black, and H. H. Rowley (ed.) *Peake's Commentary on the Bible*, London (1962) pp. 142-50.

Hoonacker, A. van, *Le lieu du culte dans la legislation rituelle des Hebreux*, Leipzig, 1894.

——, *Le Sacerdoce Lévitique*, Louvain, 1899.

——, *De compositione litteraria et de origine mosaica Hexateuchi disquisitio historico-critica*, J. Coppens (ed.) Brussel, 1949.

Hornig, G., *Die Anfänge der historisch-kritischen Theologie. Johann Salomo Semler's Schriftverständnis und seine Stellung zu Luther*, Göttingen, 1961.

Hoschander, J., "Survey of Recent Biblical Literature", *JQR* XVI (1925-1926) pp. 406-69.

Hubbard, D. A., "Priests and Levites", J. D. Douglas (ed.) *The New Bible Dictionary*, London (1962) pp. 1028-34.

Hubert, H. and Mauss, M., *Sacrifice: Its Nature and Function*, ET, Chicago, 1964.

Hügel, F. von, "The Historical Method and the Documents of the Hexateuch", *The Catholic University Bulletin* IV (1898) pp. 198-226.

Humbert, P., „Die literarische Zweiheit des Priestercodex in der Genesis", *ZAW* LVIII (1940-1941) p. 30 ff.

Hummelauer, F. de, *Commentarius in Exodum et Leviticum*, Paris, 1897.

——, *Commentarius in Numeros*, Paris, 1899.

——, *Commentarius in Deuteronomium*, Paris, 1901.

——, *Commentarius in Genesim*, Paris, 1908.

Hupfeld, H., *Die Quellen der Genesis und die Art ihrer Zusammensetzung*, Berlin, 1853.

Hurvitz, A., "The Usage of *šēš* and *būs* in the Bible and its implication for the date of P", *HTR* LX (1967) pp. 117-21.

Hyatt, J. P., "The Ras Shamra Discoveries and the Interpretation of the Old Testament", *JBR* X (1942) pp. 67-75.

——, (ed.) *The Bible in Modern Scholarship*, Nashville, 1965.

Ilgen, K. D., *Die Urkunden des Jerusalemischen Tempelarchivs in ihrer Urgestalt als Beytrag zur Berichtigung der Geschichte der Religion und Politik, Band I. Die Urkunden des ersten Buches von Mose*, Halle, 1798.

Irwin, W. A., "The Study of the Old Testament", *AJSL* LV (1938) pp. 166-82.

——, Review of J. Coppens, " 'L'Histoire critique de l'Ancien Testament' ", *JR* XIX (1939) pp. 382-86.

——, "Fifty Years of Old Testament Scholarship", *JBR* X (1942) pp. 131-35.

——, "The Significance of Julius Wellhausen", *JBR* XII (1944) pp. 160-74.

Jack, J. W., *The Ras Shamra Tablets. Their Bearing on the Old Testament*, Edinburgh, 1935.

Jackson, S. M. (ed.), "Strack", *New Schaff-Herzog Encyclopedia*, Vol. 11, New York (1911) p. 109.

Jacob, B., "Deuteronomy", *Jewish Encyclopedia* Vol. IV, London (1903) pp. 543-46.

——, "Exodus", *ibid*, Vol. V, London (1903) pp. 296-301, "Genesis", *ibid*, pp. 599-610.

Jampel, S., „Die bibelwissenschaftliche Literatur der letzten Jahre", *MGWJ* LI (1907) pp. 659-77, LII (1908) pp. 21-36, 145-61, LIII (1909) pp. 641-56.

——, „Die neuen Papyrusfunde in Elephantine", *MGWJ* LV (1911) pp. 641-65.

——, *Die Vorgeschichte des israelitischen Volkes und seiner Religion I. Teil: Die Methoden*, Frankfurt (1928), first published 1913.

Jastrow, M., *Hebrew and Babylonian Traditions*, New York, 1914.

——, "Constructive Elements in the Critical Study of the Old Testament", *JBL* XXXVI (1917) pp. 1-30.

Jepsen, A., "The Scientific Study of the Old Testament", C. Westermann (ed.) *Essays on Old Testament Interpretation*, London, 1963.

Jeremias, A., *The Old Testament in the Light of the Ancient East*, ET, 2 vols, from 2nd ed, London (1911), first published 1904.

Jerusalem, J. F. W., *Briefe über die Mosaischen Schriften und Philosophie*, Braunschweig (³1783), first published 1762.

Jones, A., *The Jerusalem Bible*, London, 1966.

Jones, D. R., "Priest and Levites", J. Hastings (ed.) *Dictionary of the Bible* (One Volume) Rev. ed, Edinburgh (1963) pp. 793-97.

Joseph, M., "Biblical Criticism and the Pulpit", *JQR* XVIII (1906) pp. 291-301.

Jowett, B., "On the Interpretation of Scripture", *Essays and Reviews*, London (³1861).

Kalisch, M. M., *Leviticus: A Historical and Critical Commentary to the Old Testament*, 2 vols, London, 1867-1872.

Kapelrud, A. S., "The date of the Priestly Code", *ASTI* III (1964) pp. 58-64.

——, "Sigmund Mowinckel and Old Testament Study", *ASTI* V (1967) pp. 4-29.

Kappeler, E., *Conrad von Orelli*, Zürich, 1916.

Kaufmann, Y. [H, J or E.] „Probleme der israelitischen-jüdischen Religionsgeschichte", Part I, *ZAW* XLVIII (1930) pp. 23-43, Part II, LI (1933) pp. 35-47.

——, *The Biblical Account of the Conquest of Palestine*, ET, Jerusalem, 1953.

——, „Der Kalender und das Alter des Priesterkodex", *VT* IV (1954) pp. 307-13.

——, *The Religion of Israel*, ET, Chicago, 1960.

Kautzsch, E. Rec. "Wellhausen J. 'Geschichte Israels' ", *ThLZ* (1879) No. 2, pp. 25-30.

——, Rec. „Baudissin ,Die Geschichte des alttestamentlichen Priestertums untersucht' ", *ThStKr* LXIII (1890) pp. 767-86.

——, *An Outline of the History of the Literature of the Old Testament*, ET, London, 1898.

——, "Religion of Israel", *HDB* Extra Vol, Edinburgh (1904) pp. 612-735. German ed, *Biblische Theologie des Alten Testaments*, Tübingen, 1911.

Kayser, A., *Das vorexilische Buch der Urgeschichte Israels und seine Erweiterungen*, Strassburg, 1874.

——, „Der gegenwärtige Stand der Pentateuchfrage", *Jahrbücher für Protestantische Theologie* VII (1881) pp. 326-65, 520-64, 630-65.

Kegel, M., *Wilhelm Vatke und die Graf-Wellhausensche Hypothese*, Gütersloh, 1911.

——, *Die Kultus-Reformation des Josia*, Leipzig, 1919.

——, *Away from Wellhausen*, ET, Nashville, 1924.

Keil, K. F., *Manual of Historico-Critical Introduction to the Canonical Scriptures of the Old Testament*, ET, from 2nd ed, Edinburgh (1869), first published 1853.

——, „Die Voraussetzungen und die Argumente der neueren Kritik des Alten Testaments", C. E. Luthardt (ed.) *ZKWL* VI (1885) pp. 169-81, 225-42.

Keller, W., *Und die Bibel hat doch recht*, Düsseldorf, 1955.

Kennett, R. H., "The History of the Jewish Church from Nebuchadnezzar to Alexander", H. B. Swete (ed.) *Cambridge Biblical Essays*, London (1909) pp. 93-135.

——, "Israel", *ERE* Vol. VII, Edinburgh (1914) pp. 439-56.

——, *The Origin of the Book of Deuteronomy*, Cambridge, 1920.

——, *Old Testament Essays*, Cambridge, 1928.

——, *The Church of Israel*, Cambridge, 1933.

Kidner, D., *Genesis* (Tyndale Commentary) London, 1967.

Kitchen, K. A., Review of "J. Vergote, 'Joseph en Égypte' ", in *JEA* XLVII (1961) pp. 158-64.

——, *Ancient Orient and the Old Testament*, London, 1966.

——, "Historical Method and Early Hebrew Tradition", *Tyndale Bulletin* XVII (1966) pp. 63-97.

Kittel, R., „Die neueste Wendung der pentateuchischen Frage", *Theologische Studien aus Württemberg* (1881) pp. 29-62, 147-69.

——, *A History of the Hebrews*, ET, 2 vols, Oxford, 1895-1896, first published 1888.

——, *The Scientific Study of the Old Testament*, ET, New York, 1910.

——, „Die Zukunft der Alttestamentlichen Wissenschaft", *ZAW* XXXIX (1921) pp. 84-99.

Kleinert, P., *Das Deuteronomium u. der Deuteronomiker*, Leipzig, 1872.

Kline, M. G., *Treaty of the Great King*, Grand Rapids, 1963.

Klostermann, A., „Beiträge zur Entstehungsgeschichte des Pentateuchs", *Zeitschrift für die gesammte Lutherische Theologie und Kirche* XXXVIII (1877) pp. 401-45; *NKZ* I (1890) pp. 618-32, 693-732, II (1891) pp. 689-711, III (1892) 421-58, 589-626, 763-797, 912-48.

——, *Der Pentateuch*, Leipzig, 1893, reprinting the above essays.

——, *Der Pentateuch*, Neu Folge, Leipzig, 1907, reprinting further essays from *NKZ*.

Knevett, E. de, „Professor Albin van Hoonacker", *ExpT* XX (1908-1909) pp. 165-66.

Koch, K., „Die Eigenart der priesterschriftlichen Sinaigesetzgebung", *ZThK* LV (1958) pp. 36-51.

——, *Die Priesterschrift von Exodus* 25 *bis Leviticus 19*, Göttingen, 1959.

——, *Was ist Formgeschichte?* Neukirchen, 1964. ET, *The Growth of the Biblical Tradition*, London, 1969.

König, E., *Die Hauptprobleme der altisraelitischen Religionsgeschichte*, Leipzig, 1884.

——, *The Religious History of Israel*, ET, Edinburgh (1885), first published 1884.

——, *Falsche Extreme in der neueren Kritik des Alten Testaments*, Leipzig, 1885.

——, "History and Method of Pentateuchal Criticism", *Expositor* 5th series IV (1896) pp. 81-99.

——, "Has a new proof of the Unity of Genesis been discovered?" *ExpT* XVI (1904-1905) pp. 524-27.

——, "The Significance of the Patriarchs in the History of Religion", *Expositor* 7th series X (1910) pp. 192-207.

——, *Die moderne Pentateuchkritik und ihre neueste Bekämpfung*, Leipzig, 1914.

——, „Der samaritanische Pentateuch und die Pentateuchkritik", *JBL* XXXIV (1915) pp. 10-16.

——, "The Burning Problem of the Hour in Old Testament Religious History", *Expositor* 8th series XXI (1921) pp. 81-106.

——, „Die sprachliche Gestalt des Pentateuchs in ihrer Beziehung zur ‚Ägyptischen Sprache' ", *JBL* XLVIII (1929) pp. 333-53.

——, „Deuteronomische Hauptfragen", *ZAW* LVIII (1930) pp. 43-66.

——, *Zentralkultstätte und Kultuszentralisierung im alten Israel*, Gütersloh, 1931.

Kraeling, E. G., *The Old Testament Since the Reformation*, London, 1955.

Kramer, S. N., "Sumerian Historiography", *IEJ* III (1953) pp. 217-32.

Kraus, H-J. *Geschichte der historisch-kritischen Erforschung des Alten Testaments*, Neukirchen, 1956.

——, *Worship in Israel*, ET, Oxford, 1966.

Külling, S. R., *Zur Datierung der „Genesis-P-Stücke"*, Namentlich des Kapitels Genesis XVII, Kampen, 1964.

Kuenen, A., *The Religion of Israel to the Fall of the Jewish State*, ET, 3 vols, London (1874-1875), first published 1869-1870.

——, *An Historico-Critical Inquiry into the Origin and Composition of the Hexateuch*, ET from the 2nd ed, London, 1886.

Kyle, M. G., *The Deciding Voice of the Monuments in Biblical Criticism*, Oberlin, 1912.

——, "A New Solution of the Pentateuchal Problem" *JBL* XXXVI (1917) pp. 31-47.

——, *Moses and the Monuments*, Oberlin, 1919.

——, *The Problem of the Pentateuch*, Oberlin, 1920.

Laessøe, J., "Literacy and Oral Tradition in Ancient Mesopotamia", *Studia Orientalia Ioanni Pedersen*, Hauniae (1953) pp. 205-18.

Lagarde, P. de, *Symmicta*, Göttingen (1877) pp. 50-57, first published *Göttingische Gelehrte Anzeigen* (1870) Stück 39, 1549-1560.

Lagrange, M. J., „La nouvelle histoire d'Israel et le prophète Osée", *RB* I (1892) pp. 203-35.

——, „Les sources du Pentateuque", *RB* VII (1898) pp. 10-32.

——, *Historical Criticism and the Old Testament*, ET, London, 1905, first published 1903.

——, *La Genèse* (Pro manuscripto) Paris, 1905.

——, „L'authenticité mosaïque de la Genèse et la théorie des documents", *RB* XLVII (1938) pp. 163-83.

Lagrange, M. J., Benoit, P. (ed.), *Père Lagrange au service de la Bible*, Souvenirs Personnels, Paris, 1968.

Lambdin, T. O., "Egyptian Loan Words in the Old Testament", *JAOS* LXXIII (1953) pp. 145-55.

Landersdorfer, S., *Studien zum biblischen Versöhnungstag*, Münster, 1924.

Lansing, G., "The Pentateuch—Egypticity and Authenticity", *Expositor* 3rd series VIII (1888) pp. 219-31, 307-17.

Lapp, P. W., "Palestine: Known But Mostly Unknown", *BA* XXVI (1963) pp. 121-34.

Lattey, C. (ed.) *Moses and the Law*, London, 1922.

Leeuwen, A. T. van, *Christianity in World History*, Edinburgh, 1964.

Lessing, G. E., „Hilkias", K. Lachmann (ed.) *Lessings Sämtliche Schriften*, Vol. XVI, Leipzig (1902) pp. 245-50.

Levie, J., *The Bible, Word of God in Words of Men*, ET, New York (1961), first published Paris, 1958.

Levy, F. A., "Contemporary Trends in Jewish Bible Study", H. R. Willoughby (ed.) *The Study of the Bible Today and Tomorrow*, Chicago (1947) pp. 98-115.

Lewy, I., *The Growth of the Pentateuch*, New York, 1955.

Lias, J. J., "Is the so-called Priestly Code Post-Exilic?", *BibSac* LXVII (1910) pp. 20-46, *ibid*, pp. 299-334.

Lichtenberger, F., *History of German Theology in the Nineteenth Century*, ET, Edinburgh, 1889.

Lieber, D., "Yehezkel Kaufmann's Contribution to Biblical Scholarship", *Jewish Education* XXXIV (1963-1964) pp. 254-61.

——, "Modern Trends in Bible Study", *Conservative Judaism* XX (1965) pp. 37-46.

Lieberman, M., "Julian Morgenstern—Scholar, Teacher and Leader", *HUCA* XXXII (1961) pp. 1-9.

Löhr, M., *Untersuchungen zum Hexateuchproblem*: I. *Der Priesterkodex in der Genesis*, Giessen, 1924.

——, "The Five Books of Moses and the Question of their Origin", H. M. du Bose (ed.) *The Aftermath Series*, Nashville (1923-1924) pp. 331-82.

——, *A History of Religion in the Old Testament*, London, 1936.

Loewenstamm, S. E., *The Tradition of the Exodus in its Development*, Jerusalem, 1965, Heb and Eng summary.

Lohfink, N., „Die Bundesurkunde des Königs Josias (Eine Frage an die Deuteronomiumsforschung)", *Biblica* XLIV (1963) pp. 261-88, 461-98.

——, *Das Hauptgebot* (Eine Untersuchung literarischer Einleitungsfragen zu Dtn 5-11), Rome, 1963.

McEleney, N. J., *The Law Given Through Moses*, New York, 1960.

M'Ewan, J., *The Bible and the Critics*, Edinburgh, 1902.

McFadyen, J. E., *Old Testament Criticism and the Christian Church*, London, 1903.

——, "Old Testament Criticism", A. S. Peake (ed.) *The People and the Book*, Oxford, 1925.

——, *The Approach to the Old Testament*, London, 1926.

——, "The Language of the Pentateuch in its Relation to Egyptian", *ExpT* XLI (1929-1930) pp. 54-58.

McKenzie, J. L., *The Two-Edged Sword*, London, 1959.

——, (ed.) *The Bible in Current Catholic Thought*, New York, 1962.

——, *Myths and Realities*, London, 1963.

——, *Dictionary of the Bible*, Milwaukee, 1965.

MacKenzie, R. A. F., "Some Problems in the Field of Inspiration", *CBQ* XXX (1958) pp. 4-5.

Maas, A. J., "Pentateuch", *Catholic Encyclopedia*, Vol. XI, London (1911) pp. 646-61.

Maisler, B., "Ancient Israelite Historiography", *IEJ* II (1952) pp. 82-88.

Maly, E. H., "Père Lagrange and the Pentateuch", in R. T. A. Murphy (ed.) *Lagrange Lectures*, Iowa (1963) pp. 70-87.

——, "Pentateuch", *New Catholic Encyclopedia*, Vol. XI, New York (1967) pp. 98-104.

Manasseh ben Israel, *The Conciliator of Manasseh ben Israel*, ET, 2 vols, London (1842), first published 1632.

Mangenot, E., „Pentateuque", *DB* Vol. V. 1 (1922) cols 50-119.

Mann, J., "The Responsa of the Babylonian Geonim as a source of Jewish History", *JQR* IX (1918-1919) pp. 139-50.

Manson, T. W., "The Failure of Liberalism to interpret the Bible as the Word of God", in C. W. Dugmore (ed.) *The Interpretation of the Bible*, London (1944) pp. 92-107.

Margoliouth, D. S., *Lines of Defence of the Biblical Revelation*, London, 1900.

Margolis, M. L., "The Scope and Methodology of Biblical Philology", *JQR* I (1910-1911) pp. 5-41.

——, *The Hebrew Scriptures in the Making*, Philadelphia, 1922.

Marston, C., *New Bible Evidence*, New York, 1934-1935.

Marti, K., „Die Spuren der sogenannten Grundschrift des Hexateuchs in den vorexilischen Propheten des Alten Testaments", *Jahrbücher für Protestantische Theologie* VI (1880) pp. 127-61, 308-54.

——, „Wellhausen's Ansicht von Geschichte und Religion des Alten Testaments", by R. Finsler, *Kirchenblatt für die reformierte Schweiz*, (1887) pp. 65-67, 69-72, 93-96.

——, *Religion of the Old Testament*, ET, London (1907), first published in this form 1897.

May, H. G., "Moses and the Sinai Inscriptions", *BA* VIII (1945) pp. 93-99.

Meinhold, L., *Wellhausen*, Leipzig, 1897.

Mendenhall, G. E., *Law and Covenant in Israel and the Ancient Near East*, Pittsburg, 1955.

Merx, A., "Aphoristische Bemerkungen über die Pentateuchkritik nebst einer Besprechung von Popper, Dr Julius, ‚Der biblische Bericht über die Stiftshütte' 1862", *Protestantische Kirchenzeitung für das evang. Deutschland* (1865) No. 17, pp. 376-87.

——, „Nachwort", A. Merx (ed.) Tuch, F. *Commentar über die Genesis*, 2nd ed. Halle (1871) pp. lxxviii-cxxii.

——, *Die Bücher Moses und Josua*, Tübingen, 1907.

Michaelis, J. D., *Commentaries on the Laws of Moses*, ET 4 vols, London (1814), first published 1770-1775.

Möller, W., *Historische-kritische Bedenken gegen die Graf-Wellhausensche Hypothese*, Gütersloh 1899.

——, *Are the Critics Right?* ET from 2nd ed, London (1903), first published 1899.

——, *Die Entwicklung der alttestamentlichen Gottesidee in vorexilischer Zeit*, Gütersloh, 1903.

——, "Genesis", J. Orr (ed.) *International Standard Bible Encyclopaedia*, Vol. II, Grand Rapids (1947) pp. 1199-1214, first published 1929, "Exodus" *ibid*, pp. 1056-1067.

Montefiore, C. G., "Recent Criticism upon Moses and the Pentateuchal Narratives of the Decalogue", *JQR* III (1891) pp. 251-91.

——, "Dr Friedländer on the Jewish Religion", *JQR* IV (1892) pp. 204-44.

Montefiore, C. G., "Some Notes on the Effect of Biblical Criticism upon the
    Jewish Religion", *JQR* IV (1892) pp. 293-306.
——, "Should Biblical criticism be spoken of in Jewish pulpits", *JQR* XVIII
    (1906) pp. 302-16.
Moore, G. F., „Alttestamentliche Studien in Amerika", *ZAW* VIII (1888)
    pp. 1-43, IX (1889) pp. 246-302.
Morgenstern, J., "The Oldest Document of the Hexateuch", *HUCA* IV (1927)
    pp. 1-138.
——, "The Book of the Covenant", Part I, *HUCA* V (1928) pp. 1-151, Part II,
    VII (1930) pp. 19-258, Part III, VIII (1931) pp. 1-150.
——, "A Chapter in the History of the High-Priesthood", *AJSL* LV (1938)
    pp. 1-24, 183-97, 360-77.
Moriarty, F. L., „Gerhard von Rad's *Genesis*", in J. L. McKenzie (ed.) *The
    Bible in Current Catholic Thought*, New York (1962) pp. 34-45.
Movers, F. C., *Kritische Untersuchungen über die biblische Chronik*, Bonn, 1834.
Mowinckel, S., *Psalmenstudien I-VI*, Kristiania, 1921-1924.
——, „Der Ursprung der Bilʿāmsage", *ZAW* XLVIII (1930) pp. 233-71.
——, *The Two Sources of the Pre-deuteronomic Primeval History (JE) in Gen. 1-11*,
    Oslo, 1937.
——, *Prophecy and Tradition*, Oslo, 1946.
——, *Zur Frage nach dokumentarischen Quellen in Josua 13-19*, Oslo, 1946.
——, "Israelite Historiography", *ASTI* II (1963) pp. 4-26.
——, „Erwägungen zur Pentateuch Quellenfrage", *Norsk Teologisk Tidsskrift*
    LXV (1964) pp. 1-138.
——, *Tetrateuch-Pentateuch-Hexateuch*, Berlin, 1964.
Mozley, J. K., *Some Tendencies in British Theology*, London, 1951.
Muilenburg, J., "Old Testament Scholarship. Fifty years in Retrospect", *JBR*
    XXVIII (1960) pp. 173-81.
Munro, J. I., *The Samaritan Pentateuch and Modern Criticism*, London, 1911.
Murphy R. T. (transl.), *Père Lagrange and the Scriptures*, Milwaukee (1946), from
    French, 1935.
——, "Moses and the Pentateuch", *CBQ* XI (1949) pp. 165-78.
Murtonen, A., "The Fixation in Writing of the Various Parts of the Pentateuch",
    VT III (1953) pp. 46-53.
Naumann, O., *Wellhausen's Methode kritisch beleuchtet*, Leipzig, 1886.
Naville, E., *Archaeology of the Old Testament*, London, 1913.
——, *Text of the Old Testament* (Schweich Lectures) London, 1916.
——, *The Law of Moses*, ET, London, 1922, first published 1920.
Neil, W., "The Criticism and Theological Use of the Bible, 1750-1950", S. L.
    Greenslade (ed.) *The Cambridge History of the Bible*, Cambridge (1963) pp. 238-93.
Neubauer, J., „Wellhausen und der heutige Stand der Bibelwissenschaft",
    Jeschurun V (1918) pp. 203-33.
Neuman, A. A. and Zeitlin, S. (ed.), *The Seventy-Fifth Anniversary Volume of the
    Jewish Quarterly Review*, Philadelphia, 1967.
Newman, F. W., *A History of the Hebrew Monarchy*, London (²1853), first published
    1847.
Nicholson, E. W., "The Centralisation of the cult in Deuteronomy", *VT* XIII
    (1963) pp. 380-89.
——, *Deuteronomy and Tradition*, Oxford, 1967.
Nielsen, E., *Oral Tradition*, London, 1954.
——, *Shechem*, Copenhagen, 1955.
——, "Some Reflections on the History of the Ark", *VTSuppl VII*, *Congress
    Volume, Oxford 1959*, Leiden (1960) pp. 61-74.

Nöldeke, T., *Untersuchungen zur Kritik des Alten Testaments*, Kiel, 1869.
North, C. R., "Living Issues in the Old Testament—The Place of Oral Tradition in the Growth of the Old Testament", *ExpT* LXI (1949-1950) pp. 292-96.
——, "Pentateuchal Criticism", H. H. Rowley (ed.) *The Old Testament and Modern Study*, Oxford (1951) pp. 48-83.
——, "Oral Tradition and Written Documents", *ExpT* LXVI (1954-1955) p. 39.
——, "Pentateuch", J. Hastings (ed.) *Dictionary of the Bible* (One Volume) Rev. ed. Edinburgh (1963) pp. 744-48.
Noth, M., „Gesetze im Pentateuch", *Gesammelte Studien zum Alten Testament*, München, (1957) pp. 9-141, first published 1940. ET now in *The Laws in the Pentateuch*, Edinburgh, 1966.
——, *Überlieferungsgeschichtliche Studien I*, Halle, 1943.
——, *Überlieferungsgeschichte des Pentateuch*, Stuttgart, 1948.
——, *The History of Israel*, ET, London, 1958, first published 1950.
——, „Hat die Bibel doch recht?" *Festschrift für Günther Dehn*, Neukirchen, 1957.
——, „Der Beitrag der Archäologie zur Geschichte Israels", *VTSuppl VII, Congress Volume, Oxford 1959*, Leiden (1960) pp. 262-82.
——, Review, Bright "History of Israel", *Interpretation* XV (1961) pp. 61-66.
——, *Die Ursprung des alten Israel in Lichte neuer Quellen*, Köln, 1961.
——, *Exodus*, *ATD*, ET, London, 1962.
——, *Developing Lines of Theological Thought in Germany*, Virginia, 1963.
——, *The Old Testament World*, ET, Philadelphia, 1966, from German ⁴1964.
——, *Leviticus*, *ATD*, ET, London, 1965.
Nyberg, H. S., *Studien zum Hoseabuche*, Uppsala, 1935.
Oettli, S., „Der Kultus bei Amos und Hosea", *Greifswalder Studien*, Gütersloh (1895) pp. 1-34.
——, *Amos und Hosea*. Zwei Zeugen gegen die Anwendung der Evolutionstheorie auf die Religion Israels, Gütersloh, 1901.
——, *Der Gegenwärtige Kampf um das Alte Testament*, Gütersloh, 1896.
Olmstead, A. T., "History, the Ancient World and the Bible", *JNES* II (1943) pp. 1-34.
Orelli, C. von, *Wider unberechtigte Machtsprüche heutiger Kritiker*, Antwort auf Prof. Meinhold's Schrift: „Wider den Kleinglauben", Düsseldorf, 1895.
——, Kappeler, E. (ed.) *Conrad von Orelli*, Zürich, 1916.
Orlinsky, H. M., "Jewish Biblical Scholarship in America", *JQR* XLV (1954-1955) pp. 374-412, XLVII (1956-1957) pp. 345-53.
Orr, J., *The Problem of the Old Testament*, London 1905.
——, *The Bible Under Trial*, London [1907].
——, "The Problem of the Old Testament Restated", *Contemporary Review* (Aug. 1907) pp. 200-12.
——, "Professor Peake on Biblical Criticism", *Interpreter* IV (1908) pp. 364-72.
Orth, J., „La tribu de Levi et la loi", *Revue de Theologie* III (1859) pp. 384-400.
——, „La centralisation du culte du Jéhovah", *ibid*, IV (1859) pp. 350-60.
Packer, J. I., '*Fundamentalism*' *and the Word of God*, Grand Rapids, 1958.
Peake, A. S, "Wellhausen and Dr Baxter", *ExpT* VII (1895-1896) pp. 400-05.
——, "A Reply to Dr Baxter", *ibid*, pp. 559-64.
——, "The Problem of the Old Testament", *Contemporary Review* (1907) pp. 493-509.
——, "Dr Orr on Biblical Criticism", *Interpreter* IV (1908) pp. 253-68.
——, *The Bible, its Origin, its Significance and its Abiding Worth*, London (⁶1920), first published 1913.
——, "Recent Developments in Old Testament Criticism", *The Servant of Yahweh*, Manchester (1931), first written 1924.

Pedersen, J., *Israel, Her Life and Culture*, ET, 2 vols, London (1926 and 1940), first published 1920 and 1934.

——, „Die Auffassung vom Alten Testament", *ZAW* XLIX (1931) pp. 161-81.

——, „Passahfest und Passahlegende", *ZAW* LII (1934) pp. 161-75.

Perles, F., *Analekten zur Textkritik des Alten Testaments*, München, 1895.

——, „Judentum und Bibelwissenschaft", A. Brüll (ed.) *Populär-wissenschaftliche Monatsblätter*, Frankfurt-am-Main, 1907.

Perlitt, L., *Vatke und Wellhausen*, Berlin, 1965.

Pfeiffer, R. H., "A Non-Israelite Source of the Book of Genesis", *ZAW* XLVIII (1930) pp. 66-73.

——, *Introduction to the Old Testament*, 2nd ed, New York (1948), first published 1942.

Pfleiderer, O., *Development of Theology in Germany since Kant and in Great Britain since 1825*, London, 1890.

Ploeg, J. van der, „Le rôle de la tradition orale dans la transmission du texte de l'ancien testament", *RB* LIV (1947) pp. 5-41.

Poels, H., *Examen critique de l'histoire du sanctuaire de l'arche*, Louvain, 1897.

Poole, R. S., "The Date of the Pentateuch", *Contemporary Review* LII (1887) pp. 350-70.

Popper, J., *Der biblische Bericht über die Stiftshütte*, Leipzig, 1862.

Porteous, N. W., "The Theology of the Old Testament", M. Black, and H. H. Rowley (ed.) *Peake's Commentary on the Bible*, London (1962) pp. 151-59.

Pritchard-Evans, E. E., *Theories of Primitive Religion*, Oxford, 1965.

Pritchard, J. B., "W. Robertson Smith, Heretic", *Crozer Quarterly* XXIV (1947) pp. 146-60.

——, Rev. "The Study of the Bible Today and Tomorrow", *JQR* XXXIX (1948-1949) pp. 103-05.

——, „Arkeologiens plats: Studiet av Gamla Testamentet", *Svensk Exegetisk Årsbok* XXX (1965) pp. 5-20.

——, "Culture and History", in J. P. Hyatt (ed.) *The Bible and Modern Scholarship*, Nashville (1965) pp. 313-24.

Rabe, V. W., "The Identity of the Priestly Tabernacle", *JNES* LXXXIII (1966) pp. 132-34.

Rad, G. von, *Das Gottesvolk in Deuteronomium*, Stuttgart, 1929.

——, *Die Priesterschrift in Hexateuch*, Stuttgart, 1934.

——, *Das Formgeschichtliche Problem des Hexateuchs*, Stuttgart, 1938. Now in *Gesammelte Studien*, München (1958) pp. 9-86. ET now in *The Problem of the Hexateuch and Other Essays*, Edinburgh, 1966.

——, „ ‚Gerechtigkeit' und ‚Leben' in der Kultsprache der Psalmen", *ibid*, pp. 225-47, first published 1950, ET, pp. 243-66.

——, „Die Anrechnung des Glaubens zur Gerechtigkeit", *ibid*, pp. 130-35, first published 1951, ET, pp. 125-30.

——, „Hexateuch oder Pentateuch", *Verkündigung und Forschung*, München (1947-1948) pp. 52-55.

——, „Literar-kritische und Überlieferungsgeschichtliche Forschung im Alten Testament", *ibid*, (1949-1950) pp. 172-94.

——, *Studies in Deuteronomy*, ET, London (1953), first published 1948.

——, "Deuteronomy", G. A. Buttrick (ed.) *The Interpreter's Dictionary of the Bible*, Vol. I, New York (1962) pp. 831-38.

——, *Old Testament Theology*, ET, 2 vols, Edinburgh, 1962-1965.

——, *Deuteronomy*, ATD, ET, London, 1966.

Rainy, R., *The Bible and Criticism*, London, 1878.

Ranke, F. H., *Untersuchungen über den Pentateuch aus dem Gebiete der höheren Kritik*, 2 vols, Erlangen, 1834 and 1840.

Rapaport, I., "The Origins of Hebrew Law", *PEQ* LXXIII (1941) pp. 158-71.

Reed, W. L., "Gibeon" in D. Winton Thomas (ed.) *Archaeology and Old Testament Study*, Oxford (1967) pp. 231-43.

Reider, J., "The Origin of Deuteronomy", *JQR* XXVII (1936-1937) pp. 349-71.

——, Reviews, *JQR* IX (1918-1919) pp. 423 ff, XII (1921-1922) pp. 195-221, XVII (1926-1927) p. 388, XIX (1928-1929) pp. 431-37.

Rendtorff, R., *Die Gesetze in der Priesterschrift*, Göttingen, 1954.

——, "Pentateuch", H. Brunotte and O. Weber (ed.) *Evangelisches Kirchen Lexikon* Vol. III, Göttingen (1958) cols 109-14.

Reuss, E., "Judenthum", J. C. Ersch, and J. G. Gruber (ed.) *Allgemeine Encyklopädie der Wissenschaften und Kunste*, Leipzig (1850) pp. 324-47.

——, *L'histoire sainte et la loi*, Paris, 1879.

——, *Die Geschichte der Heiligen Schriften Alten Testaments*, Braunschweig, 1881.

Reventlow, H. G., *Das Heiligkeitsgesetz formgeschichtlich untersucht*, Neukirchen, 1961.

——, "Die Auffassung vom Alten Testament bei Hermann Samuel Reimarus und Gotthold Ephraim Lessing", *EvTh* XXV (1965) pp. 429-48.

Richardson, A., "The Rise of Modern Biblical Scholarship", S. L. Greenslade (ed.) *The Cambridge History of the Bible*, Cambridge (1963) pp. 294-338.

Richardson, E. C., "Oral Traditions, Libraries and the Hexateuch", *Princeton Theological Review* III (1905) pp. 191-215.

Richardson, G. H., *Biblical Archaeology*, London, [1935].

Ridderbos, N. H., "Numbers", J. D. Douglas (ed.) *The New Bible Dictionary*, London (1962) pp. 899-901.

Riehm, E., *Die Gesetzgebung Mosis im Lande Moab*, Gotha, 1854.

——, Rec. „'Die geschichtlichen Bücher des Alten Testaments' von Karl Heinrich Graf", *ThStKr* XLI (1868) pp. 350-79.

——, „Die sogenannte Grundschrift des Pentateuchs", *ibid* XLV (1872) pp. 283-307.

Rigg, J. H., *The Character and Life-Work of Dr Pusey*, London, 1883.

Ringgren, H., "Oral and Written Transmission in the Old Testament", *Studia Theologica* III (1949) pp. 35-59.

——, *Sacrifice in the Bible*, ET, London, 1962.

——, *Israelite Religion*, ET, Philadelphia, 1966.

Rippner, Dr "Herder's Bibelexegese", *MGWJ* XXI (1872) pp. 16-37.

Robert, A. and Tricot, A., *Guide to the Bible I*, ET, Tournai (1951) from 1948 edition of *Initiation Biblique*, esp. pp. 94-109 "The Law" (A. Robert).

Robertson, E., *The Old Testament Problem with Two Other Essays*, Manchester, 1950, first published *Bulletin of the John Rylands Library* XX (1936) pp. 134-56, XXVI (1941-1942) pp. 182-205, XXVI (1942) pp. 369-92, XXVII (1943) pp. 359-83, XXVIII (1944) pp. 175-206, XXIX (1945) pp. 121-42, XXX (1946) pp. 91-114, XXXII (1949) pp. 19-43.

Robertson, F. W., *Notes on Genesis*, London, 1877.

Robertson, J., *The Early Religion of Israel*, Edinburgh, ²1892.

Robertson, J. M., *A History of Free Thought in the Nineteenth Century*, 2 vols, London, 1929.

Robinson, G. L., "Genesis of Deuteronomy", *Expositor* 5th series VIII (1898) pp. 241-61, 351-69; IX (1899) pp. 151-60, 271-95, 356-71.

——, "Deuteronomy", J. Orr (ed.) *International Standard Bible Encyclopaedia* Vol. II, Grand Rapids (1947) pp. 835-40, first published 1929.

Robinson, H. W., "The Contribution of Great Britain to Old Testament Scholarship", *ExpT* XLI (1929-1930) pp. 246-50.

Rome and the Study of Scripture, St. Meinrad, ⁷1964.

Roos, Fr., *Die Geschichtlichkeit des Pentateuchs ins besondere seiner Gesetzgebung*, Stuttgart, 1883.

Rosenthal, J., "Hiwi al-Balkhi—a Comparative Study", *JQR* XXXVIII (1947-1948) pp. 317-42, 419-30; XXXIX (1948-1949) pp. 79-94.

Rosmarin, T. W., "The New Trend in Biblical Criticism", *JBR* VI (1938) pp. 83-86.

Rost, L., „Zum geschichtlichen Ort der Pentateuchquellen", *ZThK* LIII (1956) pp. 1-11.

Rowley, H. H., "The Relevance of Biblical Interpretation", *Interpretation* I (1947). pp. 3-19.

——, Rev. "The Study of the Bible Today and Tomorrow" (H. R. Willoughby ed.) *Theology Today* V (1948) pp. 122-26.

——, *The Growth of the Old Testament*, London, 1950.

——, *Worship in Ancient Israel*, Its Forms and Meaning, London, 1967.

Rubaschow, S., "Bible", *Encyclopaedia Judaica* IV, Berlin (1929) cols 703-17.

Rudolph, W., *Der „Elohist" von Exodus bis Josua*, Berlin, 1938.

Rule, V. Z., *Old Testament Institutions, their Origin and Development*, London, 1910.

Ruppert, L., *Die Josepherzählung der Genesis*: Ein Beitrag zu Theologie der Pentateuchquellen, München, 1965.

Rupprecht, E., *Die Anschauung der kritischen Schule Wellhausens vom Pentateuch*, Erlangen, 1893.

——, *Der Pseudodaniel und Pseudojesaja*, Erlangen, 1894.

——, *Das Rätsel des Fünfbuches Mose und seine falsche Lösung*, Gütersloh, 1894.

——, *Des Rätsels Lösung I*, Gütersloh, 1895, II 1, (1896), II 2, (1897).

Rylaarsdam, J. C., "The Present Status of Pentateuchal Criticism", *JBR* XXII (1954) pp. 242-47.

Salm, C. L., *Studies in Salvation History*, New Jersey, 1964.

Šanda, A., *Moses und der Pentateuch*, Münster, 1924.

Sandmel, S., "The Haggada within Scripture", *JBL* LXXX (1961) pp. 105-22.

——, *The Hebrew Scriptures*, New York, 1963.

Sayce, A. H., "The Archaeological Witness to the Literary Activity of the Mosaic Age", R. V. French (ed.) *Lex Mosaica*, London, 1894.

——, *The Early History of the Hebrews*, London, 1897.

——, *Monument Facts and Higher Critical Fancies*, London, 1904.

——, *The 'Higher Criticism' and the Verdict of the Monuments*, London (⁷1910), first published 1893.

——, "The Jewish Garrison and Temple in Elephantine", *Expositor* 8th series II (1911) pp. 97-115.

——, "The Jews and their Temple at Elephantine", *ibid*, pp. 417-34.

——, *Reminiscences*, London, 1923.

Schechter, S., *Studies in Judaism*, 2 vols, London, 1896 and 1908.

——, "The Oldest Collection of Bible Difficulties, by a Jew", *JQR* XIII (1901) pp. 345-74.

Schmidt, N., "Bible Canon" *Jewish Encyclopedia* Vol. III, London (1903) pp. 140-54.

Schökel, L. A., *Understanding Biblical Research*, ET, New York, 1963.

Schrader, E. (ed.) Wette, W. M. L. de, *Lehrbuch der historisch-kritischen Einleitung*, 8th ed, Berlin, 1869.

——, *Keilinschriften und Geschichtsforschung*, Giessen, 1878.

Schultz, H., *Old Testament Theology*, ET, 2 vols, Edinburgh, 1892, from 2nd ed. 1878, first published 1869.

Schweitzer, A., *The Quest of the Historical Jesus*, ET, London, ²1911.
Segal, M. H., "Unitary Character of the Pentateuch", *Tarbiz* XXV (1955) pp. 1-10.
——, "El, Elohim and Yhwh in the Bible", *JQR* XLVI (1955-1956) pp. 89-115.
——, "The Book of Deuteronomy", *JQR* XLVIII (1957-1958) pp. 315-51.
——, "The Composition of the Pentateuch", *Scripta Hierosolymitana* VIII (1961) pp. 68-114.
——, *The Pentateuch: Its Composition and its Authorship*, Jerusalem (1967).
Sellin, E., *Introduction to the Old Testament*, ET, London (1923) first published 1910.
——, *Zur Einleitung in das Alte Testament*, Leipzig, 1912.
——, „Gehen wir einer Umwälzung auf dem Gebiete der Pentateuchkritik entgegen", *NKZ* XXIV (1913) pp. 119-48.
——, "Archaeology versus Wellhausenism", H. M. du Bose (ed.) *The Aftermath Series*, Nashville (1923-1924) pp. 227-71.
Simon, R., *A Critical History of the Old Testament*, ET, London, 1682.
Simpson, C. A., *The Early Traditions of Israel*, Oxford, 1948.
——, "The Growth of the Hexateuch", *IB* Vol. I, New York (1952) pp. 185-200, "Genesis", *ibid*, pp. 439-57.
——, "Deuteronomy", J. Hastings (ed.) *Dictionary of the Bible* (One Volume) Rev. ed, Edinburgh (1963) pp. 213-16.
Simpson, D. C., *Pentateuchal Criticism*, Oxford, 1924, first published 1914.
Singer, I, etc. (ed.) *The Jewish Encyclopedia*, Vols. III-V, London, 1902-1903.
Sinker, R., *"Higher Criticism", What is it and Where does it lead us?* London, 1899.
Skinner, J., "The Divine Names in the Pentateuch", *ExpT* XXV (1913-1914) pp. 472-73.
——, *The Divine Names in Genesis*, London, 1914.
Smart, J. D., *The Interpretation of Scripture*, Philadelphia, 1961.
Smend, R., „Ueber die von den Propheten des Achten Jahrhunderts vorausgesetzte Entwicklungstufe der israelitischen Religion", *ThStKr* XLIX (1876) pp. 599-664.
——, *Der Prophet Ezechiel*, *KEH*, Leipzig, ²1880.
——, *Die Erzählung des Hexateuchs*, Berlin, 1912.
Smend, R., „De Wette und das Verhältnis zwischen historischer Bibelkritik und philosophischem System im 19 Jahrhundert", *ThZ* XIV (1958) pp. 107-19.
——, *Wilhelm Martin Leberecht de Wettes Arbeit am Alten und am Neuen Testament*, Basel, 1958.
——, *Das Mosebild von Heinrich Ewald bis Martin Noth*, Tübingen, 1959.
——, (ed.) *Julius Wellhausen, Grundrisse zum Alten Testament*, Munich, 1965.
Smith, G. A., *Modern Criticism and the Preaching of the Old Testament*, London, 1901.
——, *The Historical Geography of the Holy Land*, 23rd ed, London, n.d.
Smith, H. P., "The theories of Julius Wellhausen", *Presbyterian Review* III (1882) pp. 356-88.
——, "Charles Augustus Briggs", *ExpT* XXV (1913-1914) pp. 294-98.
——, *Essays in Biblical Interpretation*, London, 1921.
Smith, J. M. P., *The Origin and History of Hebrew Law*, Chicago, 1931.
Smith, W. Robertson, "Bible", *EBrit*, 9th ed. Vol. III, Edinburgh (1875) pp. 634-48.
——, *Answer to the Form of Libel*, Edinburgh, 1878.
——, *Additional Answer to the Libel*, Edinburgh, 1878.
——, *Answer to the Amended Libel*, Edinburgh, 1879.
——, *An Open Letter to Principal Rainy*, Edinburgh, 1880.
——, *The Old Testament in the Jewish Church*, Edinburgh, 1881.
——, "Captain Conder and Modern Critics", *Contemporary Review* LI (1887) pp. 561-69.

Smith, W. Robertson, "Archaeology and the Date of the Pentateuch", *ibid*, LII (1887) pp. 490-503.

——, "Old Testament Study in 1876", *Lectures and Essays*, London, 1912.

Smith, W., *The Books of Moses or the Pentateuch*, Vol. I, London, 1868.

Snaith, N. H., *The Distinctive Ideas of the Old Testament*, London, 1944.

——, *Leviticus and Numbers*, London, 1967.

Soloweitschik, M., *Vom Buch das Tausend Jahre Wuchs* Berlin, 1932.

Speiser, E. A., "The Biblical Idea of History in its Common Near Eastern Setting", *IEJ* VII (1957) pp. 201-16.

——, "Leviticus and the Critics", in M. Haran (ed.) *Yehezkel Kaufmann Jubilee Volume*, Jerusalem (1960) pp. 29-45.

——, *Genesis, Anchor Bible*, New York, 1964.

Spencer, F. E., *Did Moses Write the Pentateuch after all?* London, 1892.

——, *A Short Introduction to the Old Testament*, London, 1912.

Stade, B., *Geschichte des Volkes Israel*, 2 vols, Berlin, 1887-1888.

Stähelin, J. J., *Kritische Untersuchungen über die Genesis*, Basel, 1830.

——, *Kritische Untersuchungen über den Pentateuch, die Bücher Josua, Richter, Samuels und der Könige*, Berlin, 1843.

Steinmann, J., *Les plus anciennes traditions du Pentateuque*, Paris, 1954.

——, *Biblical Criticism*, New York, 1958.

——, *Richard Simon et les origines de l'exégèse bibliques*, Paris, 1960.

——, Code Sacerdotal I. Genèse-Exode *Connaître la Bible*, Paris, 1962.

Steinmueller, J. E., *A Companion to Scripture Studies*, Vol. I, London ([7]1958), first published 1941, Vol. II, London ([8]1954), first published 1942.

Steuernagel, C., *Lehrbuch der Einleitung in das Alte Testament*, Tübingen, 1912.

Storr, V. F., *The Development of English Theology in the Nineteenth Century 1800-1860*, London, 1913.

Strack, H. L., "Pentateuch", *Realencyclopaedie für protestantische Theologie und Kirche*, Vol. XV (1904) pp. 113-24.

——, "Hexateuch", *The New Schaff-Herzog Encyclopedia of Religious Knowledge*, Vol. V (1909) pp. 260-65.

Strauss, D. F., *The Life of Jesus*, ET, London, [6]1913.

Suelzer, A., *The Pentateuch*. A Study in Salvation History, New York, 1964.

Sutcliffe, E. F. and Dyson, R. A., "Introduction to the Pentateuch", *A Catholic Commentary on Holy Scripture*, London (1953) pp. 164-76.

Thomas, D. Winton, *Archaeology and Old Testament Study*, Oxford, 1967.

Thompson, R. J., "Sacrifice and Offering", J. D. Douglas (ed.) *The New Bible Dictionary*, London (1962) pp. 1113-22.

——, *Penitence and Sacrifice in Early Israel Outside the Levitical Law*, Leiden, 1963.

Thomson, J. E. H., *The Samaritans*, London, 1919.

Thrane, J. R., *The Rise of Higher Criticism in England 1800-1870*, Microfilm, 1956.

Touzard, J., „Moïse et Josué", *Dictionnaire apologétique de la foi catholique* Vol. III, Paris (1919) cols 695-860.

Toy, C. H., "The Babylonian Element in Ezekiel", *JBL* (1881-1882) pp. 59-66.

Trattner, E. R., *Unravelling the Book of Books*, New York, 1929.

Trench, M. F. P., *The Story of Dr Pusey's Life*, London, [2]1900.

Troelstra, A., *The Name of God in the Pentateuch*, ET, London, 1912.

Tuch, F., *Commentar über die Genesis*, 2nd ed, Halle, 1871, first published 1838.

Tulloch, J. *Movements of Religious Thought During the Nineteenth Century*, London, 1885.

Tunyogi, A. C., "The Book of the Conquest", *JBL* LXXXIV (1965) pp. 374-80.

Uffenheimer, B., "On the question of centralisation of worship in ancient Israel", *Tarbiz* XXVIII (1958) pp. 138-53, Heb and Eng summary.

Urbach, E., „Neue Wege der Bibelwissenschaft", *MGWJ* LXXXII (1938) pp. 1-22.

Urie, D. M. L., "Sacrifice among the West Semites", *PEQ* LXXXI (1949) pp. 67-82.

Valk, W. M., "Moses and the Pentateuch", *Scripture* V (1952) pp. 60-67.

——, "Pentateuchal Criticism in la Bible de Jerusalem", *ibid*, pp. 99-102.

Vansina, J., *Oral Tradition*, London, 1965.

Vater, J. S., *Commentar über den Pentateuch*, 4 vols, Halle, 1802-1805.

Vatke, W., *Die Biblische Theologie I*: Die Religion des Alten Testaments, Berlin, 1835.

——, Preiss, H. G. S. (ed.) *Wilhelm Vatke's Historisch-kritische Einleitung in das Alte Testament*, Bonn, 1886.

Vaux, R. de, „Les Patriarches hébreux et les découvertes modernes", *RB* LIII (1946) pp. 321-48, LV (1948) pp. 321-47, LVI (1949) pp. 1-36.

——, *La Genèse — La Sainte Bible*, Paris, 1951.

——, „A propos du second centenaire d'Astruc-réflexions sur l'état actuel de la critique du Pentateuque", *VTSuppl I*: Congress Volume Copenhagen 1953, Leiden (1953) pp. 182-98.

——, *Ancient Israel*, ET, London, 1961, first published 1960.

——, "Hebrew Patriarchs and History", *Theology Digest* XII (1964) pp. 227-40.

——, *Studies in Old Testament Sacrifice*, Cardiff, 1964.

——, "Method in the Study of Early Hebrew History", J. P. Hyatt (ed.) *The Bible in Modern Scholarship*, Nashville (1965) pp. 15-29.

——, Review of G. R. Driver's "The Judean Scrolls" in *NTS* XIII (1966-1967) pp. 97-98.

Vergote, J., *Joseph en Égypte*, Louvain, 1959.

Vermes, G., *Scripture and Tradition in Judaism*, Leiden, 1961.

Vidler, A. R., *The Modernist Movement in the Roman Church*. Its Origins and Outcome, Cambridge, 1934.

——, *The Church in an Age of Revolution* (The Pelican History of the Church, Vol. 5) Harmondsworth, 1961.

Volz, P. and Rudolph, W., *Der Elohist als Erzähler: Ein Irrweg der Pentateuchkritik?* Giessen, 1933.

Vos, G., *The Mosaic Origin of the Pentateuchal Codes*, London, 1886.

Vries, S. J. de, "The Hexateuchal Criticism of Abraham Kuenen", *JBL* LXXXII (1963) pp. 31-57.

Vriezen, Th. C., "Twenty-Five Years of Old Testamentic Study in the Netherlands", *OTS* XIV (1965) pp. 397-416.

Wagner, N. E., "Pentateuchal Criticism: No clear Future", *Canadian Journal of Theology* XIII (1967) pp. 225-32.

Watermann, L., "A Half-Century of Biblical and Semitic Investigation", *AJSL* XXXII (1915-1916) pp. 219-29.

Waxman, M., *A History of Jewish Literature*, 5 vols, New York, ²1947.

Wedgwood, J., *The Message of Israel*, London, 1894.

Weinfeld, M., "The Source of the Idea of Reward in Deuteronomy", *Tarbiz* XXX (1960) pp. 8-15. Heb and Eng summary.

——, "The Origin of the Humanism in Deuteronomy", *JBL* LXXX (1961) pp. 241-47.

——, "Traces of Assyrian Treaty Formulae in Deuteronomy", *Biblica* XLVI (1965) pp. 417-27.

——, "Deuteronomy—The Present State of Inquiry", *JBL* LXXXVI (1967) pp. 249-62.

Weinfeld, M., "The period of the conquest and of the judges as seen by the earlier and the later sources", *VT* XVII (1967) pp. 93-113.

Weiser, A., *The Old Testament: Its Formation and Development*, ET, New York, 1961.

Welch, A. C., *The Religion of Israel under the Kingdom*, Edinburgh, 1912.

——, "The Present Position of O.T. Criticism", *Expositor* 8th series VI (1913) pp. 518-29.

——, "On the Present Position of O.T. Criticism", *Expositor* 8th series XXV (1923) pp. 344-70.

——, *The Code of Deuteronomy*, London, 1924.

——, "When was worship of Israel centralised at the Temple?" *ZAW* XLIII (1925) pp. 250-55.

——, "The Problem of Deuteronomy", *JBL* XLVIII (1929) pp. 291-306.

——, *Post-Exilic Judaism*, Edinburgh, 1935.

——, *Prophet and Priest in Old Israel*, London, 1936.

——, *The Work of the Chronicler*, Oxford, 1939.

Wellhausen, J., "Die Composition des Hexateuchs", *Jahrbücher für Deutsche Theologie* XXI (1876) pp. 392-450, 531-602, XXII (1877) pp. 407-79, reprinted in *Skizzen und Vorarbeiten* II, (1885) and with additions as *Die Composition des Hexateuchs und die Historischen Bücher des Alten Testaments*, Berlin, 1899.

——, *Prolegomena to the History of Israel*, ET, Edinburgh, 1885, from 2nd ed. 1883, first published as *Geschichte Israels I*, 1878.

——, "Israel", *EBrit* 9th ed. Vol. XIII, Edinburgh (1880) pp. 396-42.

——, "Heinrich Ewald", in *Grundrisse zum Alten Testament*, Munich (1965) pp. 120-38.

Westermann, C., *Essays on Old Testament Interpretation*, London, 1963.

Westphal, A., *Les Sources du Pentateuque*, 2 vols, Paris, 1888-1892.

——, *The Law and the Prophets*, ET, London, 1910, from the French 1903-1907.

Wette, W. M. L. de, *Dissertatio Critico-Exegetica qua Deuteronomium a prioribus Pentateuchi libris diversum alius cujusdam recentioris auctoris opus esse monstratur*, Jena, 1805.

——, *Beiträge zur Einleitung in das Alte Testament*, 2 vols, Halle, 1806-1807.

——, *Lehrbuch der historisch-kritischen Einleitung in die kanonischen und apokryphischen Bücher des Alten Testaments*, 6th ed, Berlin (1845), first published 1817. ET, 2 vols, Boston (1859), from 5th ed, 1840.

——, Rec. "Vatke, 'Relig. A.T.,' George, 'Die älteren Jüdischen Feste,' von Bohlen, 'Die Genesis' ", in *ThStKr* X (1837) pp. 947-1003.

Whitehouse, O. C., "Franz Delitzsch and August Dillmann on the Pentateuch", *Expositor* 3rd series VII (1888) pp. 132-45.

Widengren, G., *Literary and Psychological Aspects of the Hebrew Prophets*, Uppsala, 1948.

——, "Oral Tradition and Written Literature among the Hebrews in the Light of Arabic Evidence with Special Regard to Prose Narratives", *Acta Orientalia* XXIII (1959) pp. 201-62.

Wiener, H. M., *Studies in Biblical Law*, London, 1904.

——, *Notes on Hebrew Religion*, London, 1907.

——, *The Origin of the Pentateuch*, London, 1910.

——, *Essays in Pentateuchal Criticism*, London, 1910.

——, *Pentateuchal Studies*, London, 1912.

——, "Contributions to a New Theory of the Composition of the Pentateuch", *BibSac* LXXV (1918) pp. 80-103, 237-66, LXXVI (1919) pp. 193-220, LXXVII (1920) pp. 304-28, 369-402.

——, "Religion of Moses", *ibid*, LXXVI (1919) pp. 323-58.

——, "Main Problem of Deuteronomy", *ibid*, LXXVII (1920) pp. 46-82.

Wiener, H. M., "Altar", J. Orr (ed.) *International Standard Bible Encyclopaedia* Vol. I, Grand Rapids (1947) pp. 106-10, first published 1929.
——, H. Loewe, (ed.) *Posthumous Essays*, Oxford 1932.
Willey, B., *Nineteenth Century Studies*, London, 1949.
——, *More Nineteenth Century Studies*. A Group of Honest Doubters, London, 1956.
Willoughby, H. R. (ed.), *The Study of the Bible Today and Tomorrow*, Chicago, 1947.
Wilson, R., *The Bible on the Rock*. A Letter to Principal Rainy, Edinburgh, 1877.
Wilson, R. D., *A Scientific Investigation of the Old Testament*, New York, 1926.
Winckler, H., *Religionsgeschichtler und geschichtlicher Orient*, Leipzig, 1906.
Winnett, F. V., *The Mosaic Tradition*, Toronto, 1949.
——, "Re-examining the Foundations", *JBL* LXXXIV (1965) pp. 1-19.
Wise, I. M., *Pronaos to Holy Writ, Ch. VI The Authenticity of the Pentateuch*, Cincinatti, 1891.
Wiseman, D. J., "Some Trends in Biblical Archaeology", *Journal of Transactions of the Victoria Institute* LXXXII (1950) pp. 1-12.
——, "Secular Records in Confirmation of the Scriptures", *ibid*, LXXXVII (1955) pp. 25-36.
——, "Place and Progress of Biblical Archaeology", *ibid* LXXXVIII (1956) pp. 117-28.
Wiseman, P. J., "Archaeological and Literary Criticism of the Old Testament", *Journal of Transactions of the Victoria Institute* LXXVII (1945) pp. 100-11.
Wogue, L., *Histoire de la Bible et de l'exégèse biblique jusqu'à nos jours*, Paris, 1881.
Wolf, C. U., "Recent Roman Catholic Bible Study and Translation", *JBR* XXIX (1961) pp. 280-89.
Wolff, H. W., *Alttestamentliche Predigten*, 2 vols, Neukirchen, 1959.
——, „Dodekapropheton 1 Hosea", XIV/1 *BK*, Neukirchen, 1961.
Woudstra, M. H., *The Ark of the Covenant from Conquest to Kingship*, Philadelphia, 1965.
Wright, C. H. H., *Introduction to the Old Testament*, London, 1892.
Wright, G. E., "The Present State of Biblical Archeology", H. R. Willoughby (ed.) *The Study of the Bible Today and Tomorrow* (1947) pp. 74-97.
——, "Recent European Study in the Pentateuch", *JBR* XVIII (1950) pp. 216-25.
——, "Deuteronomy", *IB* Vol. II, New York, 1953.
——, "Deuteronomy", *IB* Vol. II, New York, 1953.
——, "Archeology and Old Testament Studies", *JBL* LXXVII (1958) pp. 39-51.
——, and Freedman, D. (ed.), *Biblical Archaeologist Reader*, New York, 1961.
Wright, G. E. (ed.), *The Bible and the Ancient Near East*, New York, 1961.
——, *Shechem*: The Biography of a Biblical City, New York, 1965.
Würster, P., „Zur Charakteristik und Geschichte des Priestercodex und Heiligkeitsgesetzes", *ZAW* IV (1884) pp. 112-33.
Yahuda, A. S., *The Language of the Pentateuch in its Relation to Egyptian*, ET, Oxford, 1933, first published 1929.
——, *The Accuracy of the Bible*, London, 1934.
Yamauchi, E. M., "Do the Bible's Critics use a double Standard?" *Christianity Today* X (1965) pp. 179-82.
——, *Composition and Corroboration in Classical and Biblical Studies*, Philadelphia, 1966.
Young, E. J., *An Introduction to the Old Testament*, 2nd ed, Grand Rapids (1950), first published 1949.
——, "Old Testament", C. Henry (ed.), *Contemporary Evangelical Thought*, New York (1957) pp. 11-40.
Zimmerli, W., *The Law and the Prophets*, Oxford, 1965.
Zöckler, O., *Geschichte der Beziehungen zwischen Theologie und Naturwissenschaft mit besondrer Rücksicht auf Schöpfungsgeschichte* 2 vols, Güterloh, 1877-1879.

AUTHOR INDEX

SUBJECT INDEX